TEACHING PLANS FOR

INTERNATIONAL FINANCE

TRANSACTIONS, POLICY, AND REGULATION

NINETEENTH EDITION

by

HAL S. SCOTT
Nomura Professor of International Financial Systems
Harvard Law School

And

ANNA GELPERN
Professor of Law
American University, Washington College of Law

FOUNDATION PRESS
2012

THOMSON REUTERS™

© 2012 by THOMSON REUTERS / FOUNDATION PRESS
    1 New York Plaza, 34th Floor
    New York, NY 10004
    Phone Toll Free (877) 888-1330
    Fax (646) 424-5201
    foundation-press.com
Printed in the United States of America

ISBN: 978-1-60930-186-6

Mat #41305780

TEACHING PLANS FOR

INTERNATIONAL FINANCE

TRANSACTIONS, POLICY, AND REGULATION

TABLE OF CONTENTS

PREFACE TO TEACHING PLANS

The readings in the book support more than 24 ninety-minute class sessions. While the Nineteenth Edition is now co-authored with Anna Gelpern, the teaching manual offers my plans to teach each class at Harvard Law School in the Spring of 2011 based on the Eighteenth Edition. My approach is to begin with basics, such as a simple explanation of a financial instrument, so that all students build from the same foundation. I then move to an analysis of issues, sometimes adding useful substantive information no in the readings. My experience is that the liveliest discussions come from topics about which people may reasonably differ or from puzzles juxtaposing two valid but apparently opposing observations. The teaching material for many classes is so detailed and rich that the class can easily extend beyond 90 minutes. Apart from discussion, I lecture some topics and skip others.

During the 1998-99 academic year, I began teaching with PowerPoint slides to convey data or analysis that provide the basis for discussion of questions posed on the slides. The slides help focus students' attention on key issues in what are often very complex and novel subjects.

I have included the syllabus I used, which consists of Chapters from the textbook as well as supplemental reading. The Teaching Plans are presented in the order in which I taught the Chapters. As in the past, the PowerPoint slides contain notes that support the materials on the slides.

I did not teach seven chapters from the book last year, but the materials in the textbook have been updated where required. The teaching plan for Chapter 17 (Project Finance) uses slides from the Ninth edition. The plan for Chapter 18 (Privatization and Institutional Investors) uses only the material from the Fifth edition because I did not use PowerPoint slides for that session. The slides for Chapter 20 (Financial System Reforms in Developing and Emerging Markets) are from the Thirteenth edition. The slides for Chapter 13 (Stock Market Competition) are from the Fifteenth edition. The slides for Chapters 11 (Euromarkets), 14 (Futures and Options) and 22 (Terrorism) are from the Sixteenth Edition.

Instructors who would like my digital files for the PowerPoint slides, or those Anna Gelpern used to teach the Eighteenth edition, should contact the publisher.

Syllabus: International Finance

The reading (R) will principally be taken from Scott and Gelpern, International Finance: Transactions, Policy and Regulation (Foundation Press, 18th ed. 2011) (IF). Use the detailed table of contents only, the summary table is incorrect. There will usually be some supplemental readings as well. Needless to say the regulatory response to the global financial crisis of 2008 and the Euro crisis of 2011 will be a major focus of the course. In addition, please use Davis Polk, "Summary of the Dodd-Frank Wall Street Reform and Consumer Protection Act," (DP) as a general reference summarizing the provisions of that legislation (Dodd-Frank).

This syllabus lists the topics and questions to be discussed for each class (we will not discuss the questions in IF unless the syllabus indicates otherwise). The materials will be distributed through the MyHLS course website and the Distribution Center. You will receive an email notice of any revision to the syllabus or the availability of new materials.

The teaching method is principally discussion framed by lectures with powerpoints. Copies of any powerpoints used in class will be distributed after class on the course website.

After the add-drop period is over, panelists will be assigned for each class. Your grade will consist of 25% for class participation (based on your panel performance and your additional class contributions) and 75% for your final exam.

Introduction: International Financial System

R: IF, Ch. 1, pp. 1-34.
Scott, Hal S., "How to Improve Five Important Areas of Financial Regulation." *Rules for*
> *Growth: Promoting Innovation and Growth through Legal Reform, ed* Robert E. Litan. The Kauffman Task Force on Law, Innovation, and Growth (2011), pp. 114-123.
Davis Polk, Financial Stability Oversight Council (FSOC) Releases Proposed Rules on Designation of Systemically Important Nonbank Financial Companies, October 17, 2011.
Committee on Capital Markets Regulation, Letter to FSOC on Designation of Systemically Important Nonbank Financial Companies, December 19, 2011,

http://www.capmktsreg.org/pdfs/2011.12.19_SIFI_Comment_Lett
er.pdf

Financial Stability Board, Policy Measures to Address Systemically
Important Financial Institutions, November 4, 2011.

Cleary Gottlieb, Federal Reserve Board Proposes Heightened Prudential
Requirements for Large Bank Holding Companies and Non-Bank
SIFIs, December 23, 2011.

S. Nasiripour, "MetLife to Sell Off Banking Assets," *Financial Times*,
December 28, 2011.

L. Summers, "Beware Moral Hazard Fundamentalists," *Financial Times*,
September 23, 2007.

What is the difference between a banking and securities
transaction? Which do you think is most important? What makes a
financial transaction international? What are the costs and benefits of an
increasingly global financial system?

What is systemic risk—differentiate among risks from correlation,
connectedness and contagion? Which is the most important? Dodd-Frank
gives the Fed supervision over $50 billion and plus bank holding
companies and "systemically important" institutions as identified by
FSOC—do you agree with that approach? How should SIFIs and GSIBs
be defined? How should they be regulated differently than other financial
companies?

What revisions would you make in the structure of the governance
of the international financial system?

The Global Financial Crisis of 2008 (GFC)

R: IF, Ch. 1, pp. 34-82.

Final Report of the National Commission on the Causes of the Financial
and Economic Crisis in the United States, January 2011, pp. xv-
xxviii, 441-449.

J. Stein, "Central Banking and Financial Stability," Working Papers,
October 2011, pp. 31-32.

[Contagion paper on Lehman]

What were the major causes of the GFC? How would you
apportion blame between the government and the private sector?

How would you appraise the performance of the Fed in

significantly expanding its lending facilities? Did the U.S. make the right decisions in Bear Stearns, Lehman and AIG?

Was TARP a good idea? How could it have been improved?

International Aspects of the Regulation of U.S. Capital Markets (I)

R: IF, Ch. 2, pp. 86-117, 151-161.
Committee on Capital Markets Regulation, Summary of Competitiveness Measures, Q2 2011.
Committee on Capital Markets, Statement About a Decision by the U.S. Court of Appeals on Proxy Access that Puts Dodd-Frank Implementation in Jeopardy Due to Inadequate Cost-Benefit Analysis, July 27, 2011.
X. Gao, J. Ritter and Z. Zhu, "Where Have All the IPOs Gone?, Working Paper, November 4, 2011, pp. 27-29.
G. Zuckerman and S. Pulliam, "How an SEC Crackdown Led to the Rise of 'Expert Networks,'" *The Wall Street Journal*, December 17, 2010.

What is the U.S. capital market? How competitive are public equity markets? Why should the U.S. care about public equity capital market competitiveness? What are the major factors affecting the competitiveness of public equity markets? How would you measure competitiveness of a capital market? How will UK regulatory reforms affect U.S. competitiveness?

What aspects of regulation strengthen our public markets? What aspects harm it? With respect to these questions consider (1) the overall disclosure regime; (2) Regulation FD; (3) board and auditor independence requirements under Sarbanes-Oxley; and (4) the SEC's reform of deregistration of foreign companies?

International Aspects of the Regulation of U.S. Capital Markets (II)

R: IF, Ch. 2, pp. 117-142, 162-178, 201-216.
M. Rapoport, "SEC Delays Call on Accounting Rules," *The Wall Street Journal*, December 6, 2011.
A. Ackerman and J. Eaglesham, "SEC Pushes To Toughen Penalties for Offenders," *The Wall Street Journal*, November 30, 2011.

Is SOX 404 a plus or minus for U.S. capital markets? Have the SEC and PCAOB reforms of SOX 404 gone far enough or not? Was Dodd-Frank correct in exempting small companies from SOX 404?

Was the SEC correct in allowing foreign issuers to state their accounts under international financial reporting rules (IFRS) without reconciliation to U.S. GAAP? Should the SEC permit or require U.S. firms to state their accounts under IFRS? Is the case for the SEC roadmap weakened by the financial crisis? Should the EU permit EU public companies (not just foreign companies) to state their accounts in U.S. GAAP? Should regulatory and financial reporting standards be allowed to be different?

How do the various components of the U.S. enforcement system—private enforcement, public civil enforcement by the SEC, SROs and the states, and criminal enforcement by the Department of Justice and the states—affect the competitiveness and efficiency of our public markets? What reforms would you make in these areas?

What do you think of the SEC's mutual recognition proposal? Should it be extended beyond secondary markets to allow foreign issuers to issue securities in the U.S. under their home country rules or any rules of their choice?

Securitization and the Global Financial Crisis (I)

R: IF, Ch. 12, pp. 704-728, 776-779.
Fender, Ingo and Mitchell, Janet, "The Future of Securitization," BIS Quarterly Review,
  September 2009.
D. Wu, J. Yang and H. Hong, "Securitization and Banks' Equity Risk," 39
  J. Financ. Serv. Res. 95 (2011), pp. 111-113 (without Table).
T. Riddiough, "Can Securitization Work? Economic, Structural and Policy
  Considerations," The Journal of Portfolio Management, Special
  Real Estate Issue 2011.
Testimony of Tom Deutsch, Executive Director, American Securitization
  Forum, before the U.S. Senate Banking Committee, *The State of
  the Securitization Markets,* May 18, 2011.
  (optional)
Committee on Capital Markets Regulation, Comment Letter to Six
  Agencies Regarding Risk Retention in Securitizations, July 22,
  2011.

Describe the process by which a large mortgage lender would securitize its mortgage portfolio. Does the process differ significantly from issuing a corporate bond?

Why would the mortgage lender securitize? Why would investors invest in a SPV issuing MBS (mortgage-backed securities)? What risks do various investors have? Does securitization impede mortgage modification? Overall, is securitization desirable or not?

In light of the subprime crisis, is the securitization "business model" fundamentally flawed?

Securitization and the Financial Crisis (II)

R: IF, Ch. 12, pp. 733-771.
J. Jiang, M. Stanford, and Y. Xie, "Does it Matter Who Pays for Bond
      Ratings? Historical Evidence," Working Paper, November 2, 2011,
      pp. 26-28.
A. Barker, "Barnier Backtracks on Ratings Reforms," *Financial Times*,
November 15, 2011.

How does Dodd-Frank change the securitization process? Do you agree with its approach to risk retention and loan-by-loan disclosure?

How should regulation of the ratings agencies be changed? Do you agree with the Dodd-Frank approach? In particular, do you agree with removing reliance on ratings in government regulations and heightened liability of and control over the ratings agencies?

International Aspects of the Regulation of U.S. Banking Markets (I)

R: IF, Ch.3, pp. 232-278.
Volcker, Paul A, Testimony Before the Committee on Banking, Housing, and Urban
      Affairs of the United States Senate, Washington, DC, February 2,
2010.
Scott, Hal, Testimony Before the Committee on Banking, Housing and Urban
      Affairs, United States Senate, February 4, 2010.
      (optional)
Johnson, Simon, Testimony Before the Senate Banking Committee, Hearing on

"Implications of the 'Volcker Rules' for Financial Stability," February 4, 2010.

E. Rosengren, President and Chief Executive Officer, Federal Reserve Bank of Boston, "Global Financial Intermediaries: Lessons and Continuing Challenges," Address at the Federal Reserve Bank of Boston's 56th Economic Conference: The Long-Term Effects of the Great Recession, October 19, 2011.
(optional)

Sullivan and Cromwell, Agencies Release Proposed Rule Implementing the Volcker Rule, October 12, 2011.

The Clearing House, "Understanding the Economics of Large Banks," November 7, 2011.

Independent Commission on Banking, Final Report Recommendations, Executive Summary, September 2011, pp. 9-15.
(optional)

Shearman & Sterling, The Vickers Report: What the Recommendations Mean for the Future of Banking in the UK, October 5, 2011, pp. 1-6.

How important are foreign banks in the United States? How important are U.S. banks abroad?

Should Big Banks be broken Up—how does Dodd-Frank handle this?

What are the arguments pro and con for the Volcker Rules, with respect to restrictions on proprietary trading and limits on investments in private equity and hedge funds? How would you define proprietary trading? How do the Volcker Rules apply to foreign banks?

How does the U.S. insure that foreign banks operating in the U.S. are safe and sound?

Should the U.S. prevent branches of foreign banks from offering FDIC insured deposits?

International Aspects of the Regulation of U.S. Banking Markets (II)

R: IF, pp. 278-304.

Basel Committee on Banking Supervision, Resolution Policies and Frameworks, Progress so Far, July 2011.

Federal Deposit Insurance Corporation, "The Orderly Liquidation of
   Lehman Brothers Holdings Inc. under the Dodd-Frank Act, 5
   FDIC Quarterly 1 (2011).
Credit Suisse, "Bail-in Resolution: An Approach to Reduce Systemic Risk
and End Bailouts,"
   July 2010.
Cleary Gottlieb Steen & Hamilton LLP, "A New Approach to Financial
Regulation: The End of
   The United Kingdom FSA," Alert Memo, London, August 6, 2010.
Financial Stability Board, Shadow Banking: Strengthening Oversight and
   Regulation, October 2011, pp. 27-34.
B. Masters, "Shadow Banking Surpasses Pre-Crisis Level," *Financial
   Times*, October 27, 2011.
J. Brunsden and B. Moshinsky, "Failing Banks' Short-Term Creditors
   May be Shielded From Losses in EU Plan," *Bloomberg*, November
   29, 2011.
[Contagion Paper on Resolution]

How would you reform resolution procedures? Does the Dodd-
Frank Act permit future bailouts in FDIC resolutions? Should it? What
do you think of the procedure for determining which institutions are
resolved by the FDIC and which are resolved in bankruptcy? Is there a
real difference between the bail-in and bridge bank approaches to
resolution?

What are the major problems today in handling cross-border bank
resolutions? Should the failure of financial institutions with cross-border
operations be handled on an international basis and, if so, how?

Is there a need to reorganize the U.S. federal regulatory structure?
How does its structure compare with other major countries? How do
international considerations play into that question? How would you do
it? Does the creation of FSOC make a significant contribution to
improving the U.S. regulatory structure? What is the shadow banking
system? Should we be concerned that its size is increasing?

Foreign Exchange Regimes and Sovereign Wealth Funds

R: IF, Ch. 8.
Andrew Rose, "Exchange Rate Regimes in the Modern Era: Fixed,
   Floating and Flaky," 49 J. of Economic Literature 652 (2011).
S. Rabinovitch, "China Tests U.S. with Currency Move," *Financial Times*,

October 5, 2011.

L. Wei, B. Davis and T. Nakamichi, "Tokyo and Beijing Agree on Currency Pact," *The Wall Street Journal*, December 27, 2011.

U.S. Department of the Treasury, Office of International Affairs, Report to Congress on International Economic and Exchange Rate Policies, December 27, 2011, pp.2-4, 15-21.

We will discuss the questions posed in the IF chapter.

Sovereign Debt Crises

R: IF, Ch. 19.

NML Capital Ltd. et. al. v. Banco Central de la Republica Argentina et. al., No. 10-1487- cv(L), — F.3d —, 2011 WL 2611269, at *19-20 (2d Cir. July 5, 2011).

V. Acharya, I. Drechsler, and P. Schnabi, "A Pyrrhic Victory? – Bank Bailouts and Sovereign Credit Risk," *NBER Working Paper 17136*, June 2011, pp. 36-37.

Standard & Poors, United States of America Long-Term Rating Lowered to 'AA+' On Political Risks and Rising Debt Burden; Outlook Negative, August 5, 2011.

Has the threat of contagion ever influenced the way we have dealt with a sovereign debt crisis? Could it have played a role in the response to the Asian crisis?

Are holdout creditors a substantial obstacle to dealing with sovereign debt crises?

Should some form of the IMF's proposal for a Sovereign Debt Restructuring Mechanism (SDRM) be adopted? What are its problems?

Do collective action clauses serve a useful purpose in resolving sovereign debt crises?

Should creditors' rights be strengthened to make it easier to attach sovereign assets in the event of any sovereign default, or just sovereign defaults by "rogue" debtors such as Argentina?

What do you think of the IMF's new programs adopted in response to the financial crisis?

Should the IMF enjoy seniority in sovereign debt repayments?

Was *NML Capital* (cited above) correctly decided?

The European Union Single Market in Financial Services

R: IF, Ch. 4.

> Does the EU need harmonized offering rules for securities, as under the Prospectus Directive (PD), given that most past offerings by European companies have been "offshore" in London? Should the EU restrict forum shopping under the PD? How does/should the PD be applied to foreign issuers?

> How should the EU deal with the failure of banks operating cross-EU borders? Should the EU reform its approach to deposit guarantees in light of the financial crisis?

> How would you compare the EU's approach to securitization reform with that of the U.S.?

> Have the recent EU structural reforms been a positive step for the EU?

> Will the EU mutual recognition system work internationally?

The Euro and the Eurozone Crisis (I)

R: IF, Ch. 5.

A. The Markets and the European Banks

"European Officials Round on Lagarde," *Financial Times*, August 26, 2011.

A. Jones and J. Thompson, "IASB Criticizes Greek Debt Writedowns," *Financial Times*, August 30, 2011.

J. Kapila, "EZ Banks: Scaling Potential Losses," Roubini Global Economics, September 22, 2011.

European Banking Authority, 2011 EU-Wide Stress Test, Aggregate Report, July 15, 2011, pp. 1-4.

A. Barker and P. Jenkins, "EU Bank Recap Could be Only €80 billion," *Financial Times*, October 19, 2011.

[Markets Update]

B. Default and Restructuring

R. Jenkins, "Greek Default Within the Euro is The Only Real Option," *Financial Times*, November 7, 2011.

J. Kirwin, "In A Bid to Ease Market Jitters, EU Abandons Private Sector Involvement in Future Bailouts," BNA's Banking Report, 97 BBR 1019, December 13, 2011.

C. Central Bank Liquidity Support

M. Hart, "Scope and Limits of ECB Purchases: Does Central Bank Capital Matter?," Roubini Global Economics, December 19, 2011.

Board of Governors of the Federal Reserve, Press Release [on swap lines] and FAQ: U.S. Dollar and Foreign Currency Liquidity Swaps, November 30, 2011.

G. O'Driscoll, Jr., "The Federal Reserve's Covert Bailout of Europe," *The Wall Street Journal*, December 28, 2011.

Review and Outlook, "The ECB's Backdoor Bailout," *The Wall Street Journal*, December 27, 2011.

W. Buiter and E. Rahbari, Global Economics View, The Future of the Euro Area: Fiscal Union, Break-up or Blundering Towards a "You Break it You Own Europe," September 9, 2011, pp. 21-26.

D. Eurozone Exit

N. Roubini, "Greece Should Default and Abandon the Euro," Roubini Global Economics," September 16, 2011.

[Scott Plan]

E. International Concern and Support

M. Dalton and M. Stevis, "Euro Zone Agrees to New IMF Loans," *The Wall Street Journal*, December 20, 2011.

S. Reddy, "Geithner Presses Europe for Debt Solution," *The Wall Street Journal*, December 7, 2011.

G. Dinmore, "Italy Turns to China for Help in Debt Crisis," *Financial Times*, September 12, 2011.

F. Fiscal Reform

L. Schuknecht, P. Moutot, P. Rother, and J. Stark, The Stability and Growth Pact, Crisis and Reform, European Central Bank, Occasional Paper No. 129, September 2011, pp. 13-19.

S. Fidler and C. Forelle, "EU Pushes Scenarios for Euro Bond," *The Wall Street Journal*, November 21, 2011.

M. Feldstein, *"The Euro Zone's Double Failure," The Wall Street Journal*, December 15, 2011.

W. Münchau, "Eurobonds and Fiscal Union Are the Only Way Out,"

Financial Times, September 18, 2011.

G. The December 2011 Summit Plan (and related measures)

M. Dalton, "Finance Minister Agree to EU Debt Guarantees," *The Wall Street Journal*, December 1, 2011.

M. Greene, "EU Summit: Can Successfully Kicked, but No One Too Impressed," Roubini Global Economics, December 12, 2011.

M. Stevis and F. Robinson, "Legal Uncertainty Imperils EU Agreement," *The Wall Street Journal*, December 14, 2011.

M. Wolf, "Merkozy Failed to Save the Eurozone," *Financial Times*, December 6, 2011.

H. Scott, "When the Euro Falls Apart- A Sequel," January 31, 2012 (optional)

What is the European Monetary Union?

Was it a good idea for the EU to adopt the Euro? Did the Euro strengthen the integration of EU financial markets? Should the U.K. adopt the Euro?

Did the 2005 revisions to the Stability Pact made it more effective? Would the failure of the Pact (if there is a failure) affect the viability of the Euro?

How has the viability of the Euro been affected by the sovereign debt crisis in the EU? Is this crisis an EU or Eurozone problem? Is this a sovereign debt crisis, a banking crisis or a Euro crisis? How would you compare it to the GFC of 2008?

How should the debt crisis be handled? Should the ECB greatly increase its provision of liquidity to the banks and/or the governments? Should Greece and other peripheral countries default and restructure? Should any countries leave the Eurozone? Is this possible? Should there be a more international approach to the problem? Should/can the European countries further increase the size of the bailout fund? Are the reforms of the Stability and Growth Pact sufficient? How would "Eurobonds" work? Should there be a fiscal union and what would this mean?

The Euro and the Eurozone Crisis (II)
Continue Class 12

The Japanese Financial System

R: IF, Ch. 6.

B. Aronson, "A Reassessment of Japan's Big Bang Financial Regulatory Reform," IMFS Discussion Paper Series 2011-E19, August 2011.

T. Nakamichi, "Japanese Banks Get 'Stress Tests'," *The Wall Street Journal,* January 6, 2012.

Nomura Equity Research, Assessing the Outlook for the Global Financial Industry Based on Lessons From Japan, December 9, 2011. (optional)

Why did the Japanese financial system experience a lost decade? What were the principal mistakes the Japanese made in dealing with their problems? Are there lessons from the Japanese experience that we can apply to dealing with the financial crisis?

Will the existing reform of the Postal Savings System improve the Japanese financial system? Should the reform be changed and, if so, how?

How would you compare the U.S., and Japan in terms of how they approach the regulation of financial markets and how they deal with foreign financial institutions?

What obstacles does Japan face in becoming a major international financial center? Does the financial crisis offer an opportunity or pose a threat to the Japanese financial system?

What major reforms should be made in the regulation of the Japanese financial system?

Chinese Financial Markets

R: IF, Ch. 21.

D. Lynch, "China Bank Crisis Led by Debt Seen by 61% in Global Poll," Bloomberg, December 8, 2011.

Capital Adequacy (I)

R: IF, Ch. 7, pp. 412-460.

BNA's Banking Report, "Bank Regulators Say Modified Mortgages Should Generally Retain
    Same Risk Weight," 93 BBR 1073, December 2, 2009.

Basel Committee on Banking Supervision Reforms – Basel III (Table).

Basel Committee on Banking Supervision, Progress Report on Basel III

Implementation, October 2011.

Why do governments regulate capital and why do they do so by international regulation?

Can capital regulation "level" the international playing field? Why did countries other than the G-10 adopt the Basel Accord of 1988 (Basel I)?

What is capital? Do you agree with how it is defined under Basel I? If a bank needs more capital what can it do? Do you think Basel III improves the definition?

Does the Basel Accord of 2004 (Basel II) do a better job regulating credit risk than Basel I? Do we have any evidence on this from the financial crisis?

What risk weight should residential mortgages have? How does Basel know what risk weights a given asset should have?

Capital Adequacy (II)

A. Economic Impact of Basel III

Institute of International Finance, The Cumulative Impact on the Global Economy of Changes in the Financial Regulatory Framework, September 2011, pp. 1-16.

Roubini Global Economics, "Toward Basel III: IMF Estimates Moderate Economic Impact," May 16, 2011.

McKinsey & Company, Day of Reckoning? New Regulation and Its Impact on Capital Market Business, September 2011, pp. 1-8.

S. Muñoz, "Capital Idea, Say Regulators," *The Wall Street Journal*, October 11, 2011.

B. Capital Surcharges

Bank for International Settlements, Measures For Globally Important Banks Agreed to by the Group of Governors and Heads of Supervision, June 25, 2011 (1 page).

P. Jenkins, R. Atkins and P. Spiegel, "Europe's Banks Face 9% Capital Rule," *Financial Times,* October 11, 2011.

B. Masters and N. Cohen, "EU Regulator in Bank Capital Compromise," *Financial Times.* June 29, 2011.

D. Pruzin, "Swiss Advance Implementation of 'Too Big To Fail' Requirements for UBS and Credit Suisse," BNA's Banking Report, 97 BBR 1019, December 12, 2011.

C. CoCos and Bail-Ins

L. Vaughan, "Investors May Shun CoCo Bonds," Bloomberg, December 13, 2011.

L. Becker, "FSB Admits Bail-In Weak Spot," International Financial Law Review, November 7, 2011.

L. Becker, "FSB, Deutsche Clash on CoCos," International Financial Law Review, November 2, 2011.

D. Disclosure and Market Discipline

Board of Governors of the Federal Reserve System, Enhanced Prudential Standards and Early Remediation Requirements for Covered Companies, 77 Federal Register 594-602, 625-633, January 5, 2012.

D. Fitzpatrick and V. McGrane, "Higher 'Stress' for Big Banks," *The Wall Street Journal*, November 23, 2011.

Banking Committee on Banking Supervision, Consultative Document, Definition of Capital Requirements, December 2011.

A. Zibel and V. McGrane, "Banks' Ratings Reliance Nears End," *The Wall Street Journal*, December 8, 2011.

A. Kuritzkes and H. Scott, "Markets Are the Best Judge of Bank Capital," *Financial
Times,* September 23, 2009.

Secretary of the Treasury Geithner says increased financial regulation is mainly about capital, capital, capital. Do you agree?

Do you agree with the U.S. decision to only partially implement Basel II for large banks (requiring advanced IRB)? What is the justification for a leverage ratio in addition to risk-weighted capital?

Should the U.S. implement the standardized Basel II requirements for banks other than the large banks, just refine Basel I, as it did under Basel IA, or give banks a choice between standardized Basel II or the new U.S. standardized version, Basel IB? Note this is still undecided.

How much capital does Basel III require and when does it require it? Is it too little or too much?

Do you think there should be capital buffers and/or requirements for contingent capital or the use of bail-ins? Are they the key for avoiding future financial crises?

What do you think of the SIFI 1-3% surcharges, the European 9% requirement and the Swiss Finish? Do they respond to different concerns?

Do you agree with the need for liquidity as well as capital requirements? Has Basel III taken the right approach to liquidity?

Should we rely more on market discipline or bank models to insure adequate bank capital? How could we accomplish this? Should we require periodic stress tests to insure more market discipline? What do you think of the Basel Committee's disclosure proposal? What do you think of the Fed's stress test proposal?

Should we have special accounting rules for determining regulatory capital, e.g. no fair market value accounting, or just follow normal accounting rules?

Do you agree with the Dodd-Frank provision that effectively prevents the use of credit ratings in setting capital requirements? Are the alternative methodologies being considered adequate alternatives?

What does Dodd-Frank do with respect to bank capital that departs from Basel? Do you agree with its approach?

The Large Value Dollar Payment System

R: IF, Ch. 9.
Committee on Payments and Settlement Systems, BIS, Statistics on
        Payment, Clearing and Settlement in CPSS Countries, Figures for
        2010, January 2012, Tables 9-11, pp. 403-404.

What is the difference between Fedwire and CHIPS (The Clearinghouse Interbank Payment System)? Why is the U.S. payment system so important internationally?

Why was the U.S. payment system such a potentially significant source of systemic risk? Is it still? Should regulators actively favor Agross settlement@ systems like Fedwire over "net settlement" systems like CHIPS?

What do you think of the Fed's shift from pricing to

collateralization of daylight overdrafts?

Are foreign banks discriminated against under the Federal Reserve Board's daylight overdraft policy? If so, is such discrimination justified?

Will CLS Bank eliminate most Herstatt risk?

Should central banks have any involvement in offering payments system services?

April 2: Swaps (I)

R: IF, Ch. 15, pp. 873-907.
D. Nowakowski, "Are CDS Worthless Because Greece's Exchange Won't Trigger a Credit Event?," Roubini Global Economics, November 2, 2011.

Why do banks enter into swap transactions? What is market risk? What is credit risk?

On a swap, can a party have both market and credit risk at the same time?

Why would a bank buy protection on a credit default swap (CDS)? Why would a bank sell protection on a CDS?

Should all swaps be cash settled? Can they be?

How does the auction procedure deal with the settlement problem?
Do you agree with the decision in *Lomas et. al. v. JFB Rixson, Inc.*? Why won't a Greek restructuring trigger a CDS default?

April 3 Swaps (II)

R: IF, Ch. 15, pp. 907-966
The Committee on Capital Markets Regulation, Letter to the Commodity Futures Trading
> Commission and the Securities and Exchange Commission Re: Requirements for Derivatives Clearing Organizations, Designated Contract Markets, and Swap Execution Facilities Regarding the Mitigation of Conflicts of Interest, 75 Fed. Reg. 63,732 (RIN 3038–AD01); Ownership Limitations and Governance Requirements for Security-Based Swap Clearing Agencies, Security- Based Swap Execution Facilities, and National Securities Exchanges with Respect to Security-Based Swaps under

Regulation MC, 75 Fed. Reg. 65,882 (SEC File No. S7-27-10, RIN 3235-AK74), November 15, 2010.

S. Brush and M. Leising, "CFTC Approves Rule Expanding Access to Swaps Clearinghouses," Bloomberg, October 18, 2011.

R. Hill, "New York Fed Report Says CDS Dealers Are Carrying Risk for Weeks Before Hedging," BNA's Banking Report, 967 BBR 557, October 6, 2011.

Letter from Various Trade Associations to Barnier and Geithner, Extra-Territorial Effects in EU and US Regulation of Derivatives, July 5, 2011, http://www2.isda.org/functional-areas/public-policy/europe/

A. Barker, "EU Ban on 'Naked' CDS to Become Permanent," *Financial Times*, October 19, 2011

P. Bolton and M. Ochmke, "Should Derivatives be Privileged in Bankruptcy," Working Paper, October 7, 2011, pp. 1-5.

What incentive problems are raised by CDS?

Is there a systemic risk interconnectedness problem with OTC derivatives?

How does Dodd-Frank regulate OTC derivatives? Do you agree with the requirements for central clearing and exchange or exchange-type trading? What do you think of the CFTC's proposed conflict of interest rules? The CFTC has proposed lowering minimum capital requirement for entry into a clearinghouse to $50 million—current capital requirements are closer to $50 billion. Do you agree with this?

How are and how should OTC derivatives be treated in bankruptcy or under FDIC or OLA resolution procedures?

Should Bankers Trust have been held liable, under U.S. law, in *Bankers Trust v. Dharmala?*

Clearance and Settlement

R: IF, Ch. 10.

C. Pirrong, The Economics of Central Clearing, ISDA Discussion Paper Series-Number One, May 2011.

European Parliament, Directorate General for Internal Policies, Policy Department A: Economic and Scientific Policies, Economic and Monetary Affairs, Derivatives, Central Counterparties and Trade

Repositories, Compilation and Briefing Notes, February 2011, pp. 1-21.

What is involved in the clearing of securities? How does this happen when securities are traded on an exchange? How would the following hypothetical trades on an exchange be cleared and settled: A buys 100 IBM from B at a $1 per share, B buys 50 IBM from C at $3 pershare, and C buys 40 IBM from A at $2 per share?

What risks are there to DTCC from the failure of a participant to deliver securities or pay for the securities it receives? How does DTCC protect itself from such risks? Would it be harder for a clearer to protect itself from risks associated with the trading of OTC derivatives like credit default swaps?

Suppose a US seller sells 100 IBM shares to a Japanese buyer on the Tokyo Stock Exchange, where IBM shares are cross-listed from the NYSE-Euronext. How would this trade be cleared and settled?

If a seller sold a buyer 100 IBM bonds trading at a $1 a bond, how would this be cleared and settled through Euroclear (both parties are Euroclear members)? Could/would parties want to clear a U.S. equity trade through Euroclear rather than through DTCC?

Suppose French bank buys 50 Eurobonds of a US issuer and is a Euroclear participant. Total Eurobonds issued by the US issuer are 1000 which are held by Euroclear as global custodian. Suppose French bank then sells 5 Eurobonds to UK broker acting on behalf of German investor, and that the UK broker uses the French bank as its custodian. How would this transaction be accounted for within Euroclear? What is the UK broker's rights to the securities if French bank fails? What law governs French bank's rights against Euroclear?

What is the optimal number of clearinghouses for a particular asset class, say for worldwide equities and CDSs? Should different assets classes be cleared at the same or different clearinghouses? Should we mandate that all CDS be centrally cleared and traded on an exchange?

Public and Private Pools of Capital—Mutual Funds

R: IF, Ch. 16, pp. 967-1000, 1025-1028.
Report of the President's Working Group on Financial Markets, Money Market Fund Reform

Options, October 2010.

J. Fisch and E. Roiter, "A Floating NAV for Money Market Funds," Institute for Law and Economics, Research Paper No. 11-30, August 2011.
(optional)

D. Nowakowski, "Are CDS Worthless Because Greece's Exchange Won't Trigger a Credit Event?," Roubini Global Economics, November 2, 2011.

Arnold & Porter, Comment Letter to the Financial Stability Oversight Council on Proposal to Require Supervision and Regulation of Certain Nonbank Financial Companies, December 15, 2011.

R. Stulz, Testimony before the Sucommittee on Capital Markets and Government Sponsored Enterprises, U. S. House of Representatives, June 24, 2011.

In *Union-Investment*, why was it important to the SEC that the foreign fund be incorporated in the U.S. rather than in Germany and that the managers of the fund be U.S. citizens?

Why, since 1973, have foreign funds not sought to register (even with exemptions) in the U.S.?

How would the competitiveness of U.S. mutual funds be affected by allowing U.S. investors to defer gains (as foreign investors in foreign funds can do)? Can cloning "technology" overcome the tax problem? Should the U.S. permit a "global fund" as called for in Part II of ICI's statement?

What is the correct solution to the market timing problem? Do mutual funds have the right governance structure?

What should be done, if anything, to change the regulation of money market funds in light of the financial crisis?

TEACHING PLAN FOR

CHAPTER ONE
INTRODUCTION AND GLOBAL FINANCIAL CRISIS

POWERPOINT SCREENS FOR NINETEENTH EDITION

Class One: Introduction

Introduction to International Finance
Class One Outline

- Elements of international financial transactions
- Costs and benefits of globalization
- Systemic Risk
- Governance of international financial system

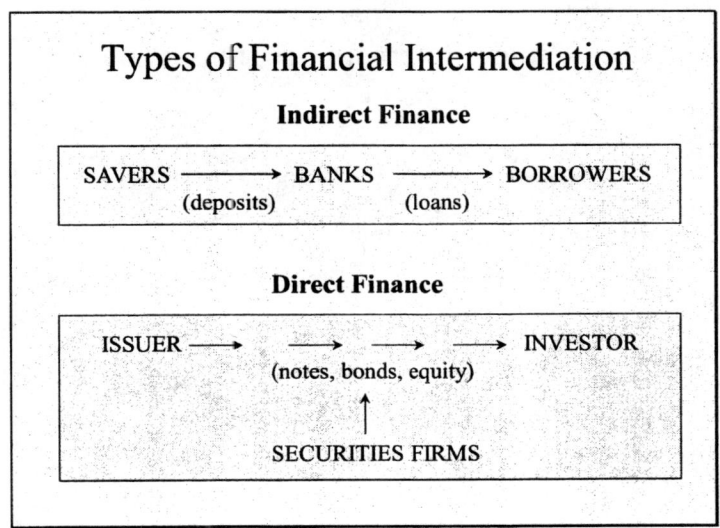

Traditionally, banks intermediate between savers and users of funds. Banks as principals have continuing obligations to depositors and bear credit risk of borrowers. Savers indirectly bear the risk of the borrowers. If the bank becomes insolvent due to borrower default, the savers may be at risk (above deposit insurance limits)

Securities companies help savers (investors) and users (issuers) transact business directly. The investor invests in the issuer by buying its securities. The security company does not normally have to hold bonds or shares very long, and has no continuing obligation to the investor or the issuer. The investor directly bears the risks of the issuer's performance.

Post-financial crisis, significant U.S. securities firms (Goldman, Morgan Stanley) have become part of bank holding companies or been acquired by bank holding companies (Bear Stearns, Merrill Lynch) or have failed (Lehman). So these are two types of transaction now generally performed by the same firms. Internationally, China and Japan, still commercial and investment bank divide, none in Europe.

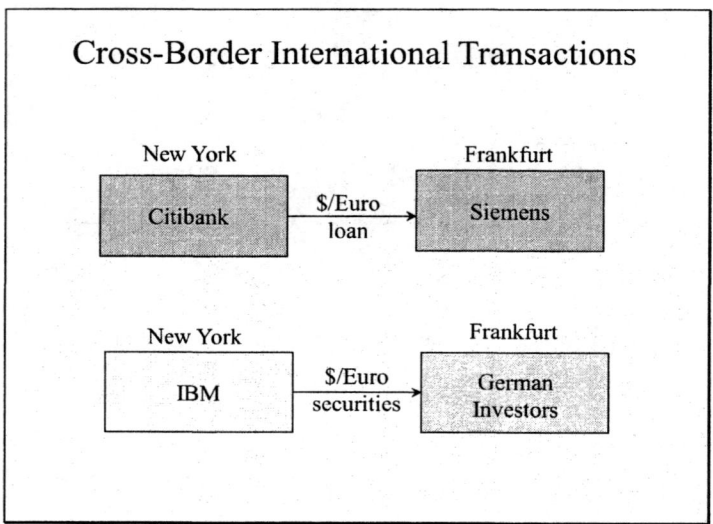

An important part of international transactions, is the international side of domestic markets. For banking, a loan by a U.S. bank to a foreign resident (depicted on top) involves a cross-border movement of funds and is an international transaction in the U.S. domestic market (and the German market as well). The same would be the case if a resident in one country made a deposit with a bank in another country.

Similarly, for securities, a sale of securities of a U.S. corporation to a foreign resident (depicted below), or a sale of the securities of a foreign corporation to a U.S. resident, would be international securities transactions involving the U.S. domestic market (and the German market as well).

When a U.S. bank loans funds to a foreign resident (Citibank to Siemens), there are really two jurisdictions involved, the country of the lender, the U.S., and the foreign country of the borrower. Those two countries have a direct interest in the transaction because it affects their residents and financial systems. So, under this view, if more than one jurisdiction is directly affected by the transfer, the transaction is international. This might be called the cross-border approach.

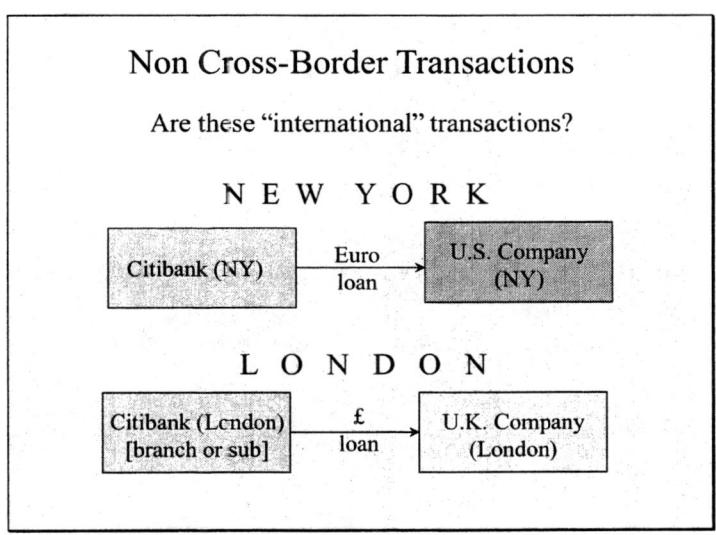

If Citibank's London branch or subsidiary (bottom transaction) makes a sterling loan to a resident of the U.K., is this an international transaction?

It does involve *nationals* of two different countries. Citibank is basically a U.S. institution (whether or not operating as a branch or sub in London) with a presence in the U.K. The U.K. could well be concerned with how foreign banks operate in London, and want to treat them differently than domestic ones. The U.S. might also be concerned with how its own banks operate abroad.

How about when Citibank NY (top transaction) loans to a U.S. company in New York in Euros, is this international?

This is actually a transaction in Euros outside the countries that have adopted the Euro. It involves activity in a foreign currency in the U.S. which might concern the U.S. or the EU could be concerned with the impact of the transaction on its own monetary policy.

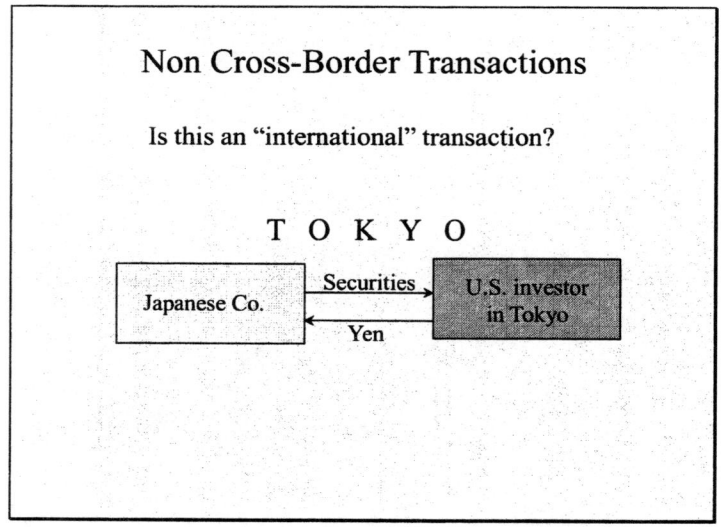

If a Japanese company sold securities in Tokyo to a U.S. investor, residing in Tokyo, Dufey and Chung say this is not international. Should it be?

Again, there is no cross-border transaction, the U.S. investor is in Tokyo when he buys the securities, but the transaction does involve an issuer from Japan selling to a U.S. investor: the nationality of the parties differs. The U.S. might have some special concern (U.S. investor buys securities not subject to U.S. disclosure regime), or the Japanese might (U.S. investors own a Japanese company). The transaction probably should be considered international for those purposes. We define international in terms of our policy concerns.

```
┌─────────────────────────────────────────┐
│            Elements of                    │
│    International Financial Transactions    │
│                                           │
│                                           │
│              Location                      │
│                                           │
│             Nationality                    │
│                                           │
│              Currency                      │
│                                           │
│                                           │
└─────────────────────────────────────────┘
```

So what is international depends on the circumstances or the concerns of the countries involved. It is not a definition in the abstract. Three factors should be taken into account in deciding whether a transaction is international:

1. Does the transaction involve residents in two different countries? (location)

2. Does the transaction involve nationals of two different countries? (nationality) We saw that nationality mattered when residency was the same for both parties; treat foreign bank lending in your country different than domestic bank lending.

3. Is the transaction in a currency other than that of the country in which the transaction takes place? (currency)

TYPES OF INTERNATIONAL LENDING
(By Location of Bank)

12/31/82

Banks In	Int'l Total	Claim on Currency	Non-res Foreign	Non-res Home	Resident Foreign	Total
Japan	11%		37%	14%	49%	100%
USA	17%		2%	98%	---	100%
UK	72%		68%	4%	28%	100%

6/30/02

Banks In	Int'l Total	Claim on Currency	Non-res Foreign	Non-res Home	Resident Foreign	Total
Japan			65%	27%	8%	100%
USA			4%	96%	---	100%
UK			69%	8%	23%	100%

Table 1A, at p. 3, types of international lending

Japan and the United States are close in 1982 (top). Both have a low international percentage of total lending. **Why?** This is because their international business is dwarfed by their large domestic economies. U.S. international business (1982 and 2002) is overwhelmingly (98-96%) dollar loans (home currency) to non-residents (foreign borrowers.

In 1982, Japan's dollar loans to non-residents and residents was pretty close, 37% as compared with 49%, but by 2002, dollar loans to non-residents dwarfed those to residents. This represents the expansion of international activity by Japanese banks in the 1980s, which then shrank back some in the 1990s. In addition, Yen loans to non-residents also increased 14% to 27%, reflecting the removal of exchange controls that had previously limited such activity.

The U.K. has a very high percentage of international lending. **Why?** It is an offshore banking center specializing in making foreign currency loans to non-residents, e.g. dollar loans to Germans. Oddly, financial activity in both the U.S. and U.K is roughly comparable, around 8% of GDP—but much more international in the UK.

Offshore Banking Centers

- Types: functional (London) or booking (Bahamas)

- Location Factors: politics (US controls), domestic regulation and enforcement (US v. UK), telecommunication/aviation, time zones, other banks

- Contribution to Host: service exports, jobs, taxes, competition, local deregulation

- International Problems: money laundering-terrorism and tax evasion, see Parmalat which operated through offshore accounts

---

Are offshore centers good or bad?

Much of the world's international financial activity goes on in offshore banking centers, like London. In fact there are very different types of offshore centers, functional versus booking. Review slide.

Domestic banks generally more profitable (exception for US foreign banks)

Increasing foreign bank market share in emerging markets (WTO process)

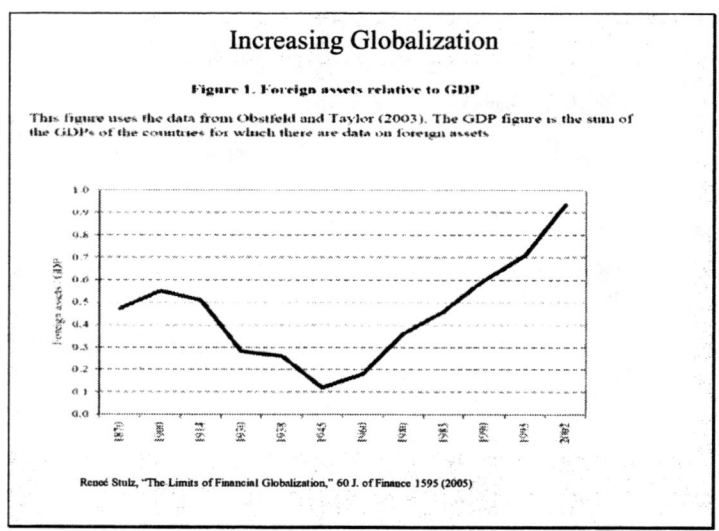

Increasing Globalization

Figure 1. Foreign assets relative to GDP

This figure uses the data from Obstfeld and Taylor (2003). The GDP figure is the sum of the GDPs of the countries for which there are data on foreign assets

Renoé Stulz, "The Limits of Financial Globalization," 60 J. of Finance 1595 (2005)

Foreign assets are assets abroad, such as a loan by a U.S. bank to a foreign borrower or investment by U.S. residents in a foreign company. This data is worldwide. By this measure globalization is increasing, and sharply since WW II.

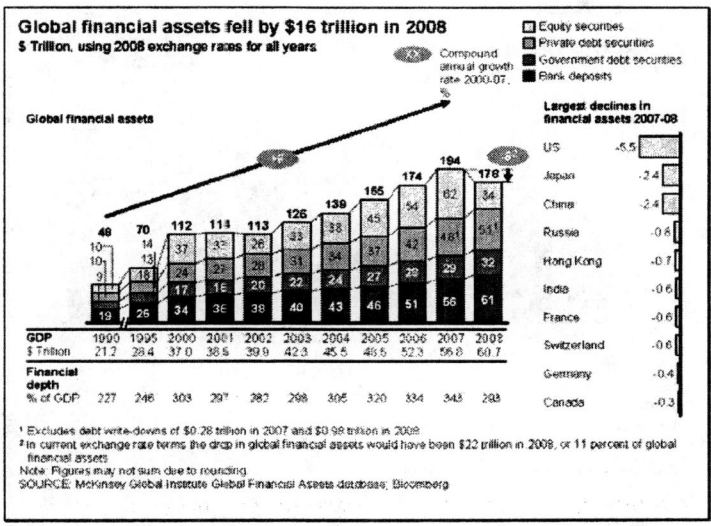

Decrease to $176 trilllon (2008) but 9% CAGR (compound annual growth rate)

The total value of the world's financial assets (including bank deposits, government debt and private debt securities, and equity securities) stood at $176 trillion at the end of 2008, down $16 trillion in 2008 due to financial crisis. No fundamental reason trend should not continue with recovery. Do not have update from McKinsey

The growth so far has been accompanied by a striking shift away from banks and toward market institutions as the primary financial intermediaries (there was a shift toward bank deposits, flight to quality in 2008, however). That change can be seen in the declining share of bank deposits in the global financial stock—to 34 percent in 2008 (61/178) from 45 percent in 1980 and in the corresponding increase in the share of debt and equity securities. The liquidity of world capital markets has increased as a result.

One can also see the dominance of the value of debt over equity in the capital markets—overall debt (public and private) was 47% in 2008, compared with equity of 19%. In 2007, however, the difference was much narrower, 39% debt compared to 31% equity. 2008 reflects low equity issuance combined with much higher debt issuance..

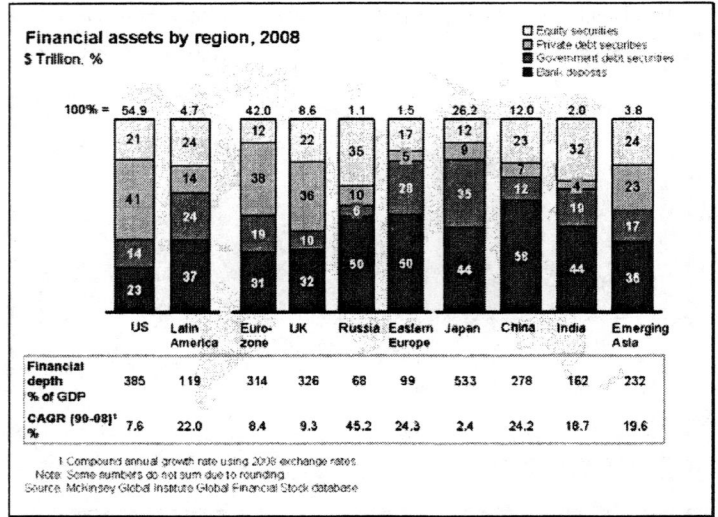

Financial assets by region, 2008
$ Trillion, %

	US	Latin America	Euro-zone	UK	Russia	Eastern Europe	Japan	China	India	Emerging Asia
100% =	54.9	4.7	42.0	8.6	1.1	1.5	26.2	12.0	2.0	3.8
Equity securities	21	24	12	22	35	17	12	23	32	24
Private debt securities	41	14	38	36	10	5	9	7	4	23
Government debt securities	14	24	19	10	6	28	35	12	19	17
Bank deposits	23	37	31	32	50	50	44	58	44	36
Financial depth % of GDP	385	119	314	326	68	99	533	278	162	232
CAGR [90-08][1] %	7.6	22.0	8.4	9.3	45.2	24.3	2.4	24.2	18.7	19.6

1 Compound annual growth rate using 2008 exchange rates.
Note: Some numbers do not sum due to rounding.
Source: McKinsey Global Institute Global Financial Stock database

CAGR = compound annual growth rate
Different profiles in different regions...

Although we talk about a global capital market, just four areas account for about 74 percent of the world's financial stock: the US, the euro zone plus the UK, Japan, and China. Furthermore, regions differ starkly. The market of the United States - which, with about $54.9 trillion in financial assets (top of bars) in 2008, accounted for 28 percent of the world's financial stock - is dominated by private debt and equity securities. The growth in the US share of financial stock has slowed recently across all asset classes, averaging 7.6 percent a year, below Eurozone of 8.4 and way below China at 24.2. Europe has a more bank centric system, bank deposits of 31 percent compared to U.S. of 23. China and Japan much more bank centric, with 58 and 44 percent.

```
┌──────────────────────────────────────────┐
│                                            │
│          Globalization of Finance          │
│                                            │
│                 Benefits?                   │
│                                            │
│                                            │
│                                            │
│                                            │
│                                            │
│                                            │
│                                            │
│                                            │
│                                            │
│                                            │
└──────────────────────────────────────────┘
```

1. **Diversification**: Korean investor can invest in U.S. and not just Korean securities. This increased country diversification can reduce overall portfolio risk if returns in Korea and the U.S. are not correlated. Ironically, if financial markets are highly integrated, the attractiveness of international portfolio diversification will weaken as returns are equalized across countries (diversification only makes sense if the asset prices in other markets are not perfectly correlated with those in the home country—why invest in Canada if it is just like the U.S.)

2. **Cheaper capital** results from increased global demand for capital. Chinese company in an international IPO has investors from all over the world competing to invest, not just those in China

3. **More flexible link between consumption and savings.** Severs the rigid link between national Savings and Investment. Czech companies can borrow from Japanese banks that take savings from Japanese citizens.

4. **Not clear that globalization contributes to economic growth**—but surprising that it would not, see Edison (2002), footnote 42, p. 20.

5. **Possibilities of dealing in other offshore markets puts constraints on national regulators.** Major theme of offshore markets.

6. **Jobs for international investment bankers and lawyers, and waiters in fancy restaurants.**

Globalization of Finance

Benefits:

- Permits more diversification (important, absent complete financial integration)
- Decreases cost of capital with more liquid markets
- Links savers and users better—across borders
- Increases global and national growth rates (mixed evidence)
- Limits powers of national regulators (regulatory competition)
- More international ibanking jobs for Harvard students

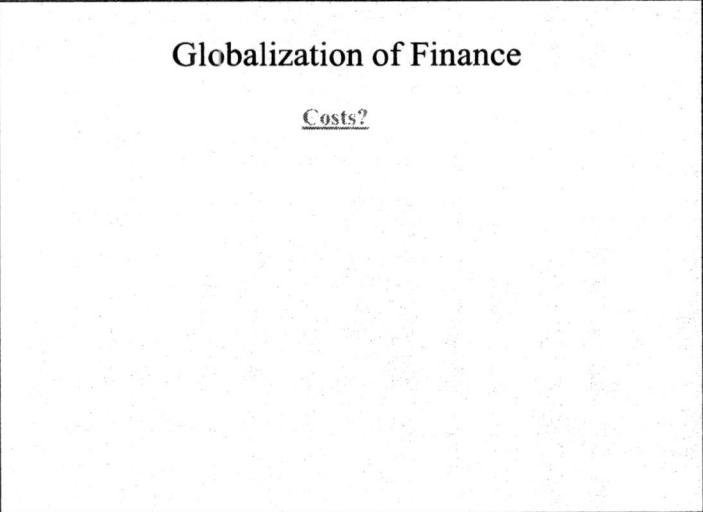

Globalization of Finance

Costs?

What are the Costs?

1. **Less autonomy for national economic policies.** Harder to manage money supply (interest rates) or foreign exchange rates. This was a major issue in the debate over European Monetary Union (Chapter 7). For smaller economies, lack of control may create volatility in domestic markets as capital comes in and out in cycles. Asian crisis, e.g. Korea.

2. **Markets are not politically correct**; poor performing economies would lose domestic funds and not attract foreign funds. Saudia Arabia may get more more funds than South Africa

3. **Leverage for creditor countries**. The US became # 1 debtor from 1984, but has compensating strengths (military and a strong economy in which people are willing to invest). Does this help China today?

4. **Systemic risk on international level**. Failure of large bank, for example in United States, could trigger bank failures in other countries. Contagion in one country affects others. Not much evidence of this in financial crisis but bailouts of major banks could have prevented.

If countries do not want globalization, what can they do to prevent it?

The "escape" to offshore markets could only have occurred with the tacit agreement of national governments. They had weapons (like foreign exchange controls) to stop this development but many did not, either because they saw value in the development or the cost of using the weapons was too high. Some, like the Japanese and Germany, did impede this development.

Globalization of Finance

Costs:

- National economic policies are less autonomous
- Markets aren't politically correct
- Creditor countries have leverage (U.S. exception)
- Systemic risk, e.g. chain reaction of bank failures, is international, contagion

Effect of Financial Crisis on Globalization?

Effect of Financial Crisis on Globalization

- Less funds for developing markets: crowding out effect of increased debt issuance by developed countries
- Multinational financial institutions pull back operations to home country (Japan during lost decade)
- Less support for globalization—like capitalism, look what it brought us, but suprisingly little economic protectionism
- Cross-border insolvencies leads to coordination and burden sharing issues
- Undermine failed international standards like Basel II and international accounting standards—some slow down in effort for harmonized standards (each country for itself), but has strengthened G20 in looking for solutions (US reforms basically consistent with European initiatives)

Elements of Systemic Risk

- Correlation: same external event creates losses for large number of important financial institutions, e.g. housing price collapse, 9-11, Eurozone sovereign debt crisis
- Connectedness (credit risk): losses of one financial institution cause losses of other major financial institutions, e.g. bilateral derivatives, payment system
- Contagion: Failure or fear of failure of financial institutions causes short-term creditors-investors to withhold-withdraw funding for financial institutions, which in turn affects other financial markets, e.g. commercial paper bought by money funds (includes liability connectedness)

Is the solution to intensively regulate "systemically important" financial institutions?

Who are they? Contrast with $50 billion+ DF bank approach, just use asset threshold. FSOC rule-making. Shadow banks? See next slide

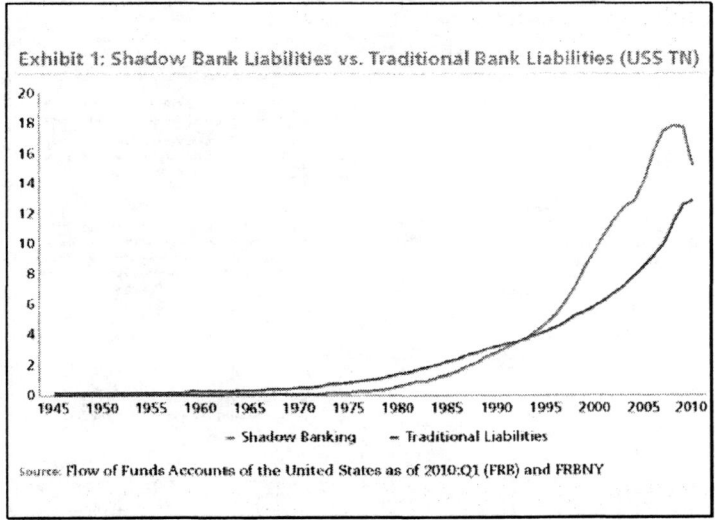

Includes money market funds, pension funds, hedge funds, securitization vehicles, insurance companies: where there is credit intermediation and transformation outside banking system

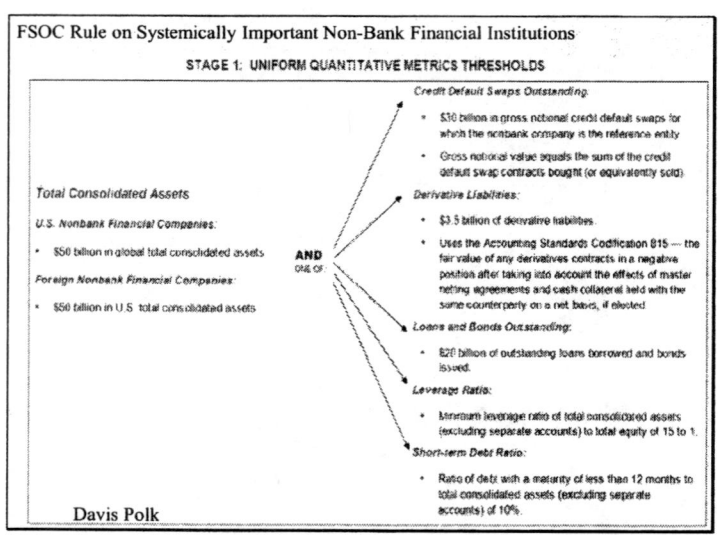

FSOC Rule of October 2011.

What do you think of $50B+ threshold (70 plus banks/thrifts)? Same as bank cutoff, but why? CCMR thinks should only be size but not same size for all FIs (if looking at $50B+, 15 insurance holding companies, 1 hedge fund manager (hedge funds?), 14 consumer finance companies, 6 private equity managers, 23 retirement funds, fewer than 20 mutual funds, including money market funds).

Size comparison (9/30/11): JPM $2.289T, GS $949B, 34 $50B+ banks now (MetLife debank could get out of $50B+bank and regulation that goes with it but might still be SIFI, $785B in assets)

CCMR believe certain companies based on activities should be ruled out because do not pose systemic risk at all: (1) real insurance companies, no short-term funding, long-term liabilities to policy holders so no risk of contagion which should be focus; (2) private equity, again no short-term funding, plus not financial investments, just private versions of IBM; (3) mutual funds, short-term funding but non-financial investments.

What about the other second stage criteria? Who knows, CDS and derivatives aimed at connectedness not contagion; loans and bonds irrelevant; leverage and dependence on short-term funding, particularly latter, are related to contagion.

FSB G-SIB Proposal November 2011

Table 1
Indicator-based measurement approach

Category (and weighting)	Individual Indicator	Indicator Weighting
Cross-jurisdictional activity (20%)	Cross-jurisdictional claims	10%
	Cross-jurisdictional liabilities	10%
Size (20%)	Total exposures as defined for use in the Basel III leverage ratio	20%
Interconnectedness (20%)	Intra-financial system assets	6.67%
	Intra-financial system liabilities	6.67%
	Wholesale funding ratio	6.67%
Substitutability/financial institution infrastructure (20%)	Assets under custody	6.67%
	Payments cleared and settled through payment systems	6.67%
	Values of underwritten transactions in debt and equity markets	6.67%
Complexity (20%)	OTC derivatives notional value	6.67%
	Level 3 assets	6.67%
	Held for trading and available for sale value	6.67%

Turn to G-SIB proposal of FSB. Different than FSOC proposal, addressed to non-banks. The FSB proposal suggests which banks should be regulated more intensively and subject to SIFI capital surcharge. Would be subset of the over 34 bank holding companies already subject to Fed regulation under DF. Fed has not yet determined

29 large banks worldwide would be subject to capital surcharges of 1-2.5% plus more intense supervision.

Note only 8 U.S. banks out of 29, huge Chinese banks not included.

What do you think of these criteria? Who knows and not related to contagion, compare FSOC, more related when comes to SIFIs..

Fed Proposal on Heightened Prudential Requirements (December 20, 2011)

- Stress Testing: all financial companies of $10 billion and plus supervised by the Fed
- Capital: covered BHCs to have a minimum of Tier I capital (Basel requirements)
- Liquidity : buffers along lines of Basel III but broader definition of what counts as a liquid asset
- Single Counterparty Credit Limits: 25% of capital and surplus; only 10% of one $500B+ financial company to another $500B+ financial company
- Heightened Prompt Corrective Action Requirements
- Leverage Limits: 15-1 where institution poses grave threat to financial system (cf. 33-1 with Basel 3% limit, or 20-1 with current Fed limit for most sound BHCs)

Applies to all banks supervised by Fed.

Governance of International Financial System

- **IMF**: monitor financial stability, lender of last resort to sovereigns, general economic analysis, review of financial regulation in developed as well as developing and emerging markets
- **Functional Regulators**: IOSCO for securities regulation (weak), Basel Committee on Banking Supervision for bank capital (strong)
- **Overall Coordination**: G-20 and Financial Stability Board

How would you revise?

G-20 Cannes Summit, November 3-4: #16: "Building on its achievements, we have agreed to reform the FSB to improve its capacity to coordinate and monitor our financial regulation agenda. This reform includes giving it legal personality and greater financial autonomy. ..."

Council on Global Financial Regulation on FSB, Report of April 14, 2011

Strengthen leadership role and clarify responsibilities of IMF and Basel etc.

Full time Chairman, Carney head of Bank of Canada

Too bank-centric

Keep track of divisions on financial regulation

Independent funding (not through BIS) and staff

Better transparency and industry consultation

The Global Financial Crisis of 2008

The Global Financial Crisis of 2008

- The major causes of the crisis and its impact
- Fed lending
- The disposition of Bear Stearns, Lehman and AIG
- TARP

Causes of Financial Crisis

- Housing price decline, bubble burst (perhaps Fed policy that permitted it to continue too long)
- Government policies to promote housing: GSEs, CRA, capital requirements (50% RW of Basel I)
- Increase in leverage of consumers and financial firms
- Inaccurate credit ratings of securitized debt pools and overexposure of financial institutions to holding such debt
- Mark-to-market accounting
- Fraudulent and predatory lending
- Other?

Impact of Financial Crisis

- Housing: decline in home values 32 percent from 2006 to 2009; 24 percent of mortgages with negative equity as of March 2010
- Total Financial System Losses: IMF estimates in April 2010, $3.4 trillion
- Recession: U.S. Real GDP fell to -2.6% in 2009 (now recovering, +2.6% in Q3 2010; unemployment rate still high at 9.1%
- Widening Spreads in Financial Markets Now Narrowed: e.g. TED (difference between three-month futures contract on LIBOR and U.S. treasuries) rose from .50 percent in 2004 to peak of 4.5 percent in October 2008
- Stock Market Collapse Most Severe Since Depression (recovered) and Securitization Grinds to Halt (still has not recovered)

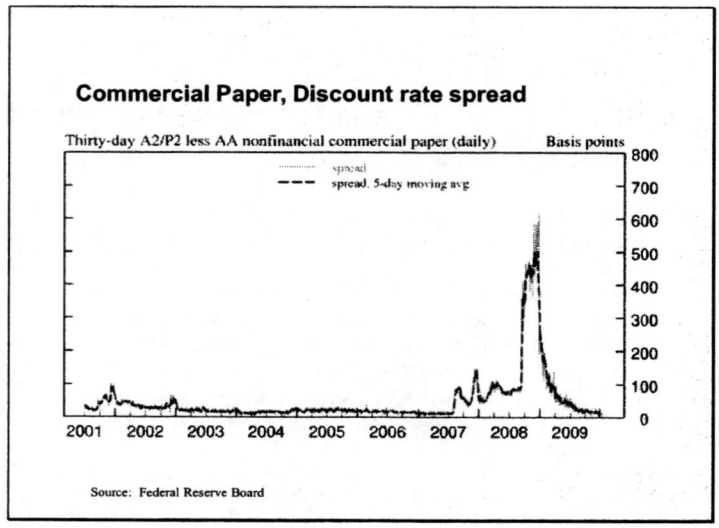

Difference between 30 day prime CP and treasuries.

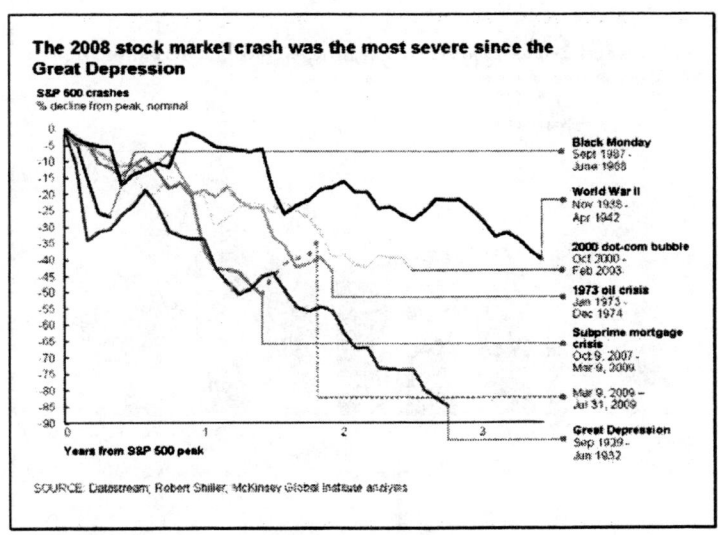

The 2008 stock market crash was the most severe since the Great Depression

S&P 500 crashes
% decline from peak, nominal

Black Monday
Sept 1987 -
June 1988

World War II
Nov 1938 -
Apr 1942

2000 dot-com bubble
Oct 2000 -
Feb 2003

1973 oil crisis
Jan 1973 -
Dec 1974

Subprime mortgage crisis
Oct 9, 2007 -
Mar 9, 2009

Mar 9, 2009 –
Jul 31, 2009

Great Depression
Sep 1929 -
Jun 1932

Years from S&P 500 peak

SOURCE: Datastream; Robert Shiller; McKinsey Global Institute analysis

S&P 500 pre-crisis, 1552 in July 2007, low of 683, March 2, 2009, now about 1318.

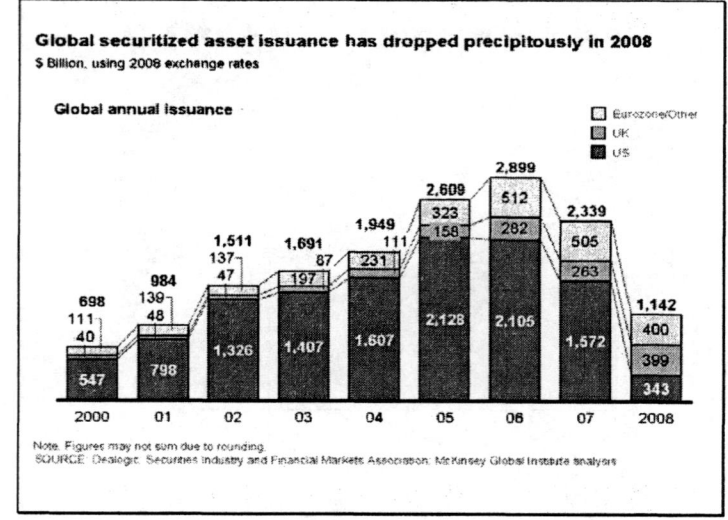

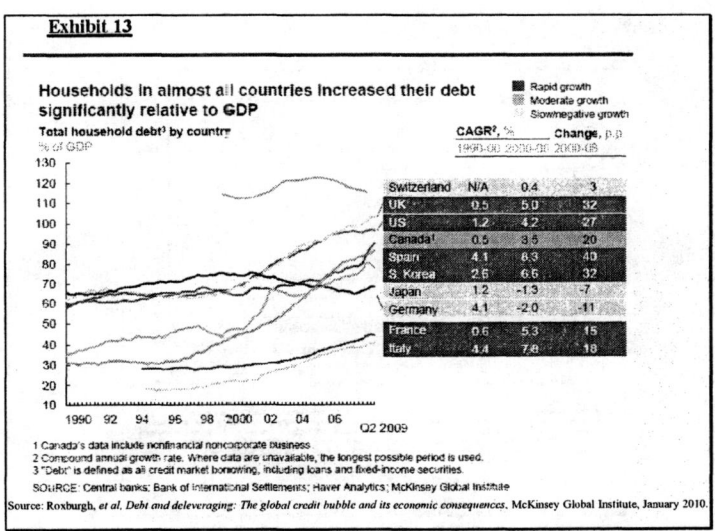

Exhibit 13

Households in almost all countries increased their debt significantly relative to GDP

Total household debt[3] by country
% of GDP

Legend: Rapid growth / Moderate growth / Slow/negative growth

	CAGR[2], % 1990-00	2000-08	Change, p.p. 2000-08
Switzerland	N/A	0.4	3
UK	0.5	5.0	32
US	1.2	4.2	27
Canada[1]	0.5	3.5	20
Spain	4.1	8.3	40
S. Korea	2.6	6.5	32
Japan	1.2	-1.3	-7
Germany	4.1	-2.0	-11
France	0.6	5.3	15
Italy	4.4	7.8	18

1 Canada's data include nonfinancial noncorporate business.
2 Compound annual growth rate. Where data are unavailable, the longest possible period is used.
3 "Debt" is defined as all credit market borrowing, including loans and fixed-income securities.

SOURCE: Central banks; Bank of International Settlements; Haver Analytics; McKinsey Global Institute

Source: Roxburgh, *et al*. *Debt and deleveraging: The global credit bubble and its economic consequences*. McKinsey Global Institute, January 2010.

So, here CAGR of U.S. ratio of debt to GDP increase from 1.2% in 1990-2000 to 4.2% in 2000-2008, change in percentage points in two periods, 27%.

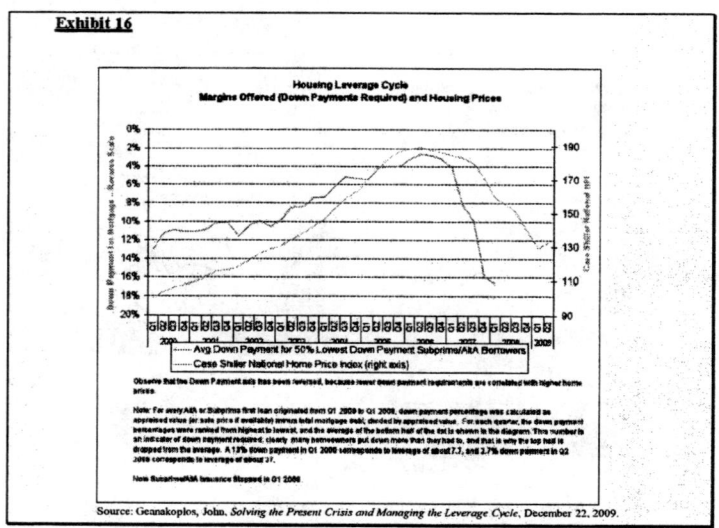

As house prices rose, mortgage leverage increased

Stabilization and the Financial Crisis

Fed Monetary Policy Since The Summer of 2007

Fed Monetary Policy

- Discount window: reduction of penalty rate from 50 to 25 BP, relaxation of collateral requirements and extension to "primary dealers" (investment banks) (now 50 again)
- Term Auction Facility (TAF): auction set amount of funds at lowest accepted interest rates (avoid window stigma) [expired]
- Term Securities Lending Facility (TSLF): Lending of securities to primary dealers (provides collateral for primary dealers to support their borrowing)[expired]
- ABCP (Asset-backed Commercial Paper) Money Market Fund Liquidity Facility (AMLF): funds supplied to depository institutions to buy ABCP (restore liquidity to ABCP market, helps money market funds with redemptions by providing market for their ABCP sales)[expired]
- Commercial Paper Funding Facility (CPFF): Fed purchases unsecured and ABCP from corporate issuers [expired]
- Money Market Investor Funding Facility (MMIFF): Fed purchases assets from money market funds (provides liquidity to money market funds) [expired]
- Term Asset-Backed Securities Loan Facility (TALF): finance purchase of AAA-rated ABS consumer and small business loans (support securitization market)
- MBS Purchase Program: purchase debt of GSEs (reduce cost of GSE debt which was being reflected in higher mortgage rates)
- Swap Lines with Foreign Central Banks (support dollar lending needs of foreign central banks) [recently renewed and increased in Euro area crisis]
- Treasury Supplementary Financing Program: Treasury issues debt to drain cash from system, aids Fed's "sterilization" of increased liquidity [not used recently]
- Payment of interest on bank reserves (additional tool to control money supply)

Roughly in order of adoption since summer of 2007.

Fed Balance Sheet: $1.9 Trillion (February 11, 2009)
($billions)

- Treasury securities   474,910   25%   (2006: 91% of 852)
- GSE securities   31,831
- MBS agency securities   7,377
- Discount Window   207,829
- Primary Dealer credit   25,805
- TAF   412,883
- CPFF   256,153
- AMLF   15,111
- AIG Credit   37,677
- Maiden Lanes (Bear/AIG)   72,065
- Central Bank $ swaps   <u>389,671</u>

Total: 1,931,312

```
Fed Balance Sheet: $2.921 Trillion (January 24, 2012)
                        ($billions)

•  Treasury securities      1,661,529  57%  (2006: 91% of 852)
•  GSE securities             101,498
•  MBS agency securities      835,624
•  Maiden Lanes (Bear/AIG)     34,174
•  Central Bank $ swaps        103,171
        Total:              2,921,869
```

What were the major changes from 2009?

Further expansion of about $1 trillion

Wind down of many emergency facilities.

Shift to support of mortgage market with GSE and MBS securities

Treasury percentage greatly increased, by 1.2T, continued easing

FDIC/Treasury Guarantees and Deposit Insurance

- Temporary Liquidity Guarantee Program (TLGP, October 14, 2008)) gave depository institutions and their holding companies authority to issue new senior unsecured debt, guaranteed by FDIC, before June 2009, for maturities up to 2012 (expired October 2009)
- In October 2009, FDIC established a new limited six-month emergency guarantee facility, upon expiration of TLGP, new guarantees ended in June 2010
- October 2008, deposit insurance limit increased from $100,000 to $250,000 (results in raise in minimum size of deposits for foreign banks, to make sure they are really "wholesale"), made permanent by Dodd-Frank §335
- October 2008, unlimited deposit insurance for transaction accounts, originally due to expire YE 2009, extended by FDIC to June 2010 and then by Dodd-Frank through 2012
- September 2008, Treasury guarantees all money market fund accounts through use of its currency stabilization fund, now expired

Big moral hazard but what is the alternative

Was TLGP real reason Goldman and Morgan Stanley became bank holding companies? Goldman sold $25 billion in bonds under the program in November 2008; similar amounts by Morgan Stanley in November-December 2008. Could have already borrowed from Fed under primary dealer facility.

Fed Monetary Policy Since The Summer of 2007

What is your overall assessment? Has it worked?

Was it appropriate for Fed to do? Who else would have acted to avoid Armaggedon?

Can Fed really lose money? Perhaps made money, $75.8 billion in remittances in 2010, largest ever, projected about $80 billion in 2011. But are they accurately accounting for Bear and AIG losses through income statement? But can lose reputation and independence.

Legal authority, next slides

Section 13(3)

In **unusual and exigent circumstances**, the Board of Governors of the Federal Reserve System, by the affirmative vote of not less than five members, may authorize any Federal reserve bank, . . . to discount for any individual, partnership, or corporation, notes, drafts, and bills of exchange when such notes, drafts, and bills of exchange are indorsed or **otherwise secured to the satisfaction of the Federal Reserve bank**: *Provided*, That before discounting any such note, draft, or bill of exchange for an individual, partnership, or corporation the Federal reserve bank shall obtain evidence that such individual, partnership, or corporation is unable to secure adequate credit from other banking institutions. . .

What do you think of this? Did Fed abuse their authority in establishing these new liquidity facilities, or in lending to AIG, or assisting Bear acquisition?

New Section 13(3) Proposed in H.R. 4173 (Section 1701)

- Federal Reserve Board can lend in "unusual and exigent circumstances" upon the written determination of the Financial Stability Oversight Council that a "liquidity event exists that could destabilize the financial system," with the written consent of the Secretary of the Treasury after certification by the President that an emergency exists and the loans are "indorsed or otherwise secured" to the satisfaction of the Fed
- Maximum amount: $4 trillion
- No member of the Board can vote for such a measure and the Secretary of the Treasury shall not provide written consent, unless the member or Secretary believes to a 99% likelihood that that the funds and all interest on such loans will be repaid
- Low quality assets cannot be used security
- No single beneficiaries (e.g. like AIG)
- Evidence of unavailability of other credit

Problems with this approach: overly constrains Fed's normal lender of last resort role. But does prevent inadequately collateralized or bailout lending.

Actual Changes in Section 13(3), Dodd-Frank, §1101

- Federal Reserve Board can lend in "exigent circumstances" with the approval of the Treasury, procedures adopted in consultation with Treasury
- No loans to single beneficiaries, e.g. AIG
- Tougher collateral policies, lendable value assigned to all collateral, and loans only to solvent borrowers
- Monitoring by Congress of all loans made (reports required within seven days)
- More rigorous audits
- Disclosure of discount window borrowers with 2 year lag

Problems with this approach: overly constrains Fed's normal lender of last resort role. But does prevent inadequately collateralized or bailout lending.

Treasury approval means less independent and approval will not be guaranteed in ant-bailout environment. Could spark contagion quickly in new crisis because not sure Fed will contain. Loss of independence could rub off on monetary policy.

Policy Toward Troubled Institutions: Arbitrary or Consistent?

- Bear Stearns (March 16, 2008): Force takeover by JP Morgan (paid $10 per share), supported by $30 billion Fed lending (against collateral of uncertain quality) without recourse to JP for over $ 1 billion. Fed refused to lend to Bear—then had no established facility for this. **Was the Fed decision correct? Was Cox right that days before the takeover Bear had adequate capital?**

- IndyMac (July 8, 2008): Put into FDIC conservatorship through a bridge bank—resulted in complete takeover of equity and power to restructure debt. Sold to PE syndicate, (FDIC and buyers share losses). **Should we be worried about PE ownership?**

- GSEs (September 8, 2008): Fannie Mae and Freddie Mac placed into Federal Housing Finance Authority (FHFA) conservatorship pursuant to legislation of July 30, 2008. Treasury invests $1 billion in each in return for preferred and equity warrants representing 79.9 percent of equity. Conservatorship gives FHFA complete control over GSEs. **What are we doing about them ($200 billion of public funds through TARP now supporting each)?**

Policy Toward Troubled Institutions: Arbitrary or Consistent?

- Lehman Brothers (September 15, 2008): allowed to file for bankruptcy, further lending refused on ground of inadequate collateral. **Was this a disaster?**

- AIG (September 17, 2008): Fed bails out by making $85 billion two-year loan to be repaid by sale of AIG assets. Fed later (October 8) lends an additional $37.8 billion through borrowing AIG securities. Later (November 10) restructured into $40 billion from Treasury and $90 billion from Fed. Treasury receives preferred stock convertible into 79.9 percent of AIG common. **Why bail them out?**

- Citigroup (October 28, 2008): Gets $25 billion in Troubled Assets Relief Program (TARP) funds (8 other banks do as well) under the Emergency Economic Stabilization Act of October 3, for preferred stock and equity warrants (worth about 2.2% of Citi common); later (November 23) $20 billion additional investment plus Treasury/FDIC/Fed guarantee of large losses on $306 billion of mortgage-related assets for additional preferred stock and equity warrants (worth another 5.5 percent of Citi common). **If insolvent why not resolve under normal FDIC procedures?**

TARP (October 3, 2008)

- $700 billion under EESA for dealing with financial system credit crisis
- First tranche was $350 billion ($250 billion immediate, additional $100 billion with certification by President). Second tranche of $350 billion required congressional approval (later given)
- First $350 billion spent on recapitalizing banks, AIG bailout and on Chrysler and General Motors
- Guaranteed losses on Citigroup ($360 billion) and Bank of America, from Merrill Lynch ($118 billion) asset pools of mortgage-backed securities
- In bank recapitalizations (Capital Purchase Program, CPP) maximum investment is lesser of 3% of risk-weighted assets or $25 billion
- TARP funds also used for mortgage relief
- Non-mortgage part of TARP will make money; banks have already more than paid back capital injections.

See next slide on status of TARP funds

Voted in after initial rejection, Administration predicted Armageddon, then supported by Democrats, most Republicans opposed and made issue in 2010 elections, hypocritical.

Executive Summary: Where We Stand

As of August 31, 2011	Maximum Allocations	Total Spent	Outstanding Investment Balance	Estimated Lifetime Cost (Gain) as of 8/31/11
Banking Programs	$ 250.46	$ 245.10	$ 19.55	$ (21.71)
Credit Market Programs	$ 27.07	$ 12.87	$ 26.40	$ (2.35)
Automotive Industry Financing Program (AIFP)	$ 79.69	$ 79.69	$ 37.17	$ 14.33
American International Group (AIG)	$ 67.84	$ 67.84	$ 50.92	$ 17.30
Treasury Housing Programs	$ 45.60	$ 2.23		$ 45.60
Total for TARP Programs	$ 470.67	$ 412.73	$ 124.04	$ 53.17
Additional AIG Common Shares Held by Treasury				$ (16.48)
Total with Additional AIG Common Shares	$ 470.67	$ 412.73	$ 124.04	$ 36.69

U.S. Treasury, Troubled Asset Relief Program Three Year Anniversary Report, October 2011

TARP Questions

- Has TARP worked?
- Would it be better to purchase mortgage-related assets, mortgages and securities, than to inject capital into banks?
- Should all banks have been eligible to receive funds?
- Did the Treasury get robbed by the banks, e.g. did the Treasury overpay for the bank securities? (COP Valuation Report)

Has TARP worked? Depends on objective, seems to have stabilized banking system from a crash but no increased lending or attraction of private capital. Treasury made money! Moral hazard cost

Better to purchase mortgage-related assets? Valuation problem, all assets in doubt, e.g. credit cards not just mortgages, so expense would be staggering. Mortgage-related assets are $6 trillion (probably only $1 trillion on bank books), total bank assets are $16 trillion. Take a long time and fraught with political controversy on pricing (capital infusion pricing less transparent, not pricing assets per se).

All banks? Hard to see reason, why go beyond systemically important? Fairness? Avoid to big too fail? Politics (each Congressman wants to save his/her bank).

Valuation on securities (next chart)

Purchase Program Participant	Valuation Date	Face Value	Total Estimated Value		
			Value	Subsidy %	Subsidy $
Capital Purchase Program					
Bank of America Corporation	10/14/08	$15.0	$12.5	17%	$2.6
Citigroup, Inc.	10/14/08	25.0	15.5	38%	9.5
JPMorgan Chase & Co.	10/14/08	25.0	20.6	18%	4.4
Morgan Stanley	10/14/08	10.0	5.8	42%	4.2
The Goldman Sachs Group, Inc.	10/14/08	10.0	7.5	25%	2.5
The PNC Financial Services Group	10/24/08	7.6	5.5	27%	2.1
U.S. Bancorp	11/03/08	6.6	6.3	5%	0.3
Wells Fargo & Company	10/14/08	25.0	23.2	7%	1.8
Subtotal		**$124.2**	**$96.9**	**22%**	**$27.3**
311 Other Transactions*		**$70.0**	**$54.6**	**22%**	**$15.4**
SSFI & TIP					
American International Group, Inc.	11/10/08	$40.0	$14.8	63%	$25.2
Citigroup, Inc.	11/24/08	20.0	10.0	50%	10.0
Subtotal		**$60.0**	**$24.8**	**59%**	**$35.2**
Total		**$254.2**	**$176.2**	**31%**	**$78.0**

Dollars in billions

* Extrapolates 22% subsidy rate from 8 studied CPP investments. See discussion in Part II.

Congressional Oversight Panel, Valuation Report (Duffy & Phelps) (February 4, 2009)

Claim $78 billion subsidy on the investments—should this be added to TARP costs?

SSFI = Systemically significant failing institution

TIP = Target Investment Program

1. Uses four methods of valuation: (1) DCF using discount rate based on market yields on publicly traded preferred stock and debt securities of each institution following Treasury's announcement of the investment; (2) DCF using discount rate inferred from credit default swaps, higher rate based on CDS spreads; (3) contingent claims analysis based on solvency forecasts (e.g. zero in bankruptcy); (4) comparable private transactions, e.g. Berkshire Hathaway in Goldman—and takes composite based on all four methods.

2. Critiques: (1) Treasury not in for the money but to stabilize banking system (non-investor related goals explicitly ignored; (2) did not go bottom up by valuing assets, perhaps Treasury had relevant information on this; (3) knocked down valuation because of provision permitting equity warrants to halve in value if preferred paid back in 5 years, designed as government exit strategy—do not want nationalized banking system; (4) standard terms for all to avoid showing some in worse shape than others

TEACHING PLAN FOR

CHAPTER TWO
INTERNATIONAL ASPECTS OF U.S. CAPITAL MARKETS

POWERPOINT SCREENS FOR NINETEENTH EDITION

U.S. Capital Markets

International Aspects of Regulation of U.S. Capital Market

- The Competitiveness of the U.S. Public Equity Capital Market
- Key Substantive Areas of Regulatory Regime: (1) disclosure; (2) independence board requirements of Sarbanes-Oxley; (3) deregistration reforms; and (4) implementation of Dodd-Frank

U.S. Capital Market: What is it?

Direct Finance as discussed in last class, so debt of various maturities (private, public), equity. Discussed mix last time. Public and private (public swamps private, combined market cap of NYSE and Nasdaq 2006 19.2T, compared to PE of less than $1T. Individuals and institutions. See next slide for increasing institutional nature.

Percentage Ownership of U.S. Equities, 1950-2011

	1950	1960	1970	1980	1990	2002	2011 (Q3)
Households	91.6	87.7	80.4	60.9	48.6	38.8	36.3
Open-End Mutual Funds	2.0	3.3	4.4	2.8	6.6	18.4	19.6
All Foreign Holders	2.0	2.1	3.0	4.2	6.3	10.3	13.6
Private Pension Funds	0.8	3.7	7.4	14.6	18.6	13.3	8.4
State-Local Government Retirement Funds	0.0	0.1	1.1	2.9	8.4	8.9	7.5
Insurance Companies	3.2	2.8	3.2	5.1	5.0	7.2	7.7
Exchange-Traded Funds						0.8	3.8
Bank-Managed Personal Trusts				7.4	5.4		
All Other Holders	0.5	0.4	0.5	2.2	1.1	2.2	3.1
Total	100.0	100.0	100.0	100.0	100.0	100.0	100.0

Notes: Values shown are year-end or quarterly dollar holdings, at market prices, as percentages of corresponding total year-end or quarterly shares outstanding. Detail may not add to totals because of rounding.

Source: Benjamin M. Friedman, "Economic Implications of Changing Share Ownership." *Journal of Portfolio Management*, 22 (Spring 1996): Board of Governors of the Federal Reserve System, Flow-of-Funds Accounts (2012).

By 2011 Q3, only 36.3% of equities were held by households, compared to 90% in the '50s and about 50% in the '90s.

Regulatory approach very retail oriented, mandated disclosures, limits on information distribution during public offerings, but private placement and 144A escape hatches.

U.S. Public Equity Capital Market

How Competitive is it?

Q3 2011 Competiveness Measures

	Measure	Historical Average	2007	2008	2009	2010	2011(Q3)
1.	U.S. Share of Equity Globally Raised in Public Markets (Thomson)	1996-2006: 32.2%	19.8%	23.6%	24.6%	30.0%	41.7%
2.	U.S. Share of Global IPOs by Foreign Companies (Broad Definition, By Value)	1996-2006: 28.7%	6.9%	1.9%	16.9%	14.2%	9.8%
3.	U.S. Share of 20 Largest Global IPOs	1996-2006: 5 of 20	0 of 20	0 of 20	2 of 20	1 of 20	3 of 20
4.	Rule 144A IPOs by Foreign Companies as % of Total Global IPOs in the U.S. (By Value)	1996-2006: 64.1%	87.9%	95.5%	70.2%	79.3%	80.1%
5.	% of IPOs by U.S. Issuers Listed Only Abroad	1996-2006: 1.3%	8.6%	20.0%	3.0%	5.2%	8.5%
6.	Equity Raised in the U.S. by Foreign Issuers via Rule 144A BONY ADRs*	2000-2006: $2.2 bn	$4.5 bn	$306 mn	$738 mn	$771 mn	$1.8bn†

† Projection based on Q3 data

Focus on a few measures (2011, Q3t):

U.S. share of global IPOs by foreign companies, 9.8% versus historical 28.7%

Most IPOs of foreign companies in U.S. are Rule 144A (see next slide), 80.1% versus 64.1%

U.S. IPOs only abroad (unheard of) 8.5% versus 0.3%

U.S. share of global market cap, 31.)% versus 45.7%, next slide

Q3 2011 Competiveness Measures

Measure	Historical Average	2007	2008	2009	2010	2011(Q3)
7. Equity Raised via Rule 144A ADRs as a % of Equity Raised by Foreign Issuers in the U.S Public Market	2000-2006: 10.2%	13.7%	5.0%	4.1%	3.8%	7.5%†
8. No. of Foreign Companies Cross-Listings in the U.S.	2000-2006: 18	5	3	5	7	12†
9. % of Foreign Companies Delisting from the NYSE	1997-2006: 4.8%	16.0%	5.0%	4.2%	6.0%	5.9%†
10. U.S. Share of Global Market Capitalization	1990-2006: 45.7%	32.8%	36.0%	32.4%	31.5%	31.0%
11. U.S. Share of the Value of Global Share Trading	1990-2006: 50.6%	50.2%	58.2%	50.2%	48.3%	48%†
12. ADR Trading Volumes as a % of Ordinary Share Trading Volumes in Home Markets	2001-2006: 17.7%	19.1%	18.3%	18.5%	22%	26.4%
13. U.S. % of Global Total of M&A Advisory and Equity/Debt Capital Market Underwriting Revenue by Client-Parent Nationality	1996-2006: 49%	42%	41%	37%	40%	40%

† Projection based on Q3 data

SUMMARY OF COMPETITIVENESS MEASURES					
Measure	Historical Average	2007	2008	2009	2010 Q1
1 U.S. Share of Equity Globally Raised in Public Markets (Thomson)	1996-2006 52.2%	19.8%	23.8%	24.6%	25.3%
2 U.S. Share of Global IPOs by Foreign Companies (Broad Definition By Value)	1996-2006 28.7%	8.9%	1.9%	16.9%	4.6%
3 U.S. Share of 20 Largest Global IPOs	1996-2006 5 of 20	0 of 20	0 of 20	2 of 20	7 of 20
4 Rule 144A IPOs by Foreign Companies as % of Total Global IPOs in the U.S.	1996-2006 64.1%	87.9%	95.5%	70.2%	64.7%
5 % of IPOs by U.S. Issuers Listed Only Abroad	1996-2006 8.3%	8.6%	20.6%	3.0%	3.4%
6 Equity Raised in the U.S. by Foreign Issuers via Rule 144A BONY ADRs*	2000-2006 $2.2 bn	$4.3 bn	$306 mn	$738 mn	$111 mn
7 Equity Raised via Rule 144A ADRs as a % of Equity Raised by Foreign Issuers in the U.S Public Market*	2000-2006 10.2%	13.7%	5.0%	4.1%	0.6%
8 No. of Foreign Companies Cross Listings in the U.S.	2000-2006 18	5	9	3	7
9 % of Foreign Companies Delisting from the NYSE	1997-2008 5.3%	18.0%	5.0%	5.1%	3.6%
10 U.S. Share of Global Market Capitalization	1996-2006 43.1%	32.6%	38.0%	32.4%	31.4%
11 U.S. Share of the Value of Global Share Trading	1990-2006 60.8%	46.0%	62.4%	58.1%	60.5%
12 ADR Trading Volumes as a % of Ordinary Share Trading Volumes in Home Markets	2001-2006 17.7%	19.0%	18.2%	18.6%	22.3%
13 U.S. % of Global Total of M&A Advisory and Equity/Debt Capital Market Underwriting Revenue by Client-Parent Nationality	1996-2006 49%	42%	41%	37%	42%

*Does not include Rule 144A equity directly issued by foreign companies. Source: Committee on Capital Markets Regulation

Focus on a few measures (2011, Q3, get new chart):

- U.S. share of global IPOs by foreign companies, 9.8% versus historical 28.7%
- Most IPOs of foreign companies in U.S. are Rule 144A (see next slide), 80.1% versus 64.1%
- U.S. IPOs only abroad (unheard of) 8.5% versus 0.3%
- U.S. share of global market cap, 31.)% versus 45.7%

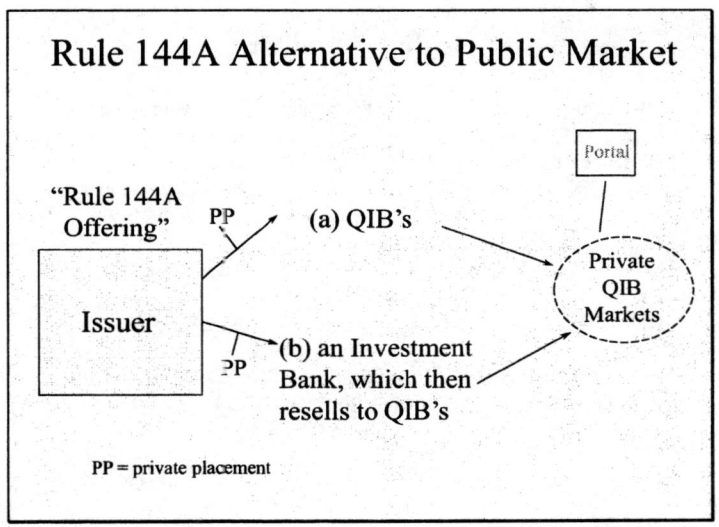

Reference

Rule 144A creates the possibility of issuing "liquid" securities in a non-public market for QIBs, institutions that invest at least $100 million on a discretionary basis in unaffiliated issuers' securities. Broker-dealers qualify if they invest $10 million or act as riskless principal for QIBs, and banks and thrifts if net worth of $25 million or more. Comment on Facebook issue with Goldman Sachs (solicitation prohibition).

Listing Premiums

- DKS 2007 find U.S. exchange listing premium (higher valuation than in U.K. Main Market) of 17% from 1990-2005 and cite as evidence of value of bonding to high U.S. standards
- Omits UK AIM market, biggest competitior for small companies (50% of AIM listings would qualify by size for U.S. listing)
- Reality: no one coming and many have left
- When control for quality of company, premium is 8% compared to 5% on OTC
- Higher premiums in competitive markets: AIM 27%, Hong Kong 80%
- Premiums do not persist (Canadian cross-listers study)
- Premiums have decreased since 2002, SOX, especially for small companies where there is a higher SOX impact

---

Listing Premiums

DKS (2007) find 17% premium. Leaves out AIM (although 25% of companies then qualified for NY listings, average capitalization in 2007 was over $50 million value of US). AIM improves regulation in 2007, beefs up Nomad regulatory system. Still pretty bad performance

Zingales (2007) shows only 3% over OTC, so not bonding

Marcelo Bianconi and Liang Tan, "Cross-Listing Premiums in the US and UK Destinations," Working Paper, January 2008, looks at cross-listings to US and UK by six Asian Pacific countries (Australia, China, India, Japan, Korea and Taiwan), and finds no difference in premiums when control for quality of firm (

Zingales and Litvak both show goes down after SOX, particularly for companies from countries with strong corporate governance—less benefit from bonding

Piotroski and Srinivasan (2007), goes down more after 2002 for small companies, disproportionate impact. Piotroski, Joseph D. and Srinivasan, Suraj, "The Sarbanes-Oxley Act and the Flow of International Listings" (April 2007),

U.S. Public Equity Capital Market

Why does the U.S. care about competitiveness?

See next slide after discussion

```
┌─────────────────────────────────────────────┐
│                                               │
│        U.S. Public Equity Capital Market      │
│                                               │
│                                               │
│        Why is it Losing Competitiveness?      │
│                                               │
│                                               │
│                                               │
│                                               │
│                                               │
│                                               │
│                                               │
└─────────────────────────────────────────────┘
```

Better foreign markets (and perhaps private markets, see Gao), more money outside U.S., litigation and regulatory system. Not time zone issue —only relevant to trading and can dual list. U.S. GAAP reconciliation was obstacle but abolished. Higher investment banking fees in primary offering, 5.6% gross spread compared to 3.5% in UK (but not material and different methodology, U.S. may result in better pricing).

Recent improvements? London cracks down (Conservatives increase regulation of City of London), flight to U.S. safety in crisis, maybe China main competitor now.

Foreign Issuers in U.S.

Why does the U.S. Care?

- Jobs and Taxes
- Canary in Coal Mine—our markets may be overly expensive for domestic companies
  - May make them uncompetitive with foreign competitors—means our issuers have higher cost of funds
  - Our own issuers may seek to do IPOs and trade elsewhere
  - May dampen venture capital due to lower rewards from public exits

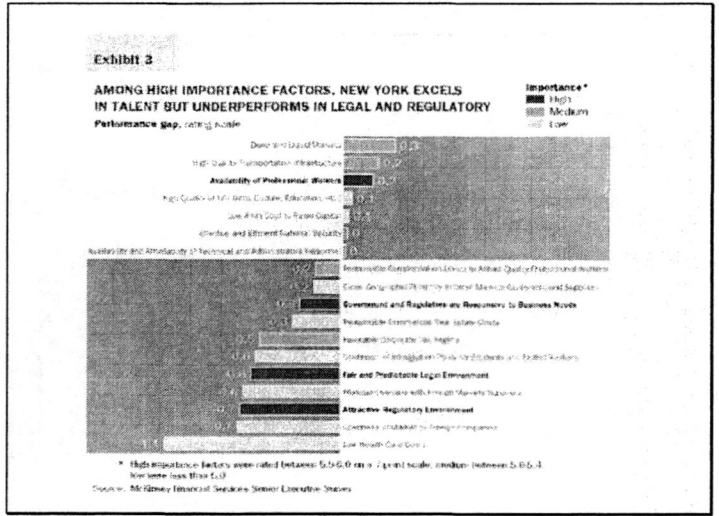

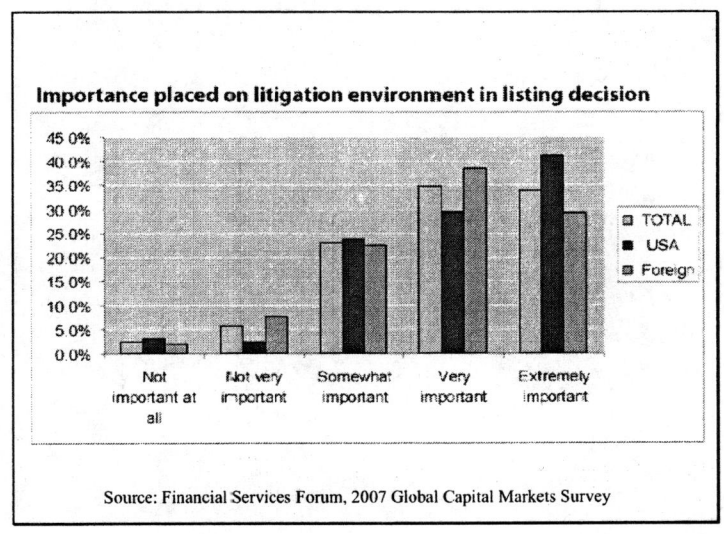

Source: Financial Services Forum, 2007 Global Capital Markets Survey

Securities class actions the major legal/regulatory issue

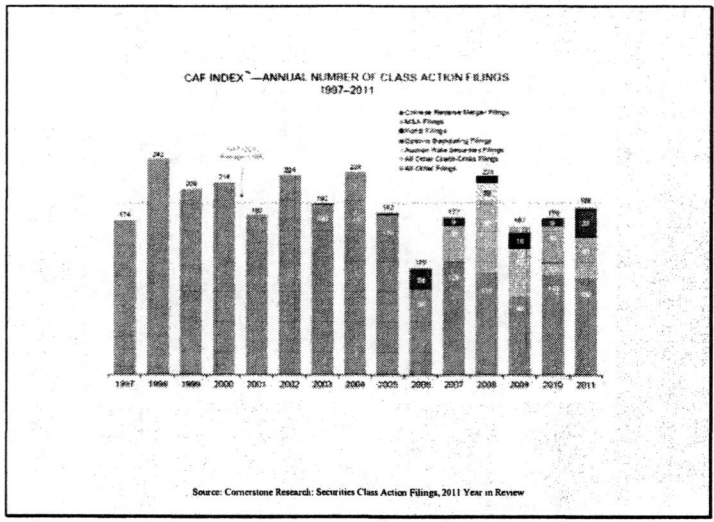

Filing have been going up again

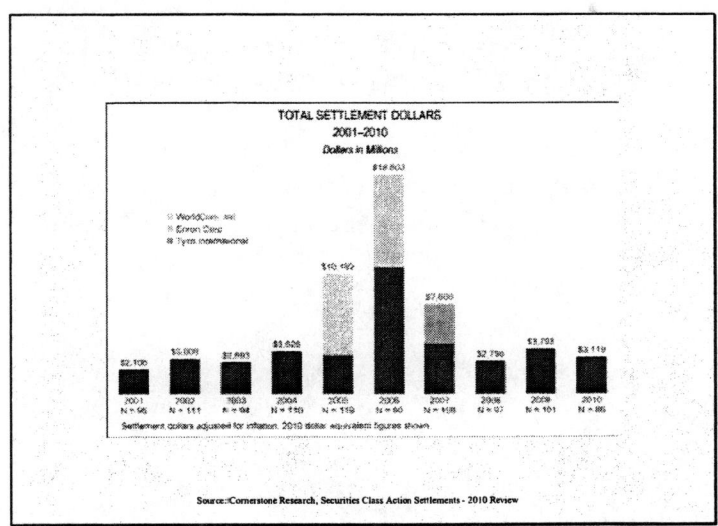

2010 settlements at $3.1 billion, down from aftermath of Enron but still significant

> The Regulatory System, Key Aspects:
> Help or Hindrance to Competitiveness?
>
> • Overall disclosure regime and Regulation FD
> • Deregistration of foreign companies
> • Board and auditor independence under SOX

- **Disclosure (fully foreign applicable)** Initial and ongoing disclosure requirements with high public enforcement. Establishes confidence, key prerequisite. Comes with high liability, so move to private markets (but more a function of litigation system than disclosure requirements). Short termism as a result of continuous disclosure (or at least earnings guidance, not required under disclosure rules).
- **Regulation FD (not foreign applicable):** Cuts off selective disclosure of material non-public information to analysts. Could result in less information, some indication that analyst coverage of small firms, particularly with complex information, has decreased. Less informed analyst forecasts. Was boon for credit rating agencies, more impact on market (now, no longer exempt under Dodd-Frank). However, studies have found no increase in volatility, indicating information flow is not less continuous. Only bars comunication by senior officials, leads to "expert networks" and possible insider trading violations (see recent prosecutions)
- **Excludes foreign issuers. Was this right decision?**
- **Deregistration** (next slide)
- **Board and Auditor Independence under SOX (modified foreign applicable).** (next slides)

SEC Foreign Company Deregistration Rule
Help or Hindrance to Competitiveness?

- Old Rule: foreign companies with more than 300 beneficial U.S. shareholders (more than 500 for companies with less than $10 million in assets) could not deregister and were subject to U.S. capital market regulation, including SOX
- New Rule (effective June 2007): allows deregistration under Old Rule (with easier methods to determine beneficial ownership) **or if issuer**
  - is reporting company for one year
  - has not made registered or unregistered offering within the last year
  - has maintained listing in home market for one year
  - and home market is primary trading market for its securities
    - Primary trading market is where 55% of average trading volume (ATV) occurs (in no more than two jurisdictions)
    - US ATV is no greater than 5% of ATV in primary trading market
- 15.1% of foreign companies (mainly European) delisted in 2007. Shows how foreign listings were inflated by blocked exit

More likely to come if leave but bad sequencing. Should have reformed our market first so that they would stay.

Sarbanes-Oxley 2002

- Most significant securities legislation since 1930s
- Many provisions, implementation through regulation
  - **Independent Audit Committees**
  - **Independence of outside auditors**
  - **Executive certification of financial statements**
  - **Disclosure of financial reporting and disclosure controls**
  - **Disgorgement of CEO and CFO compensation following restatement of financial statements**
  - **Internal controls, Section 404**
  - **Prohibition of insider loans**
  - **More continuous disclosure**
  - **Additional disclosure, e.g. code of ethics, off-balance sheet transactions**
  - **Mandated periodic SEC review of public company filings**
  - **New Accounting Oversight Board under SEC supervision**
  - **Enhanced criminal and civil liability provisions**
- Supplemented by corporate governance listing rules of the exchanges (SRO rule making), e.g. **majority of independent directors, independent committees**

Short intro to SOX, multifaceted.

NYSE Board Independence Requirements
(Manual Section 303)

- A majority of the Board must be independent (foreign companies must comply or summarily explain, approach in many foreign countries)
- Nominating, audit and compensation committees must all have only independent directors (tracks SOX): exception for foreign companies, e.g. labor representative or significant government shareholder is independent
- Every company must have a financial expert on the audit committee (applies to foreign companies—SOX only requires disclosure of whether there is an expert)
- Exceptions for controlled companies: any listed company of which more than 50% of the voting power is held by an individual, a group or another company need not have a majority of independent directors, nor compensation or nominating committees composed entirely of independent directors—must disclose its policy and that it is a controlled company
- New 2009 SEC rules requiring additional disclosures about board leadership structure, e.g. why/why not lead director, and role of board in risk oversight

How evaluate impact? By stock performance?

Performance measured by share value or Tobin's Q, basically market value/book value.

Black, no relationship (but study of UK and Canadian companies finds relationship), but may increase value in companies with dominant shareholders, might prevent abuses like backdating, e.g. avoid getting company in trouble. Basic issue of how to measure performance.

Increased costs of director fees; check the box mentality.

No other major market requires independent board, although practice followed in UK—little use of comply or explain alternative.

Non-measurable value in a crisis and in selecting CEO successor?

SEC Foreign Company Deregistration Rule
Help or Hindrance to Competitiveness?

- Old Rule: foreign companies with more than 300 beneficial U.S. shareholders (more than 500 for companies with less than $10 million in assets) could not deregister and were subject to U.S. capital market regulation, including SOX
- New Rule (effective June 2007): allows deregistration under Old Rule (with easier methods to determine beneficial ownership) **or if issuer**
  - is reporting company for one year
  - has not made registered or unregistered offering within the last year
  - has maintained listing in home market for one year
  - and home market is primary trading market for its securities
    - Primary trading market is where 55% of average trading volume (ATV) occurs (in no more than two jurisdictions)
    - US ATV is no greater than 5% of ATV in primary trading market
- 15.1% of foreign companies (mainly European) delisted in 2007. Shows how foreign listings were inflated by blocked exit

---

More likely to come if leave but bad sequencing. Should have reformed our market first so that they would stay.

Auditor Independence Requirements

- Independent from company audited
- Cannot provide auditing and consulting to same company, but can provide tax service. Some accounting firms spun off consulting (PWC), others did not (Deloitte)
- Rotation of audit partners, one year delay for acceptance of company job (considering requiring firm rotation as well)
- Strict liability with due diligence defense for public offerings
- Any auditing firm that participates in an audit of a U.S. company must register, as of January 2009, about 900. PCAOB is supposed to inspect such firms but has yet been unable to do so in China
- Partial reliance on inspections of foreign firms by foreign regulators, US relies on EU oversight

---

Do you agree with these requirements?

Hard to argue with requirement for independent auditors—market demanded long before the requirement, but unclear whether consulting limitation is good—seems to lower expertise and lead to more restatements. Independence plus concentration give auditors market power.

SOX 404

- Is SOX 404 a plus or minus for U.S. capital markets?

Start with what is SOX 404? (reference two following slides)

If costs exceed benefits may make our capital markets inefficient, burdening existing public companies, and deterring private and foreign companies from using our market. But integrity of market (will it catch fraud?).

Costs: audit and company costs, global SOX costs, concentration of auditing (reference slides)

Small companies with disproportionate impact. Small companies now covered for 2008 management certification and for outside outside audit in FY 2010.

SOX 404 Internal Controls

(a) **Rules Required** [inside auditors]

   The Commission shall prescribe rules requiring each annual report. . .to contain an internal control report, which shall—

(1) state the responsibility of management for establishing and maintaining an adequate internal control structure and procedures for financial reporting; and

(2) contain an assessment . . .of the effectiveness of the internal control structure and procedures of the issuer for financial reporting

(b) **Internal control evaluation and reporting** [outside auditors]

. . .each registered public accounting firm that issues the audit report for the issuer shall attest to and report on, the assessment made by the management of the issuer . . .

Reference

Liability

- Section 302 requires certification by CEO and CFO that they have fulfilled the obligations of Section 404
- Section 906 provides for criminal liability for knowing violation of certification requirements (up to 10 years) or for willful violation (up to 20 years)
- Auditors have long standing fraud liability for erroneous financial statements
- No private enforcement

SOX 404 Implementation for
Small, and Large Foreign, Companies

- March 2005, SEC extended compliance date for small companies (less than $75 million in market capitalization) and all foreign companies by one year, from July 15, 2005 to July 15, 2006
- September 2005, extended for another year, to **July 15, 2007**, for <u>small</u> companies, domestic and foreign; in August 2006, did same for medium sized foreign companies ($75 million to $700 million market cap)
- December 2006, extended all small companies to **December 15, 2007** [no cost-benefit study]
- February 2008, extended to 2009 results (on 2010 statements) only <u>outside</u> audit assessments for all small companies, pending cost-benefit study (follows House vote requiring this); after cost-benefit study completed in September 2009, extended one final time—the new deadline was for fiscal years ending on or after June 2010.
- **Dodd-Frank exempts small companies from outside audits**

Costs of Section 404

- SEC 2003 cost estimate, $91,000 per issuer
- The Financial Executives International survey of 217 firms with average revenues of $5 billion, found average cost of $4.51 million per firm (audit costs increase by 58%) in first year, down to $2.92 million in 2006 and to $2.74 in 2007; Zhang $1.4 trillion in market value losses from SOX
- SEC web-based survey of publicly traded companies completed in September 2009 finds pre-2007 (before reform) average cost of $2.865, post-reform $2.329, currently (2009), $2.030; 69% of costs are for internal rather than external audit. Benefits were not quantified but found to be positive.
- Management opportunity costs—spending time on controls rather than making money
- Going private and not going public distorts capital allocation
- Change business decisions—less risk, e.g. change in IT systems
- Competitive costs compared with foreign firms: countries have internal controls requirements but not certification with liability, more principled-based
- New PCAOB tougher policy on outside audit firms will further increase costs

Cost-Benefit Under Dodd-Frank

- Financial regulatory agencies, e.g. SEC or CFTC, generally have obligation to do cost-benefit analysis although the exact nature of their obligations differ
- Unlike cabinet departments, the cost-benefit analysis of independent agencies is not reviewed by the Office of Information and Regulatory Affairs (OIRA) within the Office of Management and the Budget (OMB)
- As the proxy access decision of the D.C. Circuit indicates, *Business Roundtable v. SEC*, 647 F.3d 1144 (2011), rules can be invalidated due to inadequate cost-benefit analysis.
- Of the 192 rules promulgated under Dodd-Frank as of November 16, 2011is reporting company for one year
  - 57 have no cost-benefit analysis
  - 85 have no quantitative analysis (often the agencies say they expect the costs to be minimal)
  - 50 have some quantitative analysis but the vast majority are limited to paperwork cost as compared to economic impacthas not made registered or unregistered offering within the last year
- This means that all of these rules are exposed to court invalidation resulting in vast uncertainty over the implementation of Dodd-Frank

Why so little cost-benefit analysis? Accelerated timetable, most rules had congressional deadline of one year from enactment of DF, i.e. July 2011 (but many have missed deadline with no consequences), lack of agency resources (SEC agency of lawyers), hard to do (what are quantitative benefits of financial stability but can do costs).

Audit Firm Concentration

- Serious concentration problem of top four audit firms: Deloitte & Touche, Ernst & Young, PriceWaterhouseCoopers, and KPMG audit 78% of all U.S. companies, and 97% of those with sales of more than $250 million—might result from liability and drive 404 intensity
  - Each of the 4 firms have significant claims against them that exceed their capital that are uncovered by insurance
- Means companies have very little choice in auditors (some of the 4 may not be available due to conflicts prohibited by SOX, e.g. do consulting, or would not meet independence standards)
- This gives existing auditor tremendous pricing leverage over its client for 404 and other tasks
- This also means that another "Andersen" could further concentrate the industry (see DOJ's decision not to prosecute KPMG for selling fraudulent tax shelters)
- Is new entry likely to cure this problem? Should we cap auditor liability or allow indemnity as in U.K., or permit incorporation?

Benefits of Section 404: Difficult to Quantify

- Restore investor confidence
  - Nicolaisen, ex Chief SEC accountant: "Representing to the world that a company has in place an appropriate control system, free of material weaknesses, that gathers, consolidates, and presents financial information strengthens public confidence in our markets and encourages investment in our nation's industries. If that's the case then its worth it, and it is absolutely critical that we get the internal control requirements right."
- Better credit ratings?

SOX 404

- Did the 2007 SEC and PCAOB
  implementation reforms of SOX 404 go far
  enough? What more should be done?

What are the reforms? (next slide)

Further reforms: (a) quantitative materiality standard (CCMR 5% of pre-tax gross income; (b) auditor limitation of liability through caps (with capital disclosure), indemnities, incorporation, safe harbor for professional judgment; (c) no coverage for small companies where has disproportionate impact (management as well as outside auditors) unless clearly justified by cost-benefit analysis; and (d) exempt foreign companies, if have requirement of some type in home country (mutual recognition approach).

Internal Controls, PCAOB Auditing Standard No. 5, May 2007, Major Changes

- Materiality change, top-down approach
- Tailor to type of firm
- Better guidance—focus on material controls
- No need for auditors to evaluate management process
- More permitted reliance on work of others, e.g. internal auditors and consultants
- More permitted reliance on prior audits

**Internal Controls Over Financial Reporting,
PCAOB Auditing Standard No. 2, March 9, 2004**

• Detailed provision (161 pages) describing audit standards for accountants

• **Material Weakness** is "a significant deficiency, or combination of significant deficiencies, that results in more than a <u>remote</u> <u>likelihood</u> [a reasonable possibility, AS 5] that a material misstatement of the annual or interim financial statements will not be prevented or detected."

• Materiality: reasonable person would change opinion if knew facts, not very helpful generally or with respect to internal controls

• CCMR: 5% or more impact on pre-tax income

```
┌──────────────────────────────────────────────┐
│                                                │
│              Private Enforcement               │
│                                                │
│      What reforms would you make?              │
│                                                │
│                                                │
│                                                │
│                                                │
│                                                │
│                                                │
│                                                │
│                                                │
│                                                │
└──────────────────────────────────────────────┘
```

Big impact on public capital markets based on surveys (FSF, McKinsey)

Private Enforcement

Securities class actions: weak case on compensation (present shareholders pay class shareholders, benefit went to shareholders that sold in class period); circularity for institutional shareholders; small percentage of damage in settlements, 2-3%, only small fraction of settlements actually collected by class members. Also have questionable case for deterrence: large public recoveries, criminal sanctions ($3.8 billion in 2006, $1.6 billion in 2007); between 2004-2008, SEC penalties and disgorgements were $12.9 billion (Annual Report 2008);class suits do not uncover fraud, piggyback on public investigations, do wrongdoers in company really care about prospective corporate liability, abuses (paying plaintiffs to bring suits, contributing to campaigns of potential public plaintiffs (pay-to-play).

Supreme Court cutting back: *Tellabs* (scienter in 10b-5) and *Stoneridge* (scheme liability, cites briefs that cite CCMR report)

Reforms: clarify 10b-5, allow shareholder to modify by-laws to opt-out of system (arbitration, no jury trials, no class actions, require opt-in class actions, Carlyle initiative in IPO), fee-shifting (loser pays), tighten procedures (see potpourri of reforms suggested by Financial Services Roundtable, large banks)

Public Enforcement

What reforms would you make in the various components of our public enforcement system— civil enforcement by the SEC, SROs and the states, and criminal enforcement by the Department of Justice and the states?

Civil Enforcement

SEC should be more prudential, like US bank regulators and UK FSA, needs more economists

Enforcement priorities should not be shaped solely by concerns of retail investor protection, especially in an increasingly institutional and global market; pay more attention to efficiency

Limit fines to cases of shareholder benefit and deep wrongdoing

Constrain role of states (preemption as for national banks, or defer to SEC/DOJ in matters of national importance).

Criminal

Collateral consequences of company prosecutions, Arthur Andersen—handled by deferred prosecutions (corporate monitors, reputation damage)?

Filip Memorandum: no consideration of waiver of corporate attorney-client privilege or agreement not to pay defense costs in charging (waiver held unconstitutional anyway)

Long individual sentences

Civil fines on individuals may lead to more deterrence

Federal Preemption of State Securities Laws

- State registration requirements preempted where large public offering under federal law and shares are listed on an exchange
- Most (some exceptions) securities fraud class actions must be brought under federal law (restrictive) in federal courts
- Preemption of state regulation of broker-dealers with respect to capital, custody, margin, financial responsibility, records, bonding and reporting requirements to the extent such regulation differs from or is in addition to federal law
  - based on idea that dual regulatory system was unnecessary because it is redundant, costly and ineffective

But States still have power to bring civil and criminal enforcement actions for fraud against securities firms

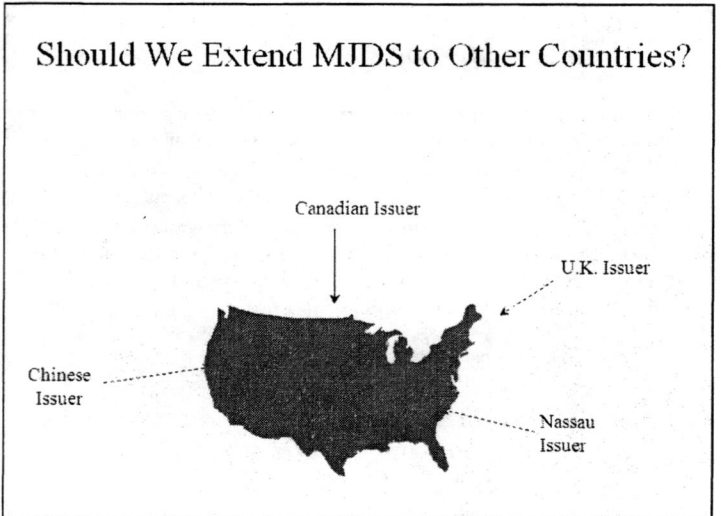

Former Governor (former AG) Spitzer

Reference

International Accounting Standards: IFRS

- EU adopted IFRS in 2005 (without provisions of IAS 39 on hedge accounting)—now home-country rules of European issuers
- EU permits foreign companies to use "equivalent" standards (previously allowed US GAAP without condition); in 2007, Commission says U.S. and other local GAAPs acceptable for countries that have adopted IFRS for foreign companies before 2011 (includes U.S.), after 2011 will have to meet equivalence standard
- December 2007, SEC decided to accept IFRS (as formulated by IASB) without reconciliation in 2008 (for 2007 results)—was this the right decision?
- SEC's November 2008 Roadmap proposes to allow certain U.S. companies (largest in industry whose foreign cohorts use IFRS) in 2010 (for fiscal year 2009), with reconcilement to US GAAP during transition. Envisions determination in 2011 as to whether to mandate IFRS for all U.S. companies in 2014 (not yet adopted)—should it do so for any or all companies? Why not yet adopted?

<u>IFRS for foreign companies without US GAAP Reconciliation-deferral to home country rules</u>

Convergence Project (will not be completed for several years, if ever). Substantial differences, and thus reported income, remain.

Will they protect U.S. investors as well as U.S. GAAP? (principles versus rules; enforcement)—not much difference, US GAAP not clearly better (see Leuz, Neuer Market study)

Will more principles-based rules work in U.S. litigation environment?

Continuing funding/independence concern of IASB; too European dominated

If not applicable to U.S. firms, comparison and competitive issue

If SEC did not do, EU would have retaliated by banning US GAAP from EU

<u>IFRS option/requirement for US companies</u>

Competitive consideration re foreign IFRS users: U.S. companies could achieve operational and cost of capital reductions

Required use: unclear general demand, good to have alternative competing systems, bad to have multiple systems for cost and comparability, small public companies will not want to incur conversion costs

Key Pending Accounting Issues
(for FASB and IASB)

- **Fair Market Value**
  - Under attack, particularly in Europe
  - Bank regulators bankers concerned with volatility (but SEC says not significant in total bank losses during financial crisis)
  - Hard to determine for non-actively traded (Level 3) assets
  - CCMR recommended dual disclosure (credit and market value), FASB (FAS 157) proposes range of disclosures—could be alternative balance sheet presentations
- **RAP v. GAAP:** former FASB Chair Hertz advocates separation, do you agree?

International Standards: IOSCO Disclosure Rules

- Adopted by U.S. in 1999: Revised Form 20-F for foreign issuers

- How significant to removing obstacles?
  - Harmonizes only basic business data
  - Key issues not harmonized, e.g. materiality, business segments, forward-looking statements
  - Did not address GAAP reconciliation
  - Does not address corporate governance, distribution and enforcement

Lecture, move to discussion of international standards

Home Country Rules: The U.S. MJDS

- MJDS generally permits Canadian issuers to issue securities in U.S. market under Canadian rules, subject to some substantial qualifications
- Also permits U.S. issuers to issue securities in Canada under Canadian rules

Lecture

MJDS: Qualifications to Home Country Rules

- Canadian foreign private issuers (real Canadians)
- Only investment grade debt
- Large portion of traded stock: Public float of > $US 75 million
- Foreign private issuer
- U.S. 10b-5 fraud liability (not Section 11)
- Supplemental disclosure
  - English translation (Quebec)
  - Corporate indemnities
- U.S. auditor independence requirements
- U.S. GAAP reconciliation (no longer)
- Sarbanes-Oxley applies in same way as to other foreign listed firms

Reference

1. Canadian issuers only. *Reason*: similar disclosure regime, large amount of foreign issues in U.S. market is Canadian (one-half of all foreign debt and equity offerings from '77-'86), close coordination between regulators.

2. Only investment grade debt. *Reason*: less risk to U.S. investors (cannot be used under DF ratings).

3. Substantial issuers and public float: as of 1993, market capitalization requirements dropped, but public float (excludes insiders) of at least $75 million U.S. (rather than Canadian, as previously). *Reason:* less non-disclosure risk to U.S. investors.

Foreign private issuer (next slide definition)

U.S. fraud liability. *Reason*: protection of U.S. investors.

Supplemental disclosure requirements where U.S. is not willing to accept Canadian regime (these narrowed as the proposal evolved)

8. Sarbanes-Oxley applies

> ## What is a Foreign Private Issuer?
>
> - More than 50% of shares owned by non-U.S. shareholders; and
> - More than 50% of Directors and Officers non-U.S. and more than 50% of Assets non-U.S. or
> Business administered principally outside U.S.
>
> Make sure company is really foreign.

Reference

Extending MJDS to Other Countries

- Major Concerns of Divergence from U.S. standards
  - Level and manner of disclosure (race to bottom)
  - Weaker and more difficult enforcement by home country, unclear role for enforcement by host country
- U.S. issuers would have tougher standards than foreign issuers
- Weak Tea: SEC 2008 Mutual Recognition approach: secondary market focus, permit U.S. investors to trade stock on foreign markets subject to home country rules and permit foreign brokers to deal with "certain" U.S. investors under foreign rules (have started with MOUs on supervision and enforcement with Australia); no progress since 2008
- Portable reciprocity: issuer can select law of any country (Choi-Guzman)—more radical than MJDS because opens up to laws of all countries on any issue

---

Regulation S: General Conditions for Exemption

• Offshore transaction

— buyer is or reasonably believed to be abroad and sale offshore, **or**

— sale on physical trading floor of an established foreign exchange (primary distributions are normally off exchanges—not a practical alternative)

• No "Directed Selling" in U.S.

Lecture

Registration is not triggered by selling to a U.S. investor, as long as the buyer is outside the U.S., one can demonstrate that the sale is outside the U.S., and that there was no attempt to get U.S. investors in the U.S. to go abroad ("directed selling efforts"). Basically, if nothing is done in the U.S., U.S. law will not apply--this is a territorial approach.

The first general condition provides that issues made abroad are never immediately available to U.S. investors in the U.S..

**Regulation S: Specific Offering and Transaction Conditions
Depend on Issuer Category: Purpose is to Prevent Sales to
U.S. Persons During Distribution**

Category	Offering Restrictions	Transaction Restrictions
I: Foreign Issuer Only: one country issue or no substantial U.S. market interest	None	None
II: Equity of Reporting foreign issuer, and Debt of a Reporting issuer or Non-reporting foreign issuer	Legends: not registered in U.S. and no sale in U.S. without registration or exemption	40 day restriction (after issue) on sales to U.S. person

Lecture

The Regulation S exemption may require the issuer to comply with additional offering or transaction restrictions if it is likely that a U.S. person (here or abroad) will actually buy foreign issued

Factors making it likely: U.S. issuer or substantial U.S. market interest (SUSMI) in the foreign issue because there is U.S. trading activity: depends whether U.S. is main market for foreign issuer's securities or whether company is already reporting company under '34 Act.

Review Categories

Restrictions: procedural safeguards to make sure no U.S. person, even if transaction is abroad, is buying the securities. For example, buyer must certify not U.S. person, legends on the securities. Strength and duration of restrictions depends on likelihood of flowback.

Even if Category I (most European issues, because trade mainly in home market) can buy immediately after IPO completion, U.S. persons still excluded from buying at fixed IPO price in primary distribution.

Regulation S (continued)		
Category	Offering Restrictions	Transaction Restrictions
III: All other issuers (including equity of all U.S. issuers)	Same as for II, plus	40 day restriction on debt sales, and 1 year for equity sales.
	-Certification by purchasers that they are not U.S. persons. -Legends barring retransfer except in accord with U.S. law. -Charter bars share registration except in accord with U.S. law.	

Does this system make sense?

Regulation S Reform

- Scott Proposal
  - Objective: provides for use of offshore markets to achieve uniform rules on disclosure and distribution (not enforcement rules)
  - Drop Regulation S for foreign issuers
  - Minimum disclosure required
  - Allow direct selling in U.S.

My proposal is another way to go for primary markets, and Steil proposal backed by Council on Foreign Relations would allow foreign exchanges to have screens in U.S. offices thereby making it easier for U.S. investors to trade shares on foreign exchanges, possible reform for secondary markets.

TEACHING PLAN FOR

CHAPTER TWELVE
ASSET SECURITIZATION AND THE CREDIT CRISIS

POWERPOINT SCREENS FOR NINETEENTH EDITION

Securitization

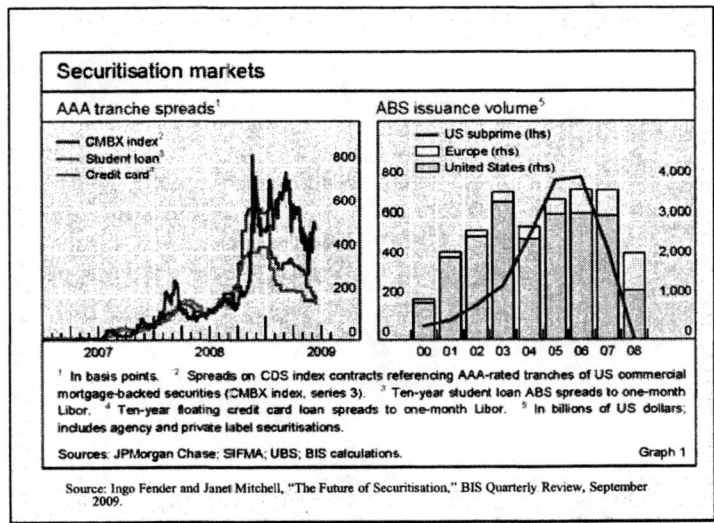

Securitisation markets

AAA tranche spreads[1]

- CMBX index[2]
- Student loan[3]
- Credit card[4]

ABS issuance volume[5]

- US subprime (lhs)
- Europe (rhs)
- United States (rhs)

[1] In basis points. [2] Spreads on CDS index contracts referencing AAA-rated tranches of US commercial mortgage-backed securities (CMBX index, series 3). [3] Ten-year student loan ABS spreads to one-month Libor. [4] Ten-year floating credit card loan spreads to one-month Libor. [5] In billions of US dollars; includes agency and private label securitisations.

Sources: JPMorgan Chase; SIFMA; UBS; BIS calculations.   Graph 1

Source: Ingo Fender and Janet Mitchell, "The Future of Securitisation," BIS Quarterly Review, September 2009.

    All asset-backed securities, mortgages, auto loans etc. Spreads in 2010 now normal, around 2007 levels, but issuance volume still down. $146 billion in 2009, $107 billion in 2010. Compare with right scale, US high over $3 trillion in 2006. Supported in November 2008 to June 2010 by Fed under TALF (term asset backed loan facility). Doing somewhat better in 2011. No subprime.

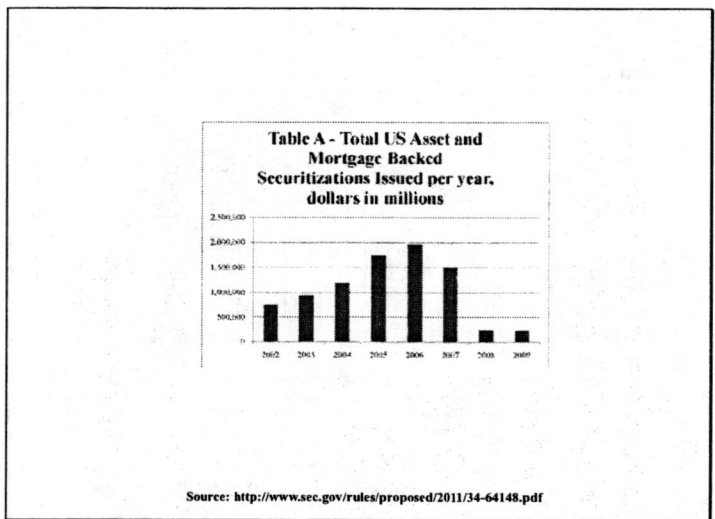

Mortgage backed securitizations way down, means less loans to home buyers, chicken or egg?

Table D - Total US Asset and Mortgage Backed Securitizations Issued per year (dollars in millions)

Source: http://www.sec.gov/rules/proposed/2011/34-64148.pdf

Mortgage securitizations not only securitizations that dropped off, e.g. credit cards down from $72.5 billion in 2006 to $6.1 billion in 2010, totals down from $1.9 trillion in 2006 to $168 billion in 2010, more than 10 fold.

Table 1: Market Description of Mortgage Categories

Attribute	Prime	Jumbo	Alt-A	Subprime
Lien Position	1st Lien	1st Lien	1st Lien	Over 90% 1st Lien
Weighted Average LTV	Low 70s	Low 70s	Low 70s	Low 80s
Borrower FICO	700~ FICO	700+ FICO	640-730 FICO	500-660 FICO
Borrower Credit History	No credit derogatories	No credit derogatories	No credit derogatories	Credit derogatories
Conforming to Agency Criteria?	Conforming	Conforming by all standards but size	Non-conforming due to documentation or LTV	Non-conforming due to FICO, credit history, or documentation
Loan-to-Value (LTV)	65-80%	65-80%	70-100%	60-100%

Source: Gorton, Gary B., The Subprime Panic (September 30, 2008). Yale ICF Working Paper No. 08-25.

Different mortgage categories

Down payment inverse of loan to value, if loan to value is 70%, down payment is 30%

Agency criteria refer to Fannie and Freddie

Table 4: Mortgage Originations and Subprime Securitization

	Total Mortgage Originations (Billions)	Subprime Originations (Billions)	Subprime Share in Total Originations (% of dollar value)	Subprime Mortgage Backed Securities (Billions)	Percent Subprime Securitized (% of dollar value)
2001	$2,215	$190	8.6%	$95	50.4%
2002	$2,885	$231	8.0%	$121	52.7%
2003	$3,945	$335	8.5%	$202	60.5%
2004	$2,920	$540	18.5%	$401	74.3%
2005	$3,120	$625	20.0%	$507	81.2%
2006	$2,980	$600	20.1%	$483	80.5%

Sources: Inside Mortgage Finance, The 2007 Mortgage Market Statistical Annual, Key Data (2006), Joint Economic Committee (October 2007).

Source: Gorton, Gary B., The Subprime Panic (September 30, 2008). Yale ICF Working Paper No. 08-25.

Over 80% of subprime securitized.

Table 2: Non-Agency MBS Outstanding

| Year | Outstandings in $ Billions | | | | | | Percent of Total MBS | | | | |
| | | | Non-Agency Outstanding | | | | | | Non-Agency Outstanding | | |
	Total MBS	Agency	Total	Jumbo	Alt-A	Subprime	Agency	Total	Jumbo	Alt-A	Subprime
2000	3,003	2,625	377	252	44	81	87%	13%	8%	1%	3%
2001	3,409	2,975	434	275	50	109	87%	13%	8%	1%	3%
2002	3,802	3,313	489	256	67	167	87%	13%	7%	2%	4%
2003	4,005	3,394	611	254	102	254	85%	15%	6%	3%	6%
2004	4,481	3,467	1,014	353	230	431	77%	23%	8%	5%	10%
2005	5,201	3,608	1,593	441	510	641	69%	31%	8%	10%	12%
2006	5,829	3,905	1,926	462	730	732	67%	33%	8%	13%	13%
2007Q1	5,984	4,021	1,963	468	765	730	67%	33%	8%	13%	12%

Source: Federal Reserve Board, Inside MBS& ABS, Loan Performance, UBS

Non-agency was up to about 33% before crisis, now negligible. 2010 non-agency was 3%. Consequences, no competition for underwriting standards, story about having enough money in your account for down payment 20 days before closing, silly underwriting standard, CYA.

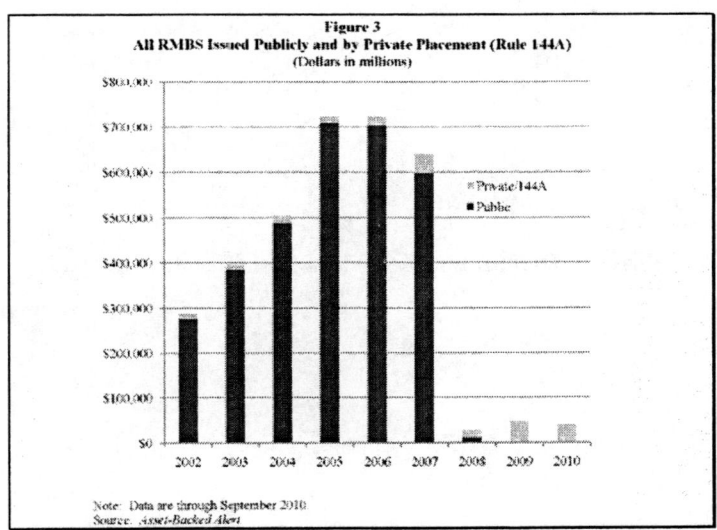

Figure 3
All RMBS Issued Publicly and by Private Placement (Rule 144A)
(Dollars in millions)

Note: Data are through September 2010
Source: *Asset-Backed Alert*

Almost all RMBS issued in public not private markets—wider range of investors; CDOs were all private market

---

Securitization and the Credit Crisis

Why Do Originators Securitize and Investors invest?

<u>Originators</u>

    Diversification but correlations of all RMBS were high

    Capital and risk reduction

    Revenue, more turnover

    Get rid of junk to unsuspecting investors

<u>Investors</u>

    Diversification

    Yield, if more risk

<u>Societal Value</u>

    Facilitates consumer borrowing (supports expansion of home ownership):

        In 2001, 61% of all mortgages were securitized; by 2007, the figure had reached 74%. Now entire market has dried up. Hinders rebound of home   prices.

    Reduces bank risk, in theory (credit crisis would be worse absent securitization)

    Tranches may increase total value through better matching of investor preferences and further reduce cost of original loans

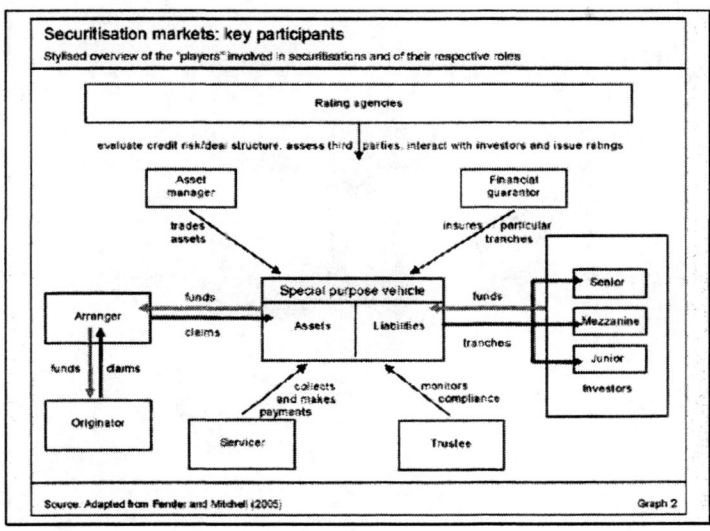

Reference to how it works

Mention possibility of overcollateralization, value of assets exceeds liabilities

What is the "waterfall" on the tranches, next chart

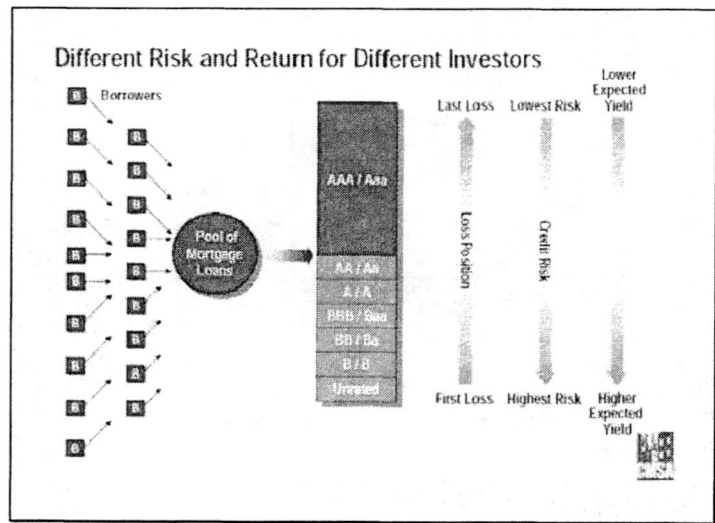

Explain chart: AAA, last loss, lowest risk and lowest expected yield; bottom of waterfall is the opposite: first loss, highest risk and highest expected yield

Initial and tracking of underlying loans

Can have AAA tranche of subprime pool because predicted default rate of pool not 100%. Percentage of the pool that can be AAA is much less than for a pool of conforming loans.

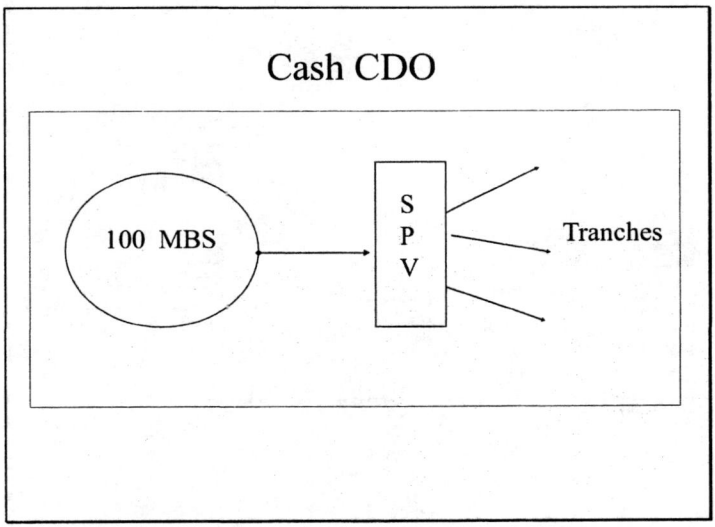

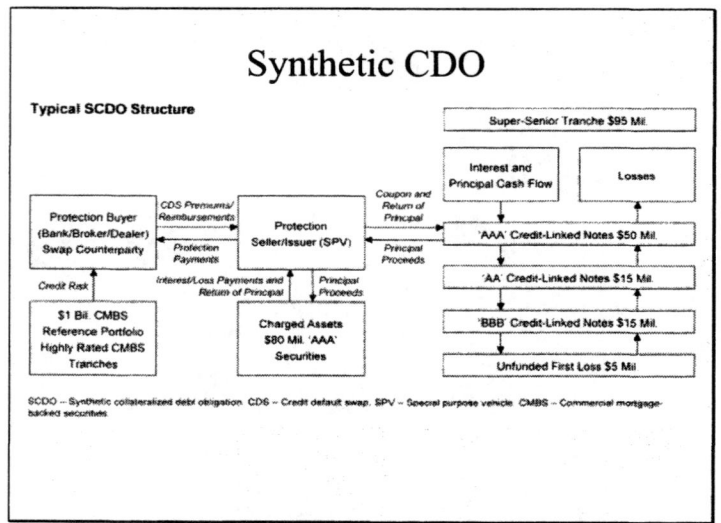

Protection buyer wants protection on CMBS portfolio—the protection seller's obligation is securitized into various tranches.

Here dealing with CMBS versus RMBS but same idea

Super Senior separate tranche (ignore): unfunded (separate collateral)

Charged assets: collateral (for risk that protection seller will not be able to honor commitment): greater to extent unfunded (investor has not actually paid)

Payments to securities holders from premiums on CDS; could lose either principal or interest if protection buyer defaults or if have to make protection payments (collateral requirements could increase as likelihood of protection increases, portfolio or reference portfolio decreases in value)

Securitization and the Credit Crisis

Is The Securitization Model Fundamentally Flawed?

Model is originate to distribute

Skin in the game problem: originators do not bear risk, so no incentive to reduce risk. But investors should police and underwriters should control. Over reliance on credit rating agencies.

Some evidence that securitized loans are riskier even with similar characteristics, e.g. the same FICO scores (but FICO scores may not be reliable). Is it bad to securitize riskier loans?

Could be improvements in disclosure, see ASF and CRA recommendations on loan-by-loan disclosures. CDO disclosure problem more difficult but solvable in digital information world. Regulation AB problem of limited scope (did not include CDOs so no standards set). Should disclosure requirements apply to Rule 144A distributions?

What about issuer pays? Viable any other way? Some empirical support that issuer pays leads to higher ratings. When Moody's switched from investor pay to issuer pay in 1971, and S&P still employed investor pay, Moody's ratings were higher by 20% of a rating grade, which could result in 10% yield decrease (but ratings may not be comparable due to different methodologies, bond market response unknown—could discount for conflict, not clear what "true" rating is, would have to look at which were more accurate in retrospect.

Perhaps biggest problem is lack of due diligence.

Also have to get capital requirements correct

Skin in the Game

- Dodd-Frank requires that regulators require originator/securitizer to retain at least 5% of the credit risk on any securitized asset [941(c) (1)] Exempts: qualified residential mortgages (debate about required down payment, 20% as proposed) and those subject to adequate "due diligence", plus further broad exemptive power entrusted to regulators
- Different methods to align incentives other than risk retention
  - Representations and warranties: hard to detect violations, issuer may be bankrupt and unable to honor (ASF trying develop third party more automatic enforcement)
  - Overcollateralization (L=100, A=110)
  - Third party guarantor: guarantor may go bankrupt (see problem during financial crisis), theory is guarantor will monitor risk
  - Conditional cash flows back to originator/servicer only if performance targets met, e.g. low delinquency rate
  - Note different asset classes have traditionally different mix of incentives
  - Credit risk retention options: 5% of each loan, 5% vertical slice of tranches, 5% slice of equity tranche, 5% of representative sample
- How about capital requirements?
- Accounting problem: under FAS 167, if originator/securitizer retains too much risk, pool could be consolidated for accounting purposes on its balance sheet (primary beneficiary test, turns on control and exposure to gains and losses), would trigger higher capital requirements

QRM: requirements at odds with the realities of today's housing market, where in 2010 only 16 percent of first-time buyers and 37 percent of repeat buyers would have qualified for QRM status.. Counting both groups together, fully 75 percent of 2010 home buyers would not have qualified for this quality of loan.

International Problems

- EU approach could differ in important respects from U.S. approach: (1) different skin in the game rules; (2) requirements to control issuer pays, e.g. investor pays or government controls ratings process; (3) no sovereign ratings in exceptional circumstances (shelved)
- How deal with differences internationally? EU says can only use ratings of foreign credit ratings agencies if their regulation is at least as stringent as EU regulation

---

QRM: requirements at odds with the realities of today's housing market, where in 2010 only 16 percent of first-time buyers and 37 percent of repeat buyers would have qualified for QRM status.. Counting both groups together, fully 75 percent of 2010 home buyers would not have qualified for this quality of loan.

The FDIC's Safe Harbor

- Uses safe-harbor from consolidating and then dishonoring obligations of SPV in a bank bankruptcy to require that asset securitizations meet certain requirments (currently based on "true sale" finding but that has been undermined by new FASB consolidation accounting rules, FAS 167)—will give way to later joint-rule-making
- Across the board 5% credit risk retention, through 5% of every loan or of vertical slice of pool
  - Same rules for different asset classes (Fed study suggests wrong)
  - Added disclosure requirements
  - Servicer rights to mitigate losses (currently none)
  - Deferred compensation for servicer based on performance
- Role of FDIC versus SEC?

Securitization and the Credit Crisis

What Should We Do About The Ratings Agencies?

Depend on market discipline, some companies and structured products no longer getting rated

Registration

More disclosure by sponsors to agencies and by agencies to public (methodology and performance), SEC September, 2009..

Increase liability: DF increases liability, 10b-5 applies with negligence standard not recklessness and Section 11 expert, so in distribution liable for bad ratings unless does due diligence. Resisted liability for years on free speech ground. More class actions, could have restricted liability to public enforcement

Business model, issuer pays promotes conflict, but would buyer pays be any better, also conflict

EU, prevent from rating sovereign debt?

Credit Ratings Purge

- Dodd-Frank (DF) §939A prohibits regulators from relying on ratings in regulations, e.g. investment grade requirement for MJDS, shelf registrations, permissible investments for MMFs, capital requirements. Is this practical?
- CCMR comment letter filed on February 3, criticizes substitute approach in capital requirements (Basel still uses credit ratings, estimated 50% less capital) for securitizations (blunt methodology, at least 20%) and sovereign debt, OECD ratings (conflict of interest)

Not in reading, part of liability story.

The Public Offering Issue

- Dodd-Frank (DF) treats credit ratings as "expertised" parts of registration statement, resulting in strict liability for the rating agencies. DF also repealed SEC Rule 436(g) which provided that ratings agencies need not consent to the inclusion of their ratings in a registration statement
- The SEC requires ratings in public offerings of ABSs but also provides that experts must consent to use of their opinions in a registration statement (with repeal of 436(g) ratings agencies were now covered by this general requirement)
- Ratings agencies refuse to give consent for fear of liability and SEC waives requirement for inclusion for six months, and has extended indefinitely
- Ratings are still provided to investors by the issuer through a "free writing prospectus" which is not, under SEC rules, incorporated into the registration statement. Exemption of certain communications from inclusion in registration statement thought to increase communication with and information for investors.

Not in reading, part of liability story.

TEACHING PLAN FOR

CHAPTER THREE
International
Aspects of
U.S. Banking Markets

POWERPOINT SCREENS FOR NINETEENTH EDITION

International Banking

International Banking

Importance of Foreign Banks in U.S.

How important are they?

- As of December 2010, 194 branches and 50 subsidiaries out of total 7,657 federally insured institutions. Held about $3 trillion in assets, 23% of total U.S. banking assets of $13 trillion, 62% of which was in branches (mainly state-chartered, 146 of 188), 31% in subsidiaries (rest in agencies).

Funded from U.S. banks, so not bringing money here—but supply cheaper lending to foreign companies whom they know better.

Size and structure of banks' foreign operations

Positions at end-2007

Banking system		BE	CA	CH	DE	ES	FR	IT	JP	NL	UK	US
Number of banks[1]		18	17	23	1,601	98	136	724	106	49	17	33
Total assets ($bn)[2]		2,218	2,437	3,810	10,985	4,341	8,390	4,180	9,845	4,649	10,696	9,984
Asset concentration[3]		94.9	72.4	89.3	60.5	62.9	96.1	70.8	62.3	92.6	75.3	58.5
Foreign claims ($bn)[4]		1,608	912	3,390	5,177	1,416	4,456	1,543	2,571	2,962	4,375	2,285
over total assets (%)		72	37	89	49	31	53	37	26	64	44	22
over annual GDP (%)		346	63	776	155	98	173	72	58	378	157	16
US dollar share (%)[5]		23	70	60	32	36	33	10	48	33	42	52
Foreign claims, by office location (%)[6]	Home entry[7]	42	23	15	44	27	54	38	75	27	44	22
	UK	4	16	30	22	28	6	6	6	20		25
	US	6	41	23	6	9	12	3	5	12	16	
	Euro Area	37	2	4	16	18	15	35	2	23	11	7
	OFC[8]	2	9	21	7	2	8	2	8	6	14	24
	Other	8	7	4	4	24	50	17	3	13	15	22
Assets booked by foreign offices (%)[9]		42	26	80	27	22	27	19	7	47	29	21

[1] Number of banking groups (headquartered in the country shown in the columns) that report in the BIS consolidated banking statistics.   [2] Total assets (including "strictly domestic assets") aggregated across BIS reporting banks. For reporting jurisdictions which do not provide this aggregate (DE, ES, FR, IT, JP), total assets are estimated by aggregating the worldwide consolidated balance sheets (from BankScope) for a similar set of large banks headquartered in the country.   [3] Share of total assets accounted for by the five largest reporting institutions.   [4] Foreign claims as reported in the BIS consolidated banking statistics (immediate borrower basis) plus foreign currency claims vis-à-vis residents of the home country booked by home offices (taken from the BIS locational banking statistics by nationality). See footnote 9 in the main text. Excludes inter-office claims.   [5] Total claims (cross-border claims plus claims on residents of the host country) booked by offices in each location over total worldwide consolidated foreign claims.   [6] Excludes banks "strictly domestic" claims, or their claims on residents of the home country in the domestic currency.   [7] Offshore financial centres: here Bahamas, Bahrain, Bermuda, the Cayman Islands, Guernsey, Hong Kong SAR, the Isle of Man, Jersey, Macao SAR, Panama and Singapore.   [8] Share of total assets (row 2) booked by offices outside the home country.

Sources: IMF IFS; BankScope; BIS consolidated statistics (immediate borrower basis); BIS locational banking statistics by nationality.

Safety and Soundness of Foreign Banks

- Safety and soundness regulation prevents or limits the effect of bank failure
  - Ex ante: examination, capital requirements, activity restrictions (e.g., limitations on loans to single borrowers, or commercial activities)
  - Ex post: Dealing with failed banks (e.g. deposit insurance, resolution procedures, bailouts)
- Adequacy of **foreign** safety and soundness regulation of foreign banks operating in the U.S. through <u>branches</u> is a major concern of U.S. since foreign banks are primarily regulated by their home countries

---

Two historical cases with foreign banks in the U.S. illustrate the difficulties a host country has regulating them and explain the evolution of safety and soundness rules for foreign bank operations in the US (and elsewhere): BCCI and Daiwa.

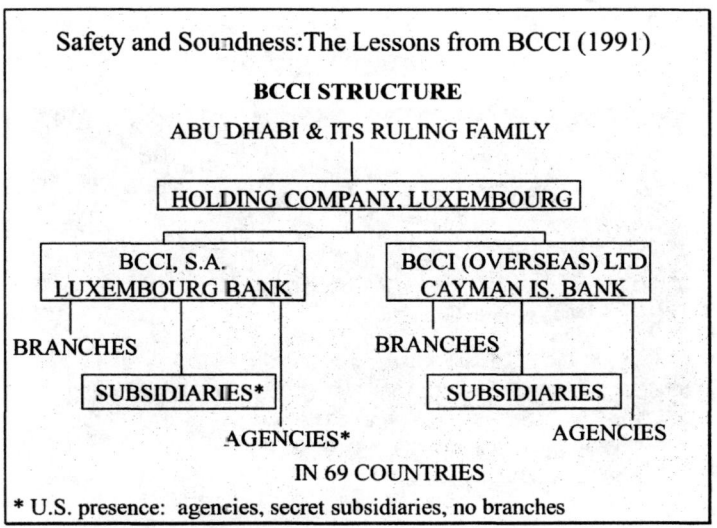

Safety and Soundness:The Lessons from BCCI (1991)

Describe organization. Both banks become insolvent even after Abu
Dhabi, owner and lender of last resort (injected capital); also injects funds
in bankruptcy to increase recovery of creditors. BCCI ownership of US
banks kept secret because Fed might not have approved. Huge
investigation in Congress of this after failure. Former Secretary of
Defense Clark Clifford was the lawyer for BCCI. No U.S. depositor
losses (agencies took wholesale deposits but liabilities covered by U.S.
assets)

Its too bad we couldn't be on a field trip today to visit one of the former
locations of its banks. Next slide.

Cayman Islands

If you look closely, you will see recent IF students making a site visit.

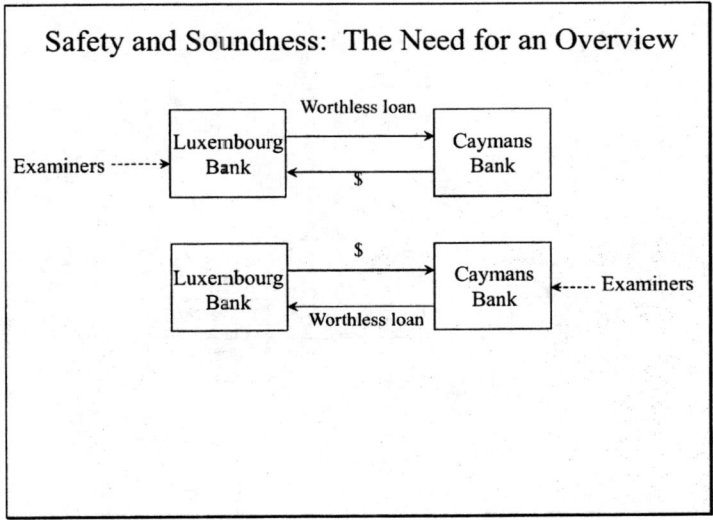

Safety and Soundness: The Need for an Overview

One problem is that each bank can help the other hide worthless loans.
BCCI did this. Plus locate in jurisdictions with poor examinations.

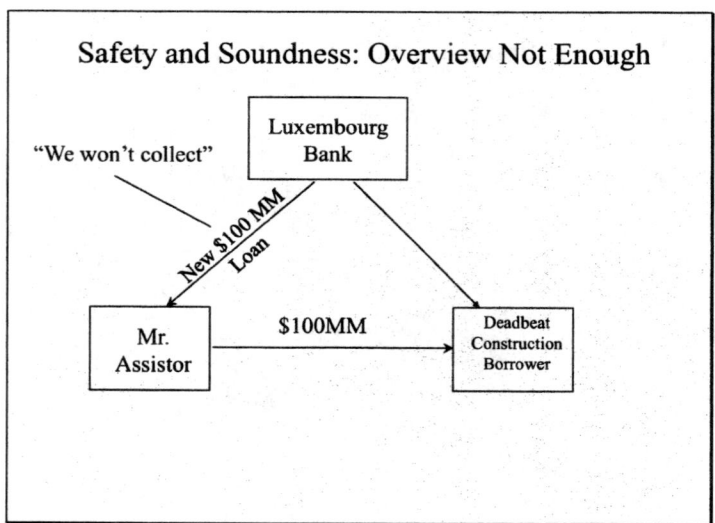

A bank can also use a friendly outsider as another way to get around the supervisors.

Here, the Luxembourg Bank has a loan that will not be repaid because of cost-overruns on construction (right side). It cannot lend more to the borrower directly because of lending limits to single or distressed borrowers, but wants to keep construction project going to avoid default, and hopes completed project will be profitable and lead to payback of loan. So it lends instead to Mr. Assistor (left side) with a promise to him not to collect from him and a promise from him to lend the funds on to Deadbeat Borrower.

Consolidated supervision cannot stop this problem. U.S. banks have been facilitators of window dressing.

What are the Lessons of BCCI?

Discuss, see next slide

What are the Lessons of BCCI?

- Concern with solvency of foreign bank
- Need for foreign bank entry/exit controls (branches particularly—U.S. adopts after BCCI)
- Need for "effective" foreign supervisors (Luxembourg had no examiners—U.S. requires after BCCI)
- Need for lender of last resort (Abu Dhabi—no formal requirement)
- Branches of foreign banks should not take U.S. insured deposits (U.S. changes regime, forces insured deposits to be taken through subsidiaries)
- Need consolidated supervisor for overview (U.S. adopts after BCCI)—next slide for problems

Consolidated Supervision Problems

- Who is the overall regulator (choice of country)?
    - Holding company incorporation (e.g. Luxembourg)
    - Major business (U.K.)
    - College approach (who is the head?)
- Role of home versus host country (Basel Concordat); home country cannot easily inspect branches
- Secrecy: How does consolidated supervisor get information on operations in Nassau?

General Discussion
Consolidated supervision:

  College of supervisors: UK, Lux, Spain, Switzerland (HK and Cay. Is. 1989). It coordinated closing BCCI July 5, 1991. Major approach in EU.
  Does Reg K solve this problem? "Effective consolidated supervision"
  Reg. K §211.24(c)(1)(ii). Foreign supervisor needs enough information about the bank's worldwide operations to assess its overall financial situation. This includes: (1) ensuring that bank has adequate monitoring procedures; (2) obtaining information about the foreign offices and subs; (3) obtaining information about intra-corporate transactions; (4) getting consolidated financial reports; and (5) evaluate prudential compliance of the bank worldwide.
  There are also discretionary standards the Fed can employ, 221.24(c)(2). Fed -- may check (1) home consent, (2) financial resources, (3) managerial resources, (4) degree bank shares information with supervisors, (5) bank's assurances it will provide information; and (6) bank's compliance with US law.
Secrecy: Big host or home countries banding together can pressure countries like Nassau to end strict secrecy requirements, and there is an ongoing effort on this. The BIS "Minimum Standards" of 1992 say home and host regulators need the "right to gather information" and allow homes to "impose restrictive measures" if necessary to get the

information. Even Nassau has announced that it will respond to demands for better information. Can cut off access to foreign markets.

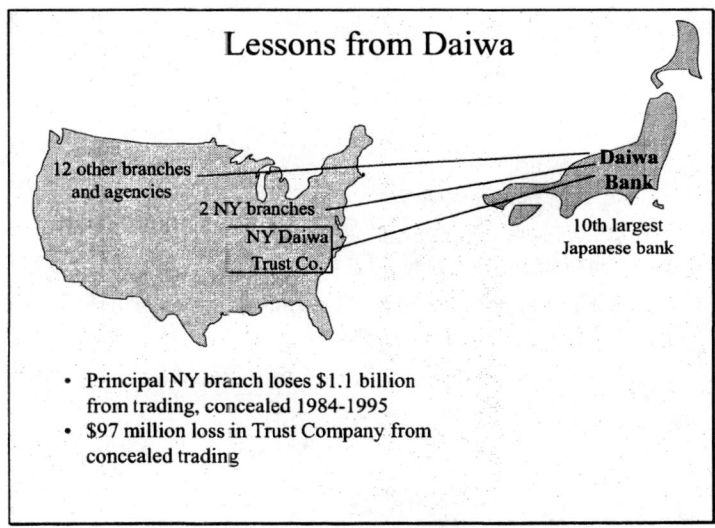

Lessons from Daiwa

12 other branches and agencies

2 NY branches

NY Daiwa Trust Co.

Daiwa Bank

10th largest Japanese bank

- Principal NY branch loses $1.1 billion from trading, concealed 1984-1995
- $97 million loss in Trust Company from concealed trading

Daiwa

- Why does U.S. care about NY branch or Trust Company losses?
- The U.S. penalties: too harsh?
  - Plea bargain on criminal charges for $340 million in fines (charged with $1.3 billion)
  - Criminal convictions (jail and fines) of branch manager and rogue trader
  - All Daiwa operations in U.S. terminated (sold to Sumitomo)

---

1. US cares about both branch and Trust: Daiwa violated US law by lying to examiners, saying they fixed the problem when they had not separated front and back office operations as they promised the regulators. Daiwa also did not promptly report the losses, but concealed them.

   But the US rules that Daiwa broke assume that the US should care about the prohibited behavior. Why? US does not insure Daiwa's deposits because wholesale branch. It might be worried about uninsured deposits, but Japan at that time guaranteed its banks' solvency and Daiwa had plenty of capital, no systemic risk
   One might argue that the US as host should rely on Japan's supervisors, who (unlike the US) could see the whole picture (eg., trading losses covered up with phony intra-corporate transactions). But Japan did not examine branches (like most countries); in effect Fed doing this for Japan.
- MOF wanted to wait until the problem was fixed before revealing it to the US. MOF could argue that it alone was responsible.
  Does all this come down to US law violation even if Daiwa did no specific harm?

   Termination of Daiwa's license is draconian. It seems aimed at MOF, which told Daiwa to delay reporting to the US. But compare this to MOF's penalties against Credit Suisse First Boston. CFSB had marketed Mr. Assistor schemes to Japanese banks with big bad loan problems. The

effect was to cover up huge bad loans of Japanese banks in a systematic way. This cost Japanese taxpayers billions. It was much more harmful to Japan than what Daiwa did in the US. Japan suspended DSFB's banking business, but not its securities license. The Fed kicked out the entire Daiwa organization.

International Rules in Banking

- Basel Concordats (BIS Committee): General Allocation of Authority Between Home and Host Countries for Subsidiaries and Branches of Foreign Banks
- International Financial Architecture Initiatives, e.g. Basel Core Principles (harmonization), mainly aimed at LDCs
- Basel Supervisors Committee Rules on Bank Capital (later in course)
- 1997 General Agreement on Trade in Services (GATS)
    - Key Purpose: remove barriers to entry for foreign financial institutions
    - Key Principle: most-favored nation (MFN)
    - Has achieved limited results

**More international than Securities: compare
IOSCO disclosure and IFRS**

Summary.

Global Financial Markets

Can you have global financial markets and national regulation?

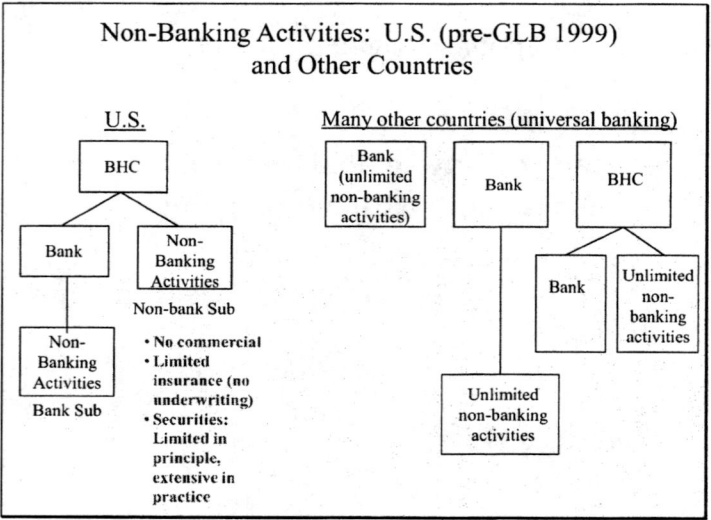

Review chart.
Extensive in practice, government securities in bank, not engaged principally in Section 20 affiliate.

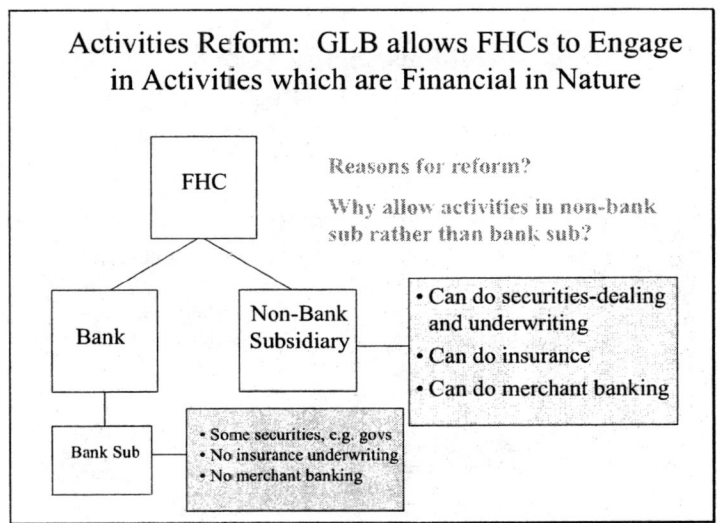

- Reasons for reform: diversification, competitiveness, not riskier than lending; Volcker against, Summers for. Volcker says insured deposits and lender of last resort should not be at risk for non-banking activities.
- Why allow activities in non-bank sub rather than bank sub? The arguments, mainly advanced by the Fed were that bank subsidiaries enjoy the subsidy of the safety net (deposit insurance, too big to fail resolutions) and that there is more risk to the bank from the failure of subsidiary than an affiliate (the latter failure just impacts the holding company). But reputational risk may result in bank rescue, see SIV rescues during financial crisis

3. Are foreign financial holding companies treated the same? Yes, generally, in U.S., but not overall. They can do most anything abroad: Under Regulation K, a QFBO (more than half of its worldwide business in banking and most of its assets and revenues outside the U.S.) can engage in virtually any activity outside the United States, e.g. own a car company.

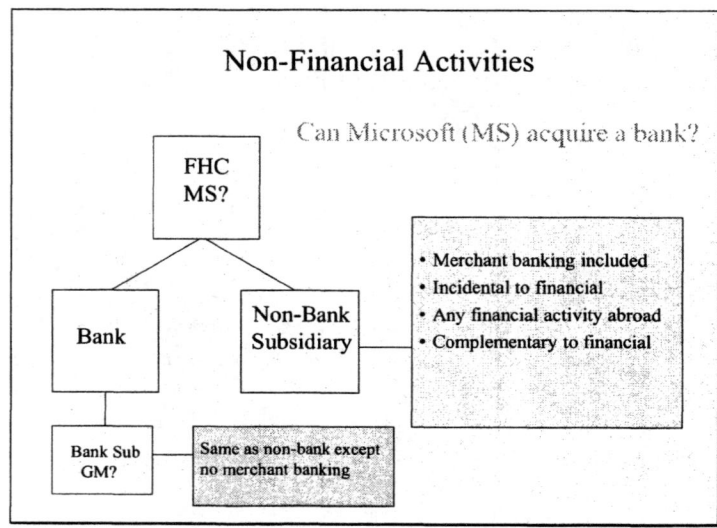

First alternative, use DP authority: Under GLB, FHC can engage in any activity in U.S. that it is allowed to engage in abroad, and it is allowed to do DP for third parties on an unlimited basis abroad (even though 30% of revenues domestically). But is MS only DP?

Second alternative, use merchant banking authority: Can hold commercial companies for over 10 years. But currently would have to deduct 50% of the cost of acquisition from FSHC capital, and up to 25% (Tier I) under the proposal. Could be show stopper if acquires big enough bank, but MS may be so well capitalized does not make a difference. FSHC generally have to have 10% capital, and commercial firms generally have to have much more.

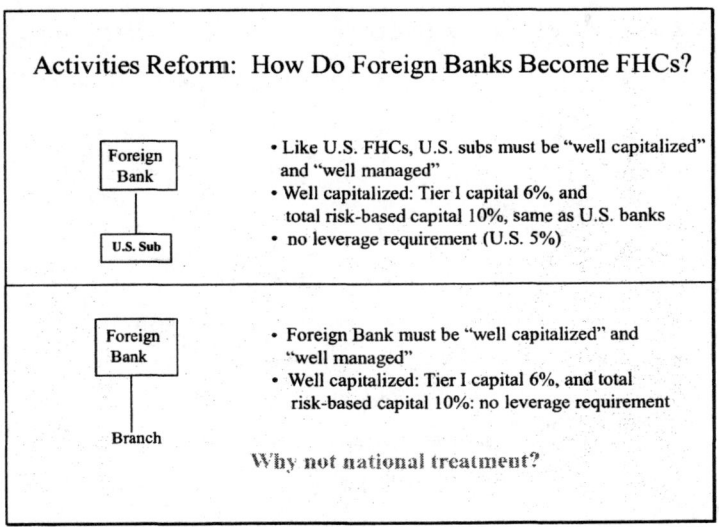

Comment on no leverage requirement. Fed originally proposed 3%, for subs as compared with normal US 5%, but dropped, December 21, 2000. Arguments: Better than national treatment, because no leverage requirement under international capital standards (changing post-crisis to 3%).

Branches operate under home country rules and no longer take insured deposits. Capital adequacy for branches is really only home country concern. Large uninsured U.S. depositors at risk if another country does not bail out (Japan has now rescinded absolute guarantee and other countries don't have one).

As of May 2010, there were 525 FHCs, 48 of which were foreign.

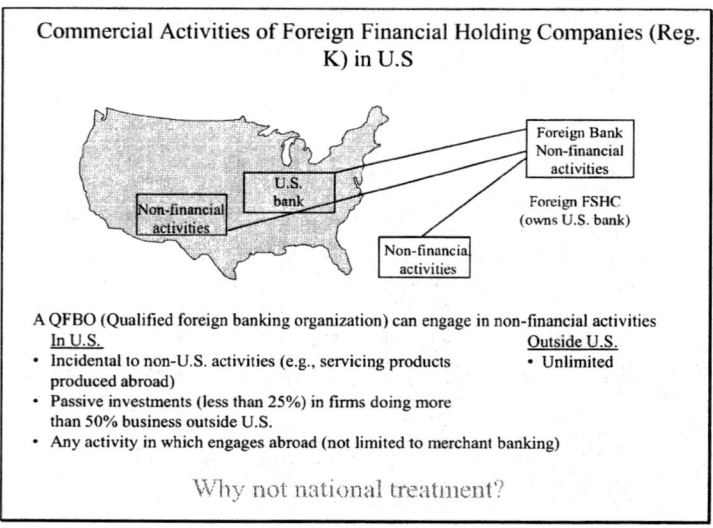

Commercial Activities of Foreign Financial Holding Companies (Reg. K) in U.S

A QFBO (Qualified foreign banking organization) can engage in non-financial activities

In U.S.
- Incidental to non-U.S. activities (e.g., servicing products produced abroad)
- Passive investments (less than 25%) in firms doing more than 50% business outside U.S.
- Any activity in which engages abroad (not limited to merchant banking)

Outside U.S.
- Unlimited

Why not national treatment?

Foreign banks can do much more in the commercial area than U.S. FSHCs, both in and outside the U.S. if they qualify as QFBOs which are banking organizations that have more than 1/2 of their business as banking (disregarding U.S. banking operations) and more than one-half of their business outside U.S. Real foreign banks (Citicorp might qualify, but Fed would probably stop). After GLB, restrictions on foreign bank financial activities have been dropped since U.S. institutions can now engage in the full range of these activities.

Volcker Rules

- The Volcker Rules, Dodd-Frank §619, prevent deposit-taking banks or their affiliates from engaging in "proprietary trading" or investing (more than 3% in a fund and overall 3% of their capital) in private equity or hedge funds, effective 12 months after date of final rules or two years after enactment (July 2012), whichever is later (applies to all transactions in U.S., including those of foreign banks)
- There were even broader proposals: McCain-Cantwell, S.2886 (December 16, 2009) would have brought back all Glass-Steagall limitations without the Section 20 ("engaged principally" affiliation loophole) and with no exception for government securities

What is the rationale for the Volcker prohibition?

- Rationale for ban on prop trading: too risky for banks, involves conflicts of interest. But residential mortgage loans were more risky, actually reduces risk through diversification, and had nothing to do with the financial crisis (estimated that it accounted for less than 5% of the 1.67 trillion in credit losses—and some banks, e.g. GS, made money on it).
- Conflicts of interest: what is it? Tell customer to go short and you go long. Are customers naïve? Do banks owe customers a fiduciary duty? Worse than lending? Make X a loan and then buy protection that exceeds value of loan? Underwriting only for companies that take loans; low price on underwriting to protect itself against risk. Business is full of conflicts of interest, put aside when Glass-Steagall repealed.

Are we just forcing activity into relatively less regulated part of financial system which can expose us more to systemic risk? (see next three slides)

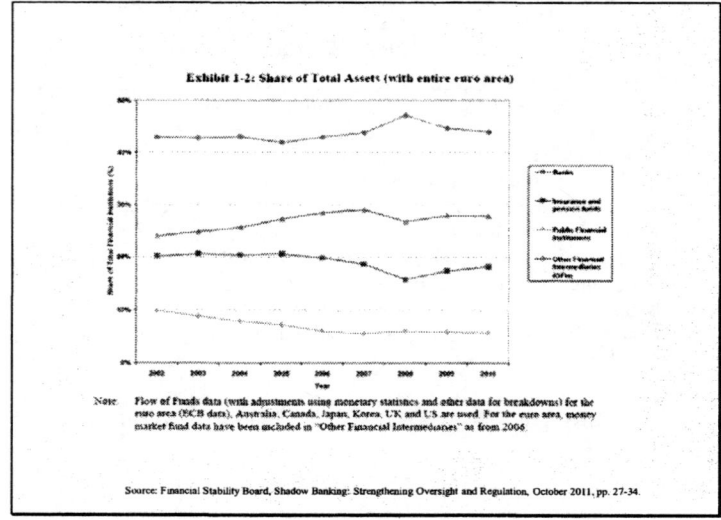

Exhibit 1-2: Share of Total Assets (with entire euro area)

Note: Flow of Funds data (with adjustments using monetary statistics and other data for breakdowns) for the euro area (ECB data), Australia, Canada, Japan, Korea, UK and US are used. For the euro area, money market fund data have been excluded in "Other Financial Intermediaries" as from 2006.

Source: Financial Stability Board, Shadow Banking: Strengthening Oversight and Regulation, October 2011, pp. 27-34.

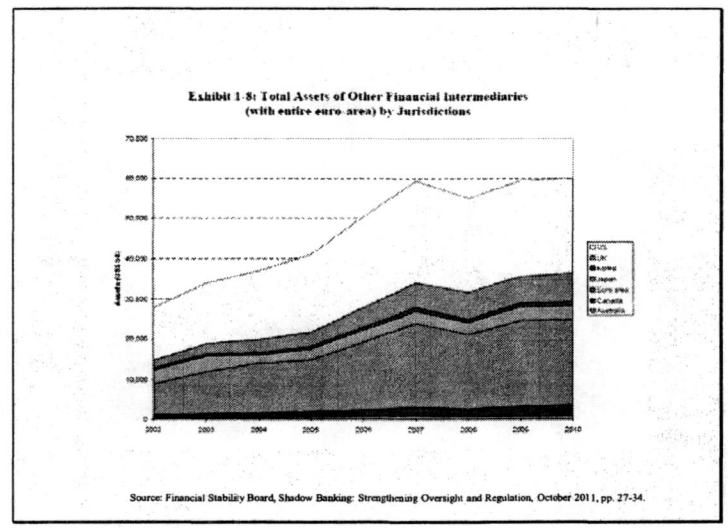

Exhibit 1-8: Total Assets of Other Financial Intermediaries
(with entire euro-area) by Jurisdictions

Source: Financial Stability Board, Shadow Banking: Strengthening Oversight and Regulation, October 2011, pp. 27-34.

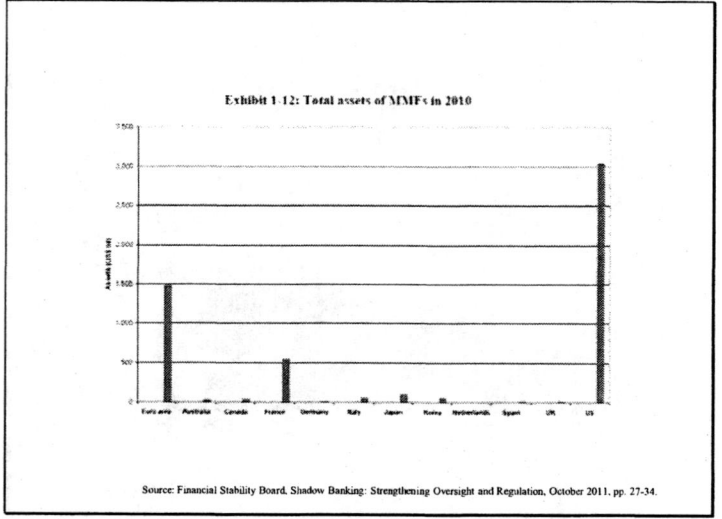

Exhibit 1-12: Total assets of MMFs in 2010

Source: Financial Stability Board, Shadow Banking: Strengthening Oversight and Regulation, October 2011, pp. 27-34.

Volcker Rules, Private Funds

- No sponsorship or investment in private equity or hedge funds
- Double 3% exception (in a fund, of total capital)
- Banks account for 10% of private equity investment, limitation could have major impact

What is the rationale of these prohibitions?

- Nothing to do with crisis, not a source of losses, not more risky than lending

Never really articulated in the legislative debate.

Volcker Rules – Proprietary Trading

- What is proprietary trading? Is it definable?
  - Engaging as a principal for the "trading account"
  - in any transaction to purchase or sell, or otherwise acquire or dispose of, any security etc.
  - Certain exclusions, e.g. market-making or hedging, make line drawing difficult—Merkley-Levin (authors) say market makers seek to profit by fees, prop traders by value of investment, and only market makers take short-term positions

---

Volcker Rules:"Trading Account,"§619(h)(4)

"(4) PROPRIETARY TRADING.—The term 'proprietary trading', when used with respect to a banking entity or nonbank financial company supervised by the Board, means engaging as a principal for the trading account of the banking entity or nonbank financial company supervised by the Board in any transaction to purchase or sell, or otherwise acquire or dispose of, any security, any derivative, any contract of sale of a commodity for future delivery, any option on any such security, derivative, or contract, or any other security or financial instrument that the appropriate Federal banking agencies, the Securities and Exchange Commission, and the Commodity Futures Trading Commission may, by rule as provided in subsection (b)(2), determine.

Defined in the rule but does not include portfolio investment, like long-term holdings of MBS, only those traded in the trading book. These are positions held for short-term price movements.

Volcker Rules: Prop Trading Exceptions, §13(d)

- Trading in U.S. government securities (foreign governments protest inclusion of their securities, does not cover many state and agencies, both could be exempted by regulation)
- Purchases for underwriting or market-making
- Risk mitigating hedging
- Transactions on behalf of customers
- Investment in small business investment corporations, or qualified rehabilitation or certified historic structure projects (investments, not trading)
- Transactions by a regulated insurance company and its affiliates for its general account

Volcker Rules: Market Making Exception

- Internal compliance program to make sure not proprietary trading
- Trading desk must hold self out as willing to buy and sell (maintain quotes on both sides with respect to liquid positions, on a "continuous" basis)
- Aimed at "near term demands" of clients, customers and counterparties (does not work for less liquid instruments or inventory needed for block trades)
- Designed to generate fees from spreads or commissions not appreciation of held position (what if net long or short?)
- Risk-neutral compensation
- Conform to extensive guidance (Appendix B)

Maybe clearer but impinges on what is regarded as market-making today

---

Volcker Rules: Economic Impact

- **Small Loss Reduction:** Will not prevent losses in financial crisis, 95% of $1.67 trillion in losses of U.S. banks not due to "proprietary trading"—those were due to bad mortgage lending or losses on ABS portfolio securities
- **Impact on Bank Earnings:** During 2006-2010 GAO finds proprietary trading .2% - 3.1% of revenues of six largest U.S. banks. Institute of International Finance says may depress bank earnings by $3.5 - $4 billion per year; limits diversification
- **Compliance Costs:** OCC estimates compliance costs will be $1 billion per year
- **Market Impact:** U.S. Chamber of Commerce estimates will impose at least a 5 basis point increase in bid-ask spreads, just measured over an $8 trillion corporate bond market, this would be $40 billion (Oliver Wyman much higher, $360 billion but methodology criticized)

What is international impact of Volcker Rules? (next slide)

Volcker Rules: International Aspects

- U.S. branches of foreign banks cannot trade in their own sovereign debt (protests from Canada, Europe and Japan)
- No banks (U.S. or foreign, in or outside of U.S.) can do proprietary trading if a party to the transaction is a U.S. resident or an execution facility is in the U.S. Thus, UBS in Switzerland could not do a proprietary trade with a U.S. hedge fund (may be changed)
- Foreign banks subject to fund investment limitations where invest in funds in turn invested in by U.S. investors even if investment takes place outside U.S.
- U.S. banks will find it difficult to compete with foreign banks abroad
- No other country has followed U.S. lead (UK through Vickers Committee permits non-retail banking in affiliate with wholesale funding), raising significant competitive problems for U.S. banks (need to offer range of services to major international customers, reason for GLB)

Volcker Rules: Process Issues

- No cost-benefit analysis in proposed rule
- Hundreds of questions in 298 page rule: specificity versus discretion
- Statute provides for latest effective date of July 2012 but implementing regulation may not be ready by then
- Two-year conformance period (from July 2012) but regulators have made recordkeeping and compliance efforts immediate (even though may not know what they are until weeks before they become effective)
- Will Republican President favor repeal and if so would Democrats in Senate block?

Should we impose size limits (not Volcker)?

See issues on next slide

Size Limits (not Volcker)

- DF provides that liabilities of a financial company cannot exceed 10% of all liabilities of such companies through mergers and acquisitions (extends 10% deposit cap for banks)
- Are U.S. banks too big to save (TBTS)? Johnson, 6 largest U.S. banks are 63% of GDP, 26 largest banks have 75% of assets
- Thrift crisis in 80's: correlation systemic risk from multiple failures of small poorly managed thrifts: takeaway was that we needed mergers
- Are certain U.S. banks too big to fail (TBTF) or too systemically important to fail or too likely to cause contagion if they fail (see FSOC, SIFI and FSB, G-SIB approach)? Should we cap total assets/GDP of individual banks? Just more capital?
- Are there economies of scale for large banks? Johnson, no economies of scale over $100 billion in assets. Clearing House Association study: per year of banks over $50 billion in assets, $20 – $45 billion in scale, $15 - $35 billion in scope, $15-35 billion in innovation, benefits continue to grow as get bigger
- International dimension: just larger foreign banks posing same risk with less U.S. control

- U.S. banks much smaller percentage of GDP than peers, at least on single bank basis

Largest U.S. banks in 2010 were Bank of America, $2.264T and JP Morgan Chase, $2.117T, each around 14% of US GDP of $14T in 2010. Compare largest bank in world, French bank BNP Paribas of $2.669T. Top 10 in 2011, next slide.

World's Largest Banks (Assets, $ trillion, 6/30/2011)

BNP Paribas	French	2.79
HSBC Holdings	UK	2.69
Deutsche Bank	German	2.68
Mitsubishi UFG	Japan	2.47
Barclays	UK	2.39
Royal Bank of Scotland	UK	2.31
Ind. & Comm'l Bk of China	China	2.30
Bank of America	US	2.26
JP Morgan Chase	US	2.24
Credit Agricole	France	2.23

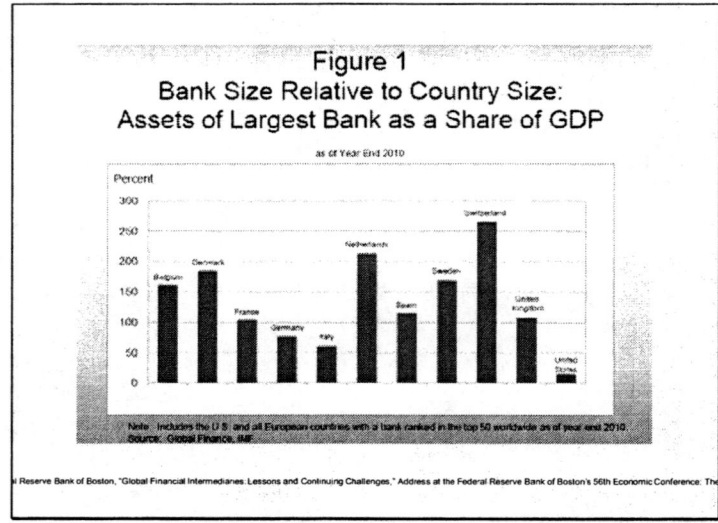

EXHIBIT 15

Benefits from large banks are distributed across product areas.

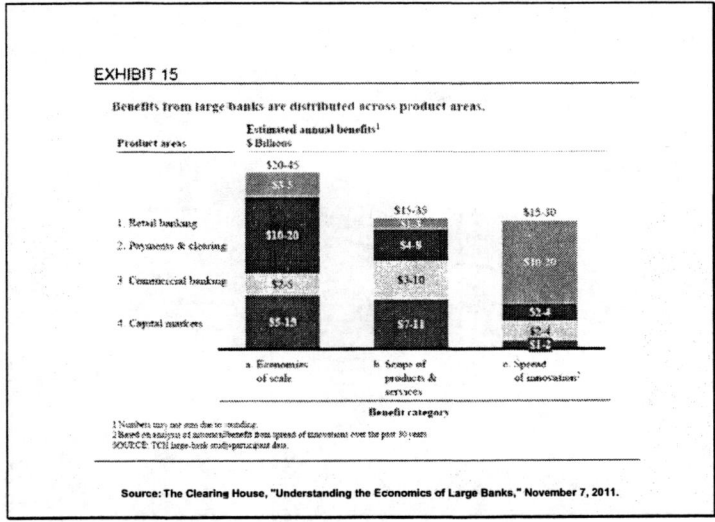

Source: The Clearing House, "Understanding the Economics of Large Banks," November 7, 2011.

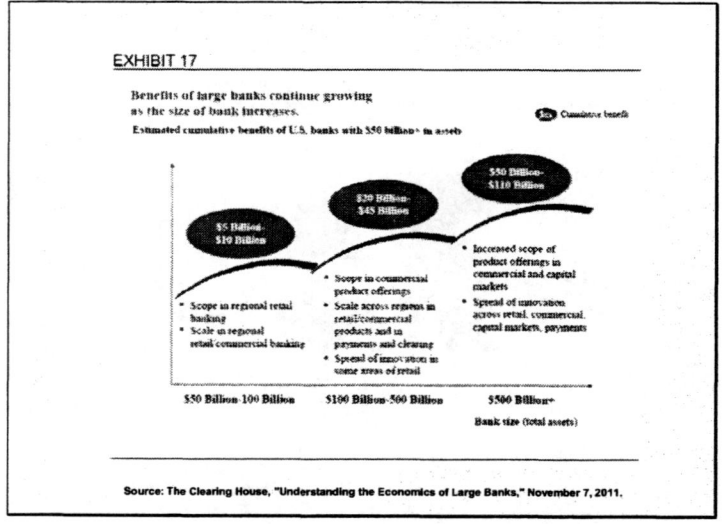

U.S. Resolution Procedures

- Prior to DF, bankruptcy procedure for non-banks (including bank holding companies) and FDIC procedure for all banks—Why dual track?
- Key Aspects of FDIC procedure
    - Receivership or conservatorship, administrative not court process
    - Insured deposits quickly transferred to solvent bank; FDIC as subrogee of insured depositors and other uninsured depositors in U.S. have a preference over other creditors
    - Derivatives contracts exempt from automatic stay (can get collateral and liquidate positions immediately) but can be transferred to third party within 24 hours to avoid close outs
    - Cross-guarantee system, bank affiliates responsible for any FDIC losses from resolution of other affiliates
    - Least cost resolution with respect to technique, "systemic risk exception" permitting open bank assistance repealed by DF

Dodd-Frank Resolution Reforms:
Orderly Liquidation Authority (OLA)

- New coverage for bank holding companies, insurers, broker-dealers and "systemically important" nonbank financial institutions, plus living wills for all firms supervised by Fed
- Systemic importance determined, on eve of resolution, by agreement of Treasury Secretary, two-thirds of boards of FDIC and Fed on basis of whether firm's failure and resolution would have "adverse effects on the financial stability of the United States" with judicial review. Why not all financial companies, like all banks under FDIC procedures? Sensible to do on eve of bankruptcy?
- Priorities similar to bankruptcy, e.g. creditors cannot receive less than they would in liquidation (Bair idea to impair secured creditors to increase monitoring rejected)
- Derivative contracts can be transferred to third parties to avoid close outs
- Cannot favor particular creditors except to maximize value for all creditors, thus cannot protect short-term unsecured creditors. What problems will this cause?
- FDIC can obtain funding from Treasury to assist in an orderly and perhaps protracted liquidation (but the longer it takes, the less value the entity may have), such funding not available in bankruptcy
- Assessments to cover taxpayer losses after the fact (no ex ante assessments like for deposit insurance). Would ex ante funding be better?

- Would Lehman have come out better under OLA than bankruptcy? Probably yes because better procedure, assuming FDIC could get in on time, discussion assumes systemically important determination has been made. Could they exercise control before this was done?

No power to favor short-term creditors and avoid contagion, the major fall out from the Lehman bankruptcy. EU rumored to provide for super priority for short-term creditors.

Bail-Ins and Contingent Capital

- Bail-Ins give regulators power to convert debt to equity based on their discretion or trigger criteria set in advance; contingent capital instruments (CoCos) provide for conversion based on contractual provisions in the instrument: aimed to preserve franchise value and avoid taxpayer funded bailouts

- Major concern is impact on cost of capital of requirement to hold such instruments (will increase due to increased risk)—further cost if contractual instruments will not count as capital (Swiss include in Swiss finish, Basel excludes)

- Major operational problem is how to set trigger. Market prices may be volatile, CDS spreads my reflect thin market

- Exemptions for short-term debt necessary to avoid setting off contagion, Lehman repeat (but will mean even more short-term credit, making system more volatile). May not be enough longer term debt to bail-in and avoid failure

- Difficult to coordinate bail-ins across borders because different regulatory regimes with different powers. Can this be avoided by having all instruments subject to one country's law?

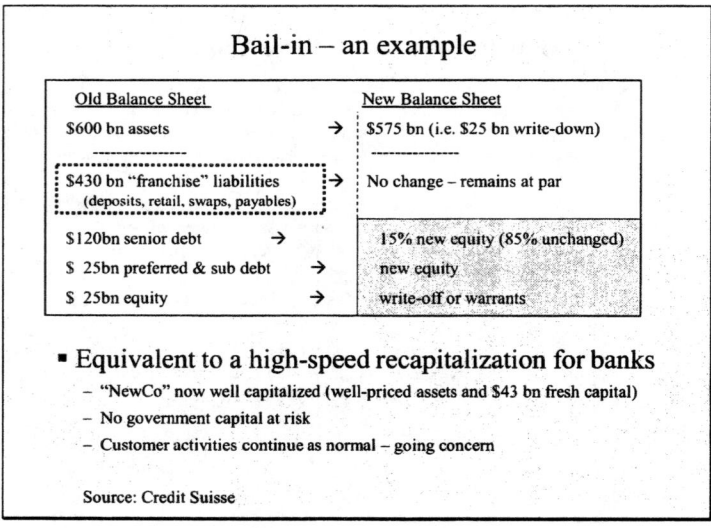

- Note that this is a very modest write down of $25 billion, only about 4% loss, 25/600
- Note also assumes plenty of debt to convert, senior debt and sub debt totaling $145 billion.
- Note requires $43 billion in conversions so that institution would have sufficient capita. The capital ratio (on a leverage basis) is 7% (Basel minimum is 3%) but what really counts is tangible common equity/risk-weighted assets.
- One time depiction, could be further losses that are much deeper.

Compare our two charts on Citigroup

Example –Impact on the System

		Actual Lehman	Bail-in Pro Forma
1)	Equity	wipe out	warrants
2)	Sub debt	wipe out	shares
3)	Senior debt	10% to 25% recovery	~par (85% + shares)
Investor Impact		~$150bn of loss	~ $25 bn loss
		(= 5x - 6x asset loss)	(= 1x asset loss)
–	Customers*:	large losses	no loss
–	Counterparties*:	large losses	no loss
–	Markets:	massive unwinds	relief rally? & deleveraging
–	Know Result?	up to 10 years	now

Source: Credit Suisse

Same idea, basic point here is that reduces creditor losses by a prompt resolution, not sure why this is.

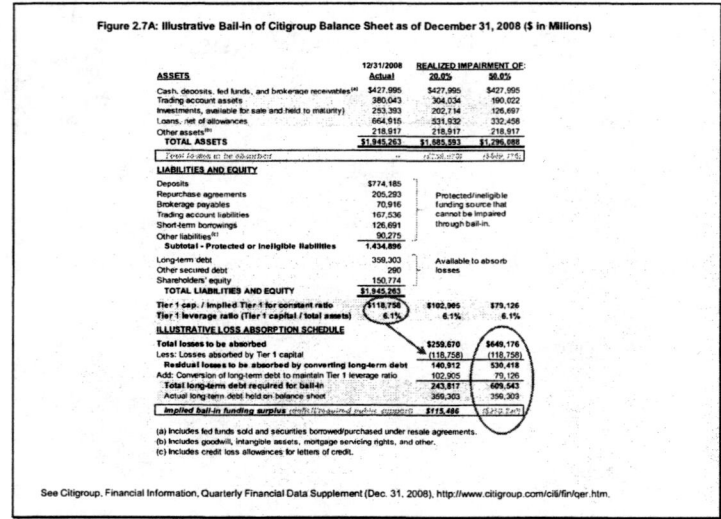

Figure 2.7A: Illustrative Bail-in of Citigroup Balance Sheet as of December 31, 2008 ($ in Millions)

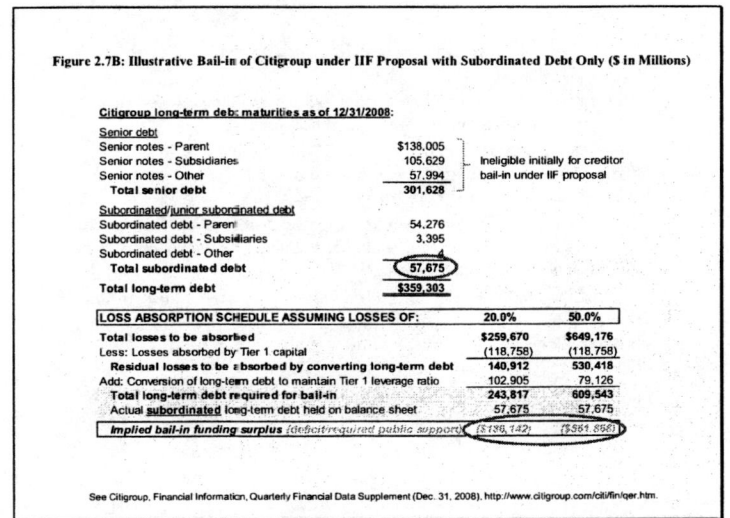

Figure 2.7B: Illustrative Bail-in of Citigroup under IIF Proposal with Subordinated Debt Only ($ in Millions)

Citigroup long-term debt maturities as of 12/31/2008:

Senior debt

Senior notes - Parent	$138,005	
Senior notes - Subsidiaries	105,629	Ineligible initially for creditor
Senior notes - Other	57,994	bail-in under IIF proposal
Total senior debt	**301,628**	

Subordinated/junior subordinated debt

Subordinated debt - Parent	54,276
Subordinated debt - Subsidiaries	3,395
Subordinated debt - Other	4
Total subordinated debt	**57,675**
Total long-term debt	**$359,303**

LOSS ABSORPTION SCHEDULE ASSUMING LOSSES OF:	20.0%	50.0%
Total losses to be absorbed	**$259,670**	**$649,176**
Less: Losses absorbed by Tier 1 capital	(118,758)	(118,758)
Residual losses to be absorbed by converting long-term debt	**140,912**	**530,418**
Add: Conversion of long-term debt to maintain Tier 1 leverage ratio	102,905	79,126
Total long-term debt required for bail-in	**243,817**	**609,543**
Actual **subordinated** long-term debt held on balance sheet	57,675	57,675
Implied bail-in funding surplus (deficit/required public support)	(\$186,142)	(\$551,868)

See Citigroup, Financial Information, Quarterly Financial Data Supplement (Dec. 31, 2008), http://www.citigroup.com/citi/fin/qer.htm.

Cross-border Resolution

- Lehman had over 2000 affiliates operating in over 40 countries—major problems in coordinating proceedings in U.S. and U.K.
- Ring-fencing of assets in country as in BCCI may interfere with value-maximizing restructuring, e.g. bail-ins and be arbitrary, e.g. Japanese clearing account in New York banks
- Policy for ring fencing much weaker if foreign bank branch deposits are uninsured by host country, e.g. no losses to public, if home country insurance is made good, cf. Iceland
- How would one allocate bail-out burden where financial institution does not fail, assuming coordinated approach that preserves holding company's affiliates? Home country pays all? What if it cannot? Proportionate to assets in country?

Regulatory Structure

Current Regulatory System

- Bank regulation at state and federal level and multiple regulators at federal level (Fed-state members and $50 billion plus banking organizations (39) under DF; OCC for national banks; FDIC for state non-member banks; NCUA for credit unions (only OTS eliminated by DF)
- FSOC identifies and Fed supervises systemically important non-bank financial institutions
- Multiple market regulators: SEC (investors in securities); CFTC (investors in commodities and derivatives, unclear line); CFPB created by DF (consumers, unclear line with investors, e.g. home), plus FTC on some consumer issues
- State-by-state insurance regulation, now have Office of Federal Insurance under DF, unclear what it will do
- Treasury (houses OCC and OCC on Board of FDIC), chairs FSOC and provides overall policy direction
- FSOC coordinates regulation

Regulatory Structure

- UK further consolidates supervision post Northern Rock: FSA (supervision) becomes Prudential Regulatory Authority (PRA) subsidiary of Bank of England and retains regulatory authority under new Consumer Protection and Markets Authority

Major Problems with Regulatory System

- Highly fragmented
- Did not function well in crisis: difficult to coordinate, gaps and regulatory arbitrage.
- US reform difficult because regulators want to survive, multiple congressional committees want to supervise them (cash cows for political campaigns), and industry likes its own regulator
- Can have great policies but will fail if do not have proper structure through which to implement them.

Reforms of Regulatory System

- Consolidate regulatory bodies on model of UK (supervisor and safety and soundness regulator (CCMR proposed USFSA—would include resolution and DI authority), market regulator and central bank, coordinated by Treasury). In UK, supervisor is subsidiary of central bank following financial crisis. Most major markets look much more like UK than US
- End state regulation of banks, securities firms and insurance companies—we have a national economy
- Debate on whether central bank should be supervisor: has expertise and needs information to conduct monetary policy/LLR function versus too much power in one agency, and supervision too political and could undercut independence (DF gives large banking organizations, systemically important, and keeps state member banks)
- Independence of regulators from government (but is not real problem today independence from Congress?)
- Funding: appropriations (SEC and CFTC), seignorage (Fed), user fees (OCC, Fed), Fed support (CFPB), FDIC (insurance premiums)
- Integrate market regulators: SEC, CFTC and CFPB, common culture on regulation and enforcement policy direction
- Role of SROs, like FINRA (ex-NASD)

Treasury Blueprint (Paulson approach, 2008):
- Market Stability Regulator – Federal Reserve (what does this mean, all or some regulation)
- Prudential Financial Regulator (merge banking regulators)
- Business Conduct Regulator (merge some SEC and CFTC and some aspect of FTC, no mention of incipient CFPB), with preemption of state regulation
- Keep separate FDIC renamed as Federal Insurance Guarantee Corporation (bow to Bair?)

Corporate Finance Regulator, corporate oversight in securities markets, e.g. disclosure function of SEC (as compared to regulation of broker-dealers), bow to SEC?

Dodd-Frank Regulatory Reorganization

- Dodd-Frank has added two new powerful agencies
- **FSOC composed of 10 members, 9 regulators and an independent presidential appointee, chaired by Treasury is given a variety of powers: monitor systemic risk, designate systemically important non-bank institutions for Fed supervision, require leverage limits for risky banks, resolution of agency disputes (only compulsory with CFTC and SEC), consult on a variety of agency proposed regulations: powerful but unwieldy**
- Bureau of Consumer Financial Protection—funded by Fed out of Fed profits ($500 million) with authority over a broad range of consumer matters, many of which were formerly entrusted to the banking agencies

Bottom line: hope that FSOC can give more overall direction to a fragmented regulatory structure

TEACHING PLAN FOR

CHAPTER EIGHT
FOREIGN EXCHANGE REGIMES

POWERPOINT SCREENS FOR NINETEENTH EDITION

Foreign Exchange Regimes

Foreign Exchange Regimes

- Functions of an exchange rate regime

- The logic of the extremes: fixed and floating

- Foreign exchange regime for Chile

- Sovereign Wealth Funds

Transition: more infrastructure after capital and payments
Lecture:
Foreign exchange markets are the largest financial markets in the world. Trades over $2.3 trillion per day. Anyone interested in international finance must understand them.
The biggest debates are about appropriate exchange regimes. Today many different exchange regimes exist side by side.
We begin by examining extreme type of exchange regimes, fixed and floating, to understand how they are supposed to work. We then turn to various types of intermediate regimes used today, some fixed (e.g., dollarized, currency board), some pegged, and others floating.
Finally, we consider what kinds of regimes countries should have today. How does a lawyer approach this subject which can quickly become very technical; it is generally what economists think of when you mention international finance? Very little international regulation; loose coordination of G-7. Regulation by countries in the form of capital and foreign exchange controls. Also, contractual drafting for various instruments requires some basic knowledge of foreign exchange rates.

Functions of an Exchange Rate Regime

- Value currencies against each other
  - As of July 2011, Big Mac in U.S. costs $4.07 and $2.335 in China: Chinese currency undervalued (should pay more for Big Macs)
- Allow a country to adjust its economy (or prices) when its trade with other countries is not in balance

---

Lecture

Function 1: Value currencies against each other reasonably well. **What is the impact of having a misvalued currency?** Will not convert $ for Yuan if can only then get about one-half of a Big Mac, but may still do so for speculation, or huge demand for unique Chinese assets, not Big Macs.

Function 2: Allow a country to adjust its economy or prices when its trade with other countries is not in balance

Both functions are important because they facilitate cross-border trade and capital movements. The second is important because it is part of the overall macroeconomic policy of a country.

Key Aspects of Fixed and Floating
FX Regimes:

1. Who sets the rate of a currency against other currencies?

2. How much can the government manage monetary policy?

- Who sets the rates: fixed-government, floating-market
- Government monetary policy: fixed-none, floating-a lot

These characteristics are like two axes of a chart (slide after next slide).

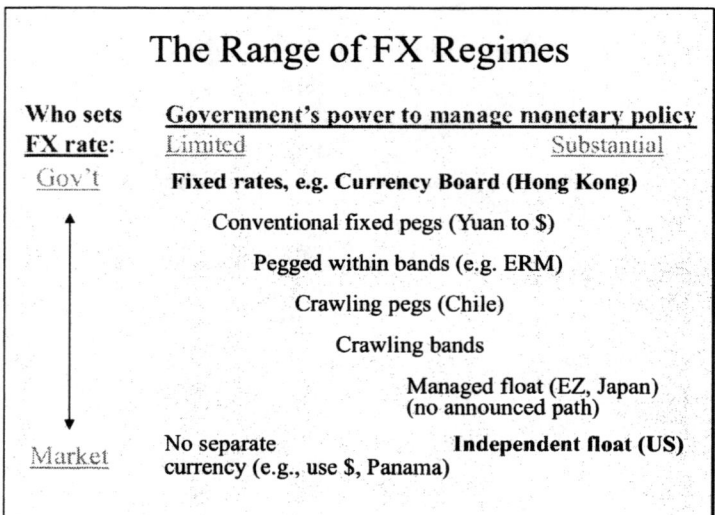

The Range of FX Regimes

Who sets FX rate:	Government's power to manage monetary policy	
	Limited	Substantial
Gov't	**Fixed rates, e.g. Currency Board (Hong Kong)**	
↑	Conventional fixed pegs (Yuan to $)	
	Pegged within bands (e.g. ERM)	
	Crawling pegs (Chile)	
	Crawling bands	
↓		Managed float (EZ, Japan) (no announced path)
Market	No separate currency (e.g., use $, Panama)	**Independent float (US)**

Lecture

The IMF identified 8 types of FX regimes, described in the reading. It categorized them by two criteria: who sets the FX rate, whether governments or the market, and how much control over its own monetary policy the regime gives the government.

We will examine the two extremes on the spectrum of Who sets the FX Rate:

fixed rates set by government and
floating rates set by the market.

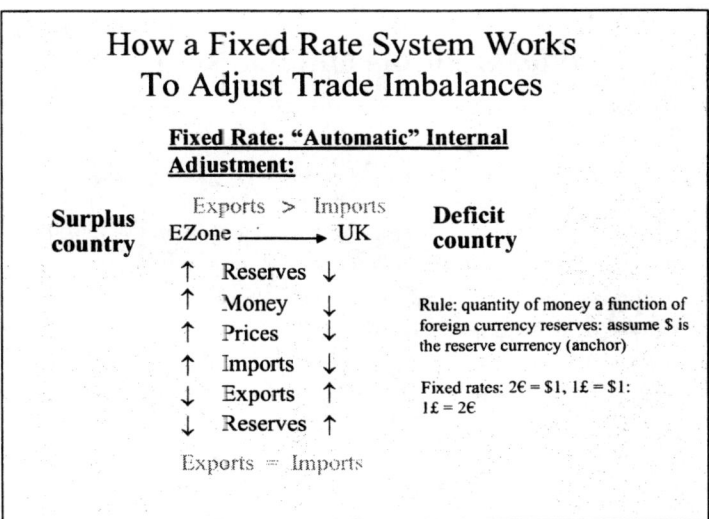

Explain Chart, start with Ezone trade surplus with UK
Discuss: why would Eurozone want to prevent adjustment?
Eurozone (EU countries with Euro) might not want to see its exports and reserves decline or its prices rise. Jobs could be lost, which is politically not popular
EZ might not want to have more imports from UK (local producers lose market share).
Why would UK want to prevent adjustment
UK consumers or businesses might not like to have to pay more for EZ imports (businesses use imports as inputs).
These motives could be very important politically, providing a strong incentive to cheat.
How could adjustment be prevented, take EZ? Price controls, restrict imports, sterilize reserves by not allowing money to increase (break rule of the game), subsidize exports. **How about the U.K?** Could borrow dollars to pay for imports. More burden on surplus country; issue of asymmetric obligations.

Capital Controls and FX Regimes

Some governments control the flow of capital into and out of their country:

- Direct controls, by administrative action
- Indirect controls, changing the price of cross-border flows to discourage them (e.g., by a tax, or multiple exchange rates)

Capital controls have become less popular, compared to the 1960s

- Developing countries, some big (China, India) still use them
- They may still be a tool to deal with FX crises (IMF more sympathetic)
- Evidence that the controls are not effective
- U.S. de facto capital controls: Regulation S (limits ability of resident U.S. investors to buy unregistered securities of foreign companies

Reference

Adjustment in a Floating Rate System

Floating Rate   **Rule:** Governments do not
"Automatic" Adjustment   intervene except to "smooth"
  Exports > Imports   the markets
EZone ————►UK

Result: Increased demand for Euro in U.K. to pay for imports from EZ

so an ↑ price of Euro against UK £ (e.g. from 1£ = €3.0 to 1.2£ = €3.0)
and an ↑ price of Ezone exports in terms of UK£ (Ezone exports more expensive)
mean a ↓ volume of Ezone's exports
Also UK exports increase to Ezone because they are cheaper

Exports = Imports

Why will the demand for Euro increase as Ezone exports increase? If the UK importer pays in Euro, must get it (sell sterling for Euro, thus increasing demand for Euro). If the UK importer pays in sterling or dollars, Ezone exporter which wants Euros will sell those currencies for Euros (increasing demand for Euros).

The increased demand for Euros triggers the adjustment mechanism, the appreciation of the Euro, which results in the elimination of the UK's trade imbalance.

Suppose the Ezone or the UK did not want to see its currency's value change against the other, what could they do? Start with EZone then U.K. (next slide hidden)

Ways EZone or UK Could Impede Adjustment in Floating Regime

Reduce Demand for Euro	Increase Supply of Euro
EZ: Lower EZ i rate *people sell Euro for £*	Lend Euro to UK residents
UK: Raise UK i rate *people sell Euro for £*	Borrow Euro
Both: Buy Sterling for Euro	Sell Euro for Sterling
Capital controls on purchase of Euro or sale of £	

Reference

Two ways to prevent adjustment: reduce demand for Euro or increase supply of Euro.

The governments would act in FX markets or on them (through monetary policy) to change the supply and demand for the two currencies. Monetary policy works on FX rates through interest rate parity, next slide.

These interventions are limited by the government's reserves and willingness to manipulate the money supply, but it can continue for quite a long time, often years, delaying the adjustments.

Interest Rate Parity Theorem

1) There is a direct relation between the interest rates in two countries and the exchange rate of their currencies.

2) A rising interest rate in country A and no change in B will mean that A's currency will attract investors and increase in value against B's currency.

Reference

What Factors Contribute to a Strong
Currency?

Why would a country want a strong currency? Purchase power and
attraction of investment..
Factors?
*   Higher interest rates in home country than abroad
*   Lower rates of inflation
*   A domestic trade surplus relative to other countries
*   Political or military unrest in other countries
*   A strong domestic financial market
*   Strong domestic economy/weaker foreign economies
*   No record of default on government debt
Sound monetary policy aimed at price stability.

What Kind of Regime Should a Country like Chile Have?

Who sets FX rate:	Government's power to manage monetary policy	
	Limited	Substantial
Gov't	Currency board	
	Conventional fixed pegs	
	Pegged within bands (e.g. ERM)	
	Crawling pegs	
	Crawling bands	
	Managed float (no announced path)	
Market	No separate currency (e.g., use $)	Independent float

1. Discuss: What kind of FX regime should a country like Chile have? Start with dollarization	
Benefits	**Costs**
1. Remove discretion in monetary policy, reducing inflation and strengthening the economy 2. Credible currency for trade and investment, end speculation	1. Lose seigniorage [next screen], 2. Lose control of monetary, FX policy, LOLR(shock absorbers) 3. Technically hard to switch: set wrong FX rate when replacing local currency with $ 4. Political damage at home
2. Discuss: Would a currency board be better?	
Get seigniorage HK succeeded	Strong domestic economic policy essential Too easy to cheat Stored up pressure results in large devaluation
3. Discuss: are pegs or bands better?	
Have discretion	Discretion is bad
4. Why not a free float?	
Market sets: no discretion	Risk too much variability and too much discretion to intervene, bad monetary policy

Seigniorage

A country that issues currency receives income from doing so:

- A person gets cash from a bank in exchange for a deposit transferred to the bank

- The bank gets the cash from the central bank: central bank debits liabilities for bank deposits (on which it may pay interest, U.S does not) and credits liabilities for cash (on which it pays no interest)

- The central bank invests the funds from the purchase of cash, realizing the income and sending it (minus expenses, including interest paid, if any on deposits) to the Government

- Also, country earns interest on foreign exchange reserves (if dollarized has no reserves)

Reference

Sovereign Wealth Funds (SWFs)

- What are SWFs? Are they significant? Different types?

- Should their investments be generally controlled?

- Should the U.S. permit them to acquire major stakes in U.S. financial institutions? If so, under what conditions?

---

1. SWFs funds owned by foreign governments, $2-3 trillion. Is this large? Compare with worldwide financial assets (McKinsey-$167 trillion, others $190 trillion), US GDP around $14 trillion. Exceed total of private equity or hedge funds.

- Different kinds—foreign exchange intervention, China, commodity exports, gulf states.

- Generally reviewed under CFIUS: national security rationale but concern with protectionism.

- Major investments in financial institutions: There were three major investments at the end of 2007 in the U.S. Abu Dhabi invested $7.5 billion in Citigroup, China invested $5 billion in Morgan Stanley, and Singapore will invest an estimated $6.2 billion in Merrill Lynch. In addition, Singapore invested $9.7 billion in UBS. Earlier in the year, there had been other notable investments, such as China's $3 billion pre-IPO investment in Blackstone and Abu Dhabi's $1.35 billion in The Carlyle Group.

- Concerns? Influence financial institutions to benefit of foreign sovereign (how)? But bailed US banks out from subprime. Dutch foundation approach (see NYSE-Euronext), seize stock, if try to influence? Covenants in preferred stock deals limit control, e.g. board seats. Aren't they exposed to our asset seizures? Should we require them to hold investments through asset managers

TEACHING PLAN FOR

CHAPTER NINETEEN
EMERGING MARKET DEBT

POWERPOINT SCREENS FOR THE NINETEENTH EDITION

Sovereign Debt

Sovereign Debt Trends from 1970-2009

- Significant growth: sovereign debt with over one year maturity increased from $46 billion in 1970 to $2.8 trillion by 2009.
- Shift from bank to bond debt: 1970 bank debt was $3.6 billion as compared to bond debt of $1.8 billion. In 2004, bond debt was $467 billion as compared to bank debt of $163 billion, about 3 times as much—by 2009 this ratio had risen to 3.4 times as much.
- Growth of IMF debt outstanding from $800 million in 1970 to $107 billion in 2003, falling to $16 billion by 2007 (payoffs and few new loans); in 2010 back up to $64 billion. Does not count Greece $39.8 billion; Portugal $34.6 billion, and Ireland $29.7 billion = $104.1 billion (non-developing).
- Shift from longer to shorter maturities, short-term was 20% of long-term in 1970 compared to 30% in 2004; short-term at over 50% in 2009 (short-term more volatile).

Note that short-term debt in 1997, the year before the Asian crisis, was 32%. Many criticized dependence on short-term debt which created more exposure in crisis—but has only decreased minimally since 1997.

Techniques for Dealing with
Sovereign Debt from 1970 - 2000

- 1980s: Repetitive Moratoria and Debt Reschedulings of bank debt (IMF/countries only loan if banks give new money and reschedule)
- Early 1990s: Securitization, collateralization and reduction of bank debt through the Brady Plan
- Mid 1990s: Mainly bailouts, some restructurings and defaults
  - <u>Bailouts</u>: e.g. *Mexico* 1994, *Asia* 1997
  - <u>Restructurings</u>: *Ecuador* 1999: Restructures $6.6B dollar bond debt through exchange offer and exit amendments; limited IMF role. Also *Ukraine* and *Pakistan*
  - <u>Defaults</u>: *Russia* 1998: no IMF money, write-offs and debt discrimination (favors eurobonds); *Argentina* 2001

Policy in the 2000s: Bush Administration

- Argentina 2002-2005: IMF grants $12.5 billion stand-by in September 2003 and permits $3.1 billion rollover of payment in March 2004; U.S. does not oppose highly unfavorable bond exchange for creditors and does oppose efforts of holdout creditors in courts

- Turkey: 2001: $30B pledge, of IMF ($19B) and U.S. ($11B), assistance to deal with domestic lira debt before any agreement of private creditors to reschedule

- Brazil: 2002: $45B support to deal with Real devaluation and political unrest; no private debt rescheduling, more like LLR

Senior Treasury officials (Taylor, O'Neill) in the Bush administration opposed bailouts and use of the IMF before taking office.
What policy were they following? Interest group politics, foreign policy and success of Mexico (re Brazil).

Debt Crises

What are the principal lessons from the debt crises of 1982-2006?

See next slide for lessons.

Principal Lessons 1982-2000

Need to Cut Back IMF and Official Lending, plus alter conditionality approach
- Large expenditure of public funds
  - Not always paid back—rescheduling in Paris Club
  - Argentina default on WB loan, avoids IMF default by rollover (without meaningful conditions) of $12.5 billion on 9-11-03, but repays in 2006
  - Lending at subsidized rates
  - $310 billion increase since 1990 (all public creditors), but goes down after 2005
- Emergence of IMF as lender of last resort with access to increasing country resources (around 2000% of quota used in Korea and Turkey)
- Increase in creditor moral hazard (bond spread studies following bailouts inconclusive—sometimes decrease, sometimes do not)
- Failure of IMF conditionality policies (policies do not work, Stiglitz v. Rogoff debate)

Contagion
- Concern with contagion: Mexico in 1980s, Asian crisis (within Asia) 1997, Europe 2010-
- Market uncertainty due to ad hoc responses

Need to Improve Restructuring Process
- Dispersed bond debt makes restructurings more difficult (compare with bank debt in 1980s) but less threat to banking system
- Debtor discrimination among private creditors (Russia and Ecuador)
- Holdouts: good or bad?

Need to Improve Creditor Rights
- Few rights (attachments do not work), little success of attachments
- No future market discipline

Table 13. Summary of Evidence

Effect of Default on:	Immediate Effect	Long-Run Effect
GDP growth	• Negative effect ranging between 0.6 and 2.5 percentage points • If quarterly data are used no statistically significant effect in the quarter after the default	No statistically significant effect after the year in which the default takes place
Exclusion from capital market	Almost full exclusion	There is no permanent exclusion. Access is regained between four and eight years after the default.
Credit rating	Negative effect of about one notch in the three years after the default	No statistically significant effect after three years
Borrowing cost	• 250 to 400 basis-point increase in the two years after the default • This includes the effect of credit rating downgrade (the effect on spread is smaller and often not statistically significant if credit ratings are included in the regression)	No statistically significant effect after two years
Trade	• Net decrease of bilateral trade (about 8 percent) • Negative effect on export-oriented industries	• The negative effect on bilateral trade lasts for approximately 15 years • The effect on export-oriented industries lasts for two to three years
Trade credit	Decline of 0.5 percentage points in the year of the default and the year after the default	Some evidence of an effect up to four years after the default
Banking crises	An increase in the probability of a banking crisis of approximately 11 percentage points	
Politicians and policymakers	• A 16 percent decrease in support of the ruling party in the first election after a default • A 50 percent increase in the probability of replacing the head of the executive • A 33 percent increase in the probability of replacing the minister of finance or the head of the central bank	

Note: This table is based on the various articles surveyed in this paper and on the various econometric experiments included in this paper.

Eduardo Borensztein and Ugo Panizza, "The Costs of Sovereign Default," IMF Staff Papers (International Monetary Fund), Vol. 59, 2009, pp. 723.

A truly crucial issue is whether debt default has a significant cost for the defaulting country, i.e. by restricting their market access to international markets. This is very debatable. A recent piece by Gelos, Sahay and Sanleris, "Sovereign Borrowing by Developing Countries: What Determinbes Market Access?," 83 J. of International Economics 243 (2011) argues no or little cost—easier to borrow once reduce debt, markets look to future not past. More reason to strengthen creditor rights.

Debt Crises

Are Holdout Creditors a Substantial Obstacle to Dealing with Sovereign Debt Crises?

Background on Argentina
- Next slide gives background for Argentina although question is more general
- Any assets to seize (next slides)

Impact on the process: good or bad (negotiation leverage or blocking)

Don't cry for me, Argentina!

Argentina Default

- Largest sovereign default in history: $141 billion in external debt in late December 2001—mostly bond debt, significant number of retail investors in Italy and Japan
- Many bondholders (e.g. Dart $600 million) got judgments that Argentina owed them the value of their debt but very few assets were attached, e.g. some New York real estate: Argentina moved its assets outside the U.S., e.g. reserves into BIS
- June 2004 bond exchange offer for $81.8 billon of its bond debt (plus $20 billion in past due interest)—76% acceptance by cut-off in March 2005, or $62.3 billion (historical acceptance rate over 90%; given 40% of debt held by domestic creditors, much lower foreign acceptance rate, my calculation is about 53% of foreign creditors)
  - Offer worth about 25 cents on the dollar when made (but bonds traded at 32 cents on the dollar when tendered) compared to average of 64 cents in other restructurings in the 1990s; GDP kicker on interest rates pays off
  - Creditors argued Argentina did not negotiate with them in good faith and could afford to pay more given 7% GDP growth and 5% inflation rate in 2004
  - Bonds rated B- by S&P, one notch above C, the rating for a country expected to default within a year (inconsistent with creditors claims that Argentina could afford to pay more? Just another mistake by ratings agencies?)
  - Argentine legislature passes law stating could not make better offer to holdouts, rescinded when did second exchange later)
  - Exchange completed in June 2005 after old bond attachment suit rejected by Second Circuit
- Argentina in June 2010 did a second bond exchange (with slightly better terms than the old exchange) for holdouts. The $18.3 billion that remained in default—Italians held $4.5 and "vultures" $3 billion. Of this $12.1 billion tendered. Argentina still negotiating over $6.5 billion outstanding to Paris Club

Sovereign Debt Issues: Holdout Creditors

- Sovereigns owe creditors money on defaulted obligations, *Westover*; the issue is whether they can enforce judgments
- Sovereigns have few attachable fixed assets abroad, e.g. bank accounts or companies (but see alter ego SOEs, banks and central banks, Argentine pension fund nationalization)
- Sovereigns do have lots of flows, e.g. payments for exports (inflow, e.g. Congo oil where no prepayment), payments on debt (outflow)
- Seizure of debt service flows—*pari passu* clause (language differs), case pending in District Court against Argentina
  - Elliot: claims on loans rank "at least pari passu <u>in right and priority of payment</u> with the claims of other creditors..."
  - Other example: "bonds will rank pari passu, without any preference among themselves" with all other creditors
  - Argentine dollar-denominated Boden bonds avoid problem by having flow take place in Argentina
- *Elliot* court in Belgium (2000) allows seizure of incoming funds at Euroclear (results in settlement), triggers Belgian statute to protect Euroclear

NML Capital v. Argentina (July 2011)

- US District Court (SDNY) decides that holdout creditors can attach $100 million of Argentine central bank (BCRA) deposits with the Federal Reserve Bank of New York (FRBNY). District court finds that BCRA is "alter ego" of Argentina because not independent and does its bidding.
- Second Circuit reverses, July 5, 2011: BRCA is not Argentina and therefore entitled to central bank immunity because immunity is presumed when funds are held in a bank in name of BRCA and presumption cannot be overcome because inadequate showing that funds were not used for central bank activities (see p. 35)—its independence is irrelevant (many central banks are not independent and were not at time of passage of FSIA in 1976).
- Do you agree with the activities finding? What about the district court holding that Argentina had previously directed BRCA to repay IMF loan by acquiring $8.4 - $9.5 billion in dollar reserves (through issuance of pesos)?
- Amicus (Scott versus Treasury and Federal Reserve Bank of New York) battle: (1) Will the value of the dollar be affected or (2) will other foreign central banks withdraw their dollars from FRBNY, if the attachment is allowed? Why does U.S. side with Argentina against U.S. creditors?

EM LTD. V. Republic of Argentina, 389 Fed. Appx. 38 (CA2 2010), cert. denied 2011: permits attachment of proceeds received by a trust in connection with the privatization of a state-owned Argentine bank—bank is Argentina and trust does not insulate attachment, $90 million.

Note most of the BCRA foreign exchange reserves, $2.1B, previously transferred to BIS but needed some transaction money in New York.

Principal Reform Proposals

- Two major reforms proposed in 2001-2002
  - an international agreement establishing a sovereign debt restructuring mechanism (SDRM), a type of bankruptcy procedure, advanced by Anne Kreuger, then deputy managing director of the IMF
  - use of collective action clauses in sovereign bonds, promoted by John Taylor, then U.S. Undersecretary of Treasury, endorsed by G-7 (organized drafting of "model" clauses)
- CACs have been implemented, SDRM dropped (U.S. opposition, few subsequent debt defaults)

Collective Action Clauses (CACs)

- Major focus has been on clauses permitting a majority of creditors to change the financial terms of debt instruments in a restructuring:
  - bonds issued under U.S. law (about 70% in 2001) traditionally required unanimity to change payment terms
    - Only non-payment terms, like waiver of sovereign immunity or listing permissions, can be changed by exit consents in bond swaps; payment terms cannot
    - Restrictions on changing terms spring from concern that majority of creditors can abuse minority (TIA of 1939 for corporate bonds, not applicable to sovereign bonds)
  - bonds issued under British law generally permit 2/3 majority to change any terms (of those voting—voting quorum can be as low as 25%, so might allow 16.7% (.25 x .66) majority to control
- G-7 CACs have higher percentage requirement than British bonds
  - 75% (IIF, creditors group, wanted 90%)
  - Exclude domestic institutions, e.g. state owned banks, controlled by sovereign, from vote, e.g. Uruguay 2003
  - Percentages of all credit outstanding (no lower quorum requirements)
  - Not used by developed countries (but see Greece retroactive clauses)

Are Majority Action Clauses the Solution to Resolving Sovereign Debt Crises?

1. <u>Cost to issuer</u>
    Could increase debt cost: empirical studies on costs mixed, but some show higher issuance cost because clauses facilitate default and restructuring (Moody and Eichengreen, 2000)
    May be first mover cost, as country that changes covenant signals that it may be more likely to default (did not materialize)
    Mexico used 75% clause in $1 billion international bond offering in 2-03. Cost dispute, street reports 20 basis points, Australia Reserve Bank study says no cost--yield consistent with yields on outstanding bonds of same maturity
    No cost because ineffective
2. <u>No change because of high effective requirement</u>: creditors only want clauses with very high "majority" requirement, e.g. 90%, to preserve negotiation leverage. But this undermines the very objective, to make restructuring easier.
3. <u>Abuse</u>: if lower, possibility that majority abuses minority, TIA concern
4. <u>Aggregation</u>: Will not work across different instruments: loans or bond without same requirement: this is why we have bankruptcy laws: private contract is not sufficient to structure bankruptcy, given different creditors not in privity interacting with a debtor over time (private contracts only work in shadow of default bankruptcy procedure)
<u>IMF</u>: does not restrain its lending

The SDRM (a modified Chapter 11 procedure)

- At debtor's request, majority of creditors can impose a standstill on payments and a stay of creditor litigation for fixed duration, potentially renewable—IMF may impose in short-term transition, e.g. for 90 days.
- Super-majority of creditors supplying new financing during procedure could subordinate existing claims (DIP financing)
- Priority creditors (multilaterals like IMF and World Bank, and possibly countries) would still be paid outside of the restructuring, but some parallel restructuring would occur
- Restructuring plan approved by super-majority of creditors in all classes (no cram down), informed by IMF's view of sustainability of debt burden (future IMF debt conditional on sustainability finding)
- Independent tribunal (maybe judicial organ) would adjudicate issues like lack of equitable treatment or valuation of claims
- Will not preclude IMF lending: "Under an SDRM, the nature of the financing decisions that the IMF would need to make before, during and after a debt restructuring would not change." (Anne Kreuger, Deputy Managing Director of IMF)
- Adopted by amendment to IMF Articles of Agreement: requires 3/5ths of members having 85% of votes (U.S. must approve since has over 15% of votes)

Basic approach.

```
+------------------------------------------+
|                                          |
|                                          |
|                                          |
|        Could the SDRM Be The Solution?   |
|                                          |
|                                          |
|                                          |
|                                          |
|                                          |
|                                          |
|                                          |
|                                          |
|                                          |
+------------------------------------------+
```

- Debtors and creditors oppose: existence will make credit more expensive, as creditors' existing rights will be impaired (both sides prefer existing bailout system, taxpayers are real parties in interest)
- Increase of IMF power: keeps lending and heavily involved in SDRM: imposes short-term stay, makes judgment of debt sustainability for approval of plan, may be the tribunal adjudicating disputes (although conflict of interest as existing lender); IMF as information provider?
- No benchmark like liquidation value in Chapter 11, need to know what is sustainable debt (different models say different things)
- Unfair exclusion of certain creditors (multilaterals)—same problem with CACs, discrimination problem.
- Exclusion of domestic debt
- Lack of cram down makes resolution under the procedure less likely, requires majority of creditors in all classes to agree
- Not clear such a structure is needed to deal with holdout creditors (issue of how important this threat is--also justification for CACs)
- Prospect will mean earlier withdrawals of credit in anticipation of imposition of SDRM (raises preference and clawback issues)

Could be applied to developed countries even if only covered foreign currency debt (Sweden, 22%, other countries as well, U.K., Canada and Italy), might lead them to oppose or restrict coverage

**Should Creditors Rights be
Strengthened?
How?**

TEACHING PLAN FOR

CHAPTER FOUR
THE EUROPEAN UNION: THE SINGLE MARKET IN FINANCIAL SERVICES

POWERPOINT SCREENS FOR NINETEENTH EDITION

European Union

EU Single Market

- Creation of A Single Internal Market
- Securities Markets (major focus)
  - Offerings
  - Firms

Complicated by new 12 members—small percentage of GDP, 12.7% of the old (2007); more bank based, 73% financial assets are held by banks compared with 52% of old, 70% of banking assets held by foreign banks as compared to 19% of old.

How compare E.U. to U.S. and Japanese financial system?

- Not one country
- Not one currency
- Not one political system? U.S. federalism contrast

Economy size of US and size of financial systems comparable (2009: US/EU GDP, 14.3/14.5; 2006 financial assets 56-37T, Japan 19; EU/Japan more bank centric, U.S. more capital markets)

Creation of Single Internal Market

- Major international issue: integration within EU as opposed to global integration (major issue in formation of GATT)
- Single Market in goods and services was a fundamental objective of the creation of the EEC which became the EU—goods first and then services
- Requires removal of explicit (de jure) barriers to offering services cross border
  - E.g. prohibiting foreign EU banks from taking cross-border deposits or acquiring local banks (Italian problem)
  - Hard to know what it is—protectionism versus investor/consumer protection, and safety and soundness concerns; concerns require new cooperative arrangements
  - "General good" exception for host state construed narrowly by European Court of Justice
- Also requires removal of implicit (de facto) barriers
  - E.g. restrictive national treatment rules on what products can be offered within a country
  - State subsidies to banks (1999, Commission fines Landesbanks $834 million), state-owned banks but see credit crisis (are implicit guarantees subsidies?)
  - Difficult to do

The Italian Problem

- Bank of Italy in 2005 blocks ABN Amro (large Dutch bank) acquisition of Banca Antonveneta (9th largest Italian bank) and encourages counter bid by Banco Populare (BPI)(10th largest Italian bank, weak financial condition)

- Bank of Italy in 2005 blocks attempted takeover by BBVA (large Spanish bank) of Banca Nazionale del Lavoro (6th largest Italian bank) by requiring BBVA to get 50% of the shares.

- 2005 Unicredito (largest Italian bank) acquires Germany's second largest bank HVB—merger results in largest Polish bank, blocked by Poland, then goes through.

In 2006, Fazio, Bank of Italy head, resigns as does Finance Minister Domenica Siniscalco. New head of Bank is Mario Draghi, also head of FSB, statutory reform, cross-border bank mergers then go through.

The Bank of Italy Affair: Antonio Fazio

Wiretapped home call on the nights July 11 and 12
Fazio to Fiorani (BPI) "Did I wake you up?" Mr Fiorani replies,"No, no, look I'm still here in Milan talking to my collaborators". Mr Fazio goes on,"All right, I've just signed it" [BPI approval]. Fiorani: "Ah Tony... I'm moved. I've got goose bumps. Thank you, thank you...I'd kiss you right now, on the forehead but I can't...". Fazio: "We must not make a single wrong move now." Fazio's wife to Fiorani: You must, until tomorrow be silent, don't speak with anyone. Stay C_A_L_M.

BPI counter bidder to ABN Amro for Banco Antonveneta.

EU: Degree of Integration

How integrated is the EU? Briefly review slides, Euro does not add much to integration. Not great studies on this.

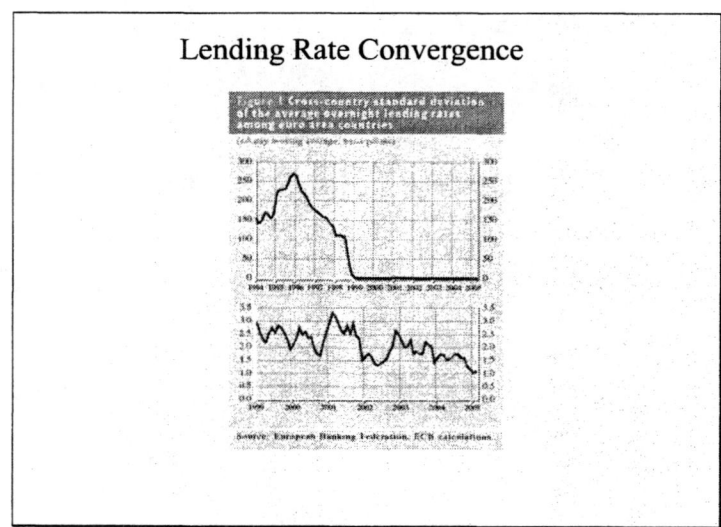

After 1999, it appears difference is less than 2.5 bp. EU more integrated, but maybe more EU than Euro

Cross-Border Lending

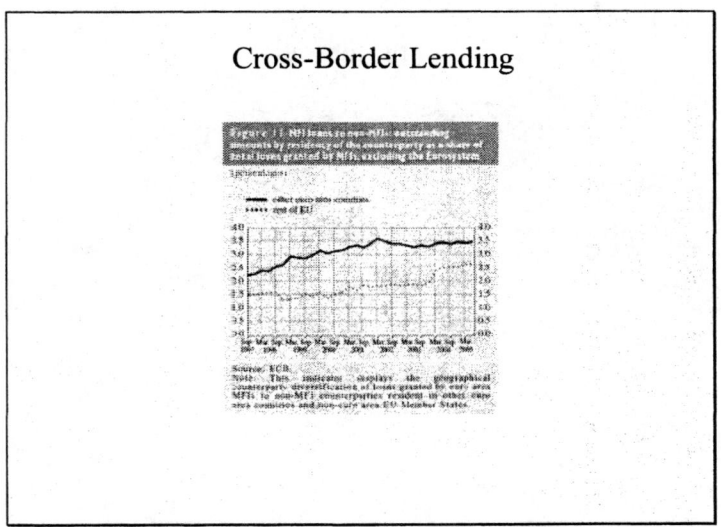

Low amount of cross-border lending. MFI is monetary financial institution, basically a bank. Bank business regional in U.S.

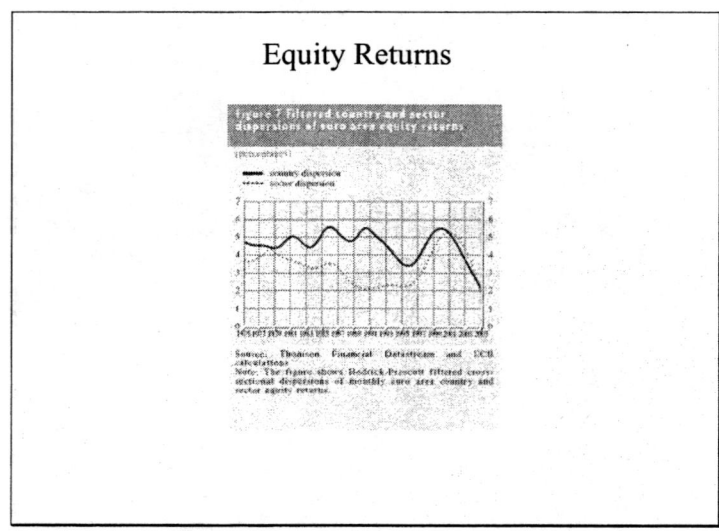

Equity Returns

Country returns becoming closer

The Men Behind The Single Internal Market

Jonathan Faull

European Commission Director General Internal Market and Services

Michel Barnier

European Commissioner for Internal Market and Services

Now in 2010, Irish to French flavor (previous Commissioner was Charlie McGreevy).

**Does the EU Need Harmonized
Offering Rules for Securities?**

Offering Rules for Securities

- Harmonization approach in 1970-1980s failed: too difficult to harmonize rules of 15 countries
- 1990s Single Passport system (for bank/securities firm branches, and securities offerings): home country rules subject to minimum harmonization (agreed list for banks) and cooperative supervision, with host country enforcement
- Works reasonably well for banks but not for public capital markets—Deutsche Telekom only pan-European offering
  - Concern about race to bottom even with minimum harmonization
  - Offering of securities still subject to local disclosure rules, e.g. use of local language
  - Different home country rules confusing to investors: need detailed harmonization (CESR)
  - No EU enforcement, all at member state level
- As a practical matter, European offerings were done in London—the investor came to the issue rather than the issue coming to the investor (mostly institutional, and uneven prohibition on cross-border advertising/solicitation)

Does the EU need harmonized offering rules?
Offshore illustration on next page.

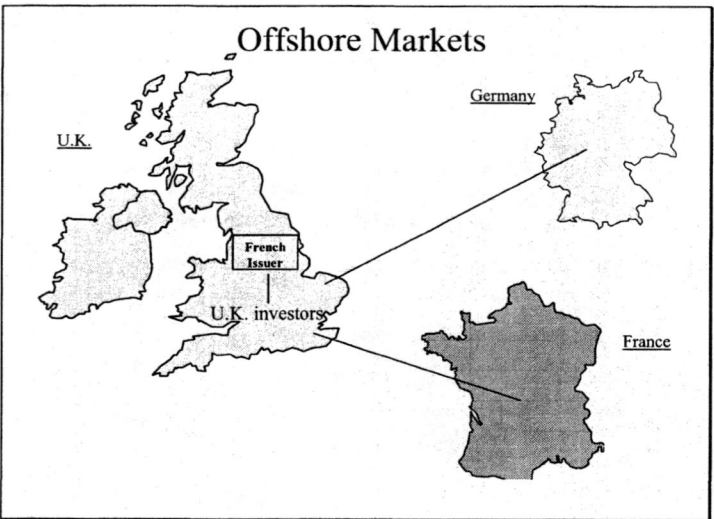

Given modern technology there is no need to sell within a particular territory. Indeed, it would be cheaper not to have widespread distribution within countries. This assumes that offshore offerings can be advertised in countries other than that of issue. If this is true, Maughan's conception may be flawed. In a global regime, everything will be done in the most efficient place, and everyone will come there electronically.

The November 2003 Prospectus Directive
Changes

What does it do that is
different than the past?

See next slides for items

The 2003 Prospectus Directive - 1

- Use of Lamfalussy Comitology (detailed implementation through CESR)
- Covers securities offered to public or listed on a "regulated market" (Eurobonds, not sold to public but listed on regulated market, gets wholesale exemptions from rules)
- Limits use of offshore public markets by prohibiting advertising of securities not covered by prospectus directive—harder to get offshore retail integration
- Harmonizes disclosure standards (common prospectus, IOSCO based), not clear what is left for home country rules
- Prospectus in "language customary in international finance," i.e. English, summary in local language
- Covers resales to public—Eurobonds cannot be sold to "Belgian dentists" without registration

Came into force in July 2005, still very limited, if any, pan-European equity offerings other than in special cases, e.g. rights offerings

---

The 2003 Prospectus Directive - 2

- Private placements and shelf registration concepts introduced ("qualified investor" defined differently in different countries, broadened in 2010)
- Public enforcement by home country; different host country private liability regimes
- Non-EU issuers: equity and small debt offerings subject to rules of country in which make first offering, large debt offerings can pick jurisdiction for each offering
- Plus: continuous material disclosure forced by Market Abuse Directive of January 2003; Transparency Directive of 2004 only requires biannual reports of material transactions and general description of financial position and performance (compare with much broader quarterly reports in U.S.)

Comitology, next slide

Focus on:

- Harmonization, choice of law does not really matter except for enforcement
- Treatment of non-EU issuers, why not always give choice? National treatment?
- Major problem: diverse liability regimes

Technical amendments in 2010 (Cleary reading)

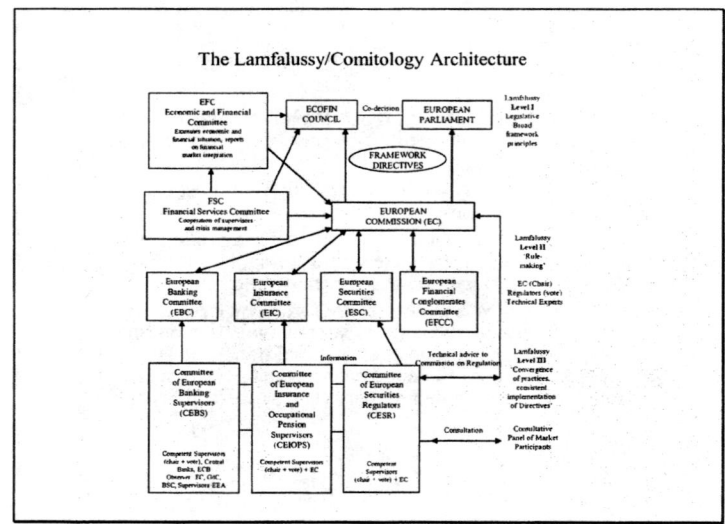

Reference

In the past, there was only the top row of law-making, Level I generating Framework Directives. Next step in evolution was to create Level II, where technical committees give input to Commission Directive process. And there is Level III, where the action is—implementation of directives by specialized groups of regulators in each country.

Beyond Lamfaloussy (2011)

Figure 2: the European System for Financial Supervision (ESFS)

Current institutional setting		ESFS
Coordination of the three committees on the basis of a Joint Protocol	**Cross-sectoral**	Joint Committee of European Supervisory Authorities
Committee of European Banking Supervisors (CEBS)	**Banking**	European Banking Authority (EBA)
Committee of European Insurance and Occupational Pension Supervisors (CEIOPS)	**Insurance**	European Insurance and Occupational Pensions Authority (EIOPA)
Committee of European Securities Regulators (CESR)	**Securities**	European Securities and Markets Authority (ESMA)
Colleges of supervisors for banking and insurance groups		
National supervisors		

Source: Recine, Fabio and Teixeira, Pedro Gustavo, The New Financial Stability Architecture in the EU (November 2009). Paolo Baffi Centre Research Paper No. 2009-62. Available at SSRN: http://ssrn.com/abstract=1509304

Came into existence on January 1, 2011

Beyond Lamfalussy 2011

Figure 3: The toolbox of the European Supervisory Authorities

	Tools
1	Guidelines and recommendations for the consistent supervisory practices and application of EU law
2	Specific recommendations to national supervisors failing to ensure compliance of financial institutions with EU law
3	Last resort decisions addressed to individual financial institutions not in compliance with EU law
4	Decisions addressed to national supervisors in crisis situations
5	Last resort decisions addressed to individual financial institutions in crisis situations
6	Collection of information and setting-up of central database
7	Mediation of disagreements between national supervisors, including the possibility to address decisions to national supervisors to take or refrain from taking action

Source: Recine, Fabio and Teixeira, Pedro Gustavo, The New Financial Stability Architecture in the EU (November 2009). Paolo Baffi Centre Research Paper No. 2009-62. Available at SSRN: http://ssrn.com/abstract=1509304

Beyond Lamfalussuy, 2011 (same source)

Figure 4: The toolbox of the European Systemic Risk Board

Tools
1 Issuance of risk warnings
2 Issuance of recommendations with a specified timeline for policy response addressed to the Community as a whole, to one or more Member States, to one or more of the European Supervisory Authorities, or to one or more national supervisors, and also to the Commission in respect of Community legislation.
3 Publication of risk warnings and recommendations
4 Monitoring of the follow-up to the ESRB recommendations; in particular, the addressees have the obligation to communicate to the ESRB their policy response or to explain why they have not acted ("act or explain").
5 If the ESRB decides that its recommendation has not been followed and that the addressees have failed to explain their inaction appropriately, it shall inform the Council and, where relevant, the European Supervisory Authorities concerned.
6 The ESRB may request information from the European Supervisory Authorities in summary or collective form, such that individual financial institutions cannot be identified. If the requested data are not available to those Authorities or are not made available in a timely manner, the ESRB may request the data from national supervisory authorities, national central banks or other authorities of Member States. The ESRB may address a reasoned request to the European Supervisory Authorities to provide data that are not in summary or collective form.

Compare with U.S. regulatory system?

Old Investment Services Directive: Key Securities Markets Provisions

- Direct EU wide access for banks and securities firms to all exchanges (not just through local subsidiaries) (Article 15)

- Block trading exception to normal prompt price reporting for exchanges (Article 21)

- Trading only on "regulated" markets (Article 14)—concentration rule, with investor opt-out

Lets look at the regulated markets issue, we have already looked at securities offerings

---

Investment Services Directive: Key Firm Provisions

- Single license: if authorized in any member state, investment firm may operate in another (minimum prudential standards and CAD, Arts. 3.3, 10)
- Home state services (if services on agreed list, Annex A)
- Host state "rules of conduct", e.g. custody of securities (Art. 11)
- Forum shopping limited by definitions of "home member state"? (Art 1.6(b))

   where the investment firm is a legal person, [the home member state is] the Member State in which its registered office is situated [many states require registration in state of head office, but U.S. choice of incorporation system may be emerging through Court of Justice decisions] or, if under its national law it has no registered office, the Member State in which its head office is situated.

Moving from transactions to firms.
How do host states satisfy themselves about the safety and soundness of securities firms authorized by another state? (Similar approach and more important for banking, systemic risk)

1. Article 3.3 requires that the "competent authorities shall not grant authorization" (host country) unless the firm has minimum initial capital under CAD and persons of good repute running business.

2. Article 10 requires home states to meet prudential standards.

3. Article 11 allows host states to impose "rules of conduct" in general and makes specific mention of non-core services in Annex, Section C, e.g. safekeeping and custody (worried about local investors having securities stolen, or misused as in Maxwell affair). This host country power can create some conflicts with general home country control principle.
May not work internationally as well because of lack of institutional framework, e.g. CESR, CEBS, courts, Commission, ECB.

Trading on "Regulated" Market Requirement

Definition (Art. 1.13), e.g. Euronext in Paris

- Market for specified securities (includes most securities)
- On list of market's home state
- Functions regularly
- Regulated by home state as to
  - operations
  - access
  - trading rules
- Transparency (block exception)

When Member States can Require (Art. 14.3)

- If investor resident of member state (French investor)
- Investment firm carries out transactions in member state (broker does French business)
- Securities dealt with on regulated market in member state (Euronext is regulated)
- **But Investor may waive**

So what this says is if the Paris Bourse, part of Euronext, is a regulated market—which it is—investor buying French stocks through a firm authorized to trade on the Bourse, must buy that stock on the Bourse, rather than in London (where might be cross-listed), subject to the proviso that the investor may opt out. **What do you think of this?** Seen as method to limit UK competition for continental markets.

Directive on Markets in Financial Instruments, MiFID, April 21, 2004 (effective 11-07)

- Replaces Investment Services Directive
- Abolition of requirement for trading on "regulated markets"
- Transparency: publish order books or quotes; depth of book for regulated markets (large block exemption)
- Specific rules for regulated markets: admission, suspension and removal of instruments from trading
- Legitimizing of more lightly regulated MTFs (electronic communication networks, ECNs)
- Controls on internalization (firms must publish quotes on liquid shares traded on regulated market, large block exemption)
- Best execution requirements (not just price)
- Firm regulation: organization (risk), conflicts of interest, investment research (regulation but no separation from investment banking), suitability, client communications

ISD was thoroughly revised in 2004. It has evolved from a single passport regime into a market structure framework
Atos estimates $1 billion cost to implement in UK
Country coordination problem.
Counterpart but different than Regulation NMS in U.S.

Directive on Markets in Financial Instruments, MiFID, December 2010 Proposals

- Access of non-EU firms to EU markets to be based on equivalence
- Tightened regulation of derivatives (on OTC derivatives, mirrors proposed European Market Infrastructure Regulation)
  - non-discriminatory access to central clearing
  - pre- and post-trade transparency
  - report transaction data to central repositories
  - dedicated facilities for trade execution
  - supervision strengthened
- New "organized trading facility" regulation
- More harmonized transaction reporting to regulators
- Strengthening of investor protection

Securitization and Credit Rating Reforms Compared to U.S.

- 5% retention but more retention options (proposed)
- No mitigation, e.g. for due diligence or QRM (proposed)
- More detailed control of credit ratings agencies
- Mandatory rotation, 4-7 years
- Client disclosure
- Cannot use normal ratings symbols for structured finance
- No ratings where not reliable data on structure
- Foreign credit ratings agencies must have at least as stringent regulation

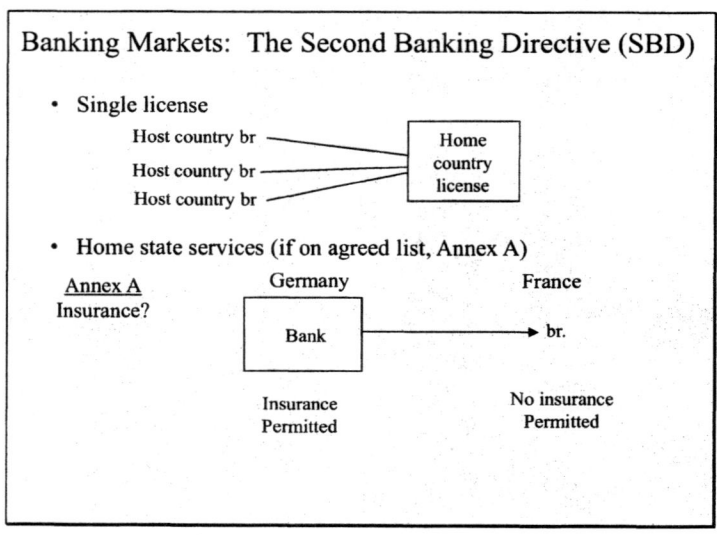

What is the idea of a single license?

If a bank is incorporated in one state (home state), it can offer in another state (host state) any service it can offer in its home state and will be supervised by the home state authorities.

Does this mean a German bank could offer insurance in France even if French banks could not do so? How could French banks survive?

Actually, this could not happen. Insurance is not on the agreed list in the Annex. The only activities that are subject to this "mutual recognition" regime are those agreed in the Annex. If the activity were on the list, for example, securities activities, and host country institutions could not offer the service (item on list probably means most countries do permit) then host country will have to change rules in order to avoid discriminating against local banks--this is regulatory convergence.

What if a Greek bank could not do financial leasing (on Annex A) in Greece but wanted to do so in Germany even though German banks could not offer the service. What could it do? Could it offer the service through a Spanish bank subsidiary which was allowed to do financial leasing in Spain?

The "whereas" clause, (as consistent with Article 3, as amended) says the bank's home state will be deemed to be the state of its registered office (Spain) and that member states must require that the registered office be in the same state as the head office. Does this refer to the head office of the banking organization (Greece) or of the bank subsidiary (Spain)? Probably Spain if buys an existing bank, but maybe Greece if de novo bank the only purpose of which is to offer financial leasing services in Germany.

Could the Greek bank offer the service in Greece through a branch of the Spanish bank, a roundtrip strategy? Not very likely in light of the policy in the Whereas clause.

Colleges of Supervisors

- Where significant banking institutions operate in multiple European countries, supervised by a "college" of supervisors from those countries

- Extends to European Economic Area (Iceland, Norway and Lichtenstein in addition to EU countries)

- College chaired in EU by consolidating supervisor of group (required in EU by capital adequacy rules)

- 31 colleges, CEBS (Committee of European Bank Supervisors) peer review of 2010 focused on 17 of 31 colleges

- Review focused on information exchange, risk assessment (top down or bottoms up) and planning and coordination (particularly of credit models)

- Uneven performance, worst colleges were for National Bank of Greece and Royal Bank of Scotland, bad on all three criteria

- Peer review fails to mention failure in cases of Icelandic and Irish banks

- Stress tests prompted by sovereign debt crisis do not have scenario of default (only look at losses in trading book, narrow portion of portfolio)

- Mention new stress tests, last year's tests derided (bad stress tests worse than no stress tests), what counts as core capital differs among countries, as compared with Tier I standard which is too capacious.

TEACHING PLAN FOR

CHAPTER FIVE
EUROPE'S ECONOMIC AND MONETARY UNION

POWERPOINT SCREENS FOR NINETEENTH EDITION

European Monetary Union

European Monetary Union

- Key Features of EMU
  - Not coextensive with EU
  - One currency, floats against other non EMU currencies
  - One monetary policy (ESCBs) (stable prices only goal) and separate fiscal policies—controlled by Stability and Growth Pact

EMU Membership

17 EMU Members:

Austria	Italy
Belgium	Luxembourg
Germany	Netherlands
Finland	Portugal
France	Spain
Ireland	Greece (01)
Slovenia (06)	Cyprus (07)
Malta (07)	Slovakia (09) Estonia (11)

10 EU Non-Members:

Denmark	**Sweden**
U.K.	**+ new 7**

EMU: Exchange Rate System in Stage 3

1) A national currency unit (NCU) had a fixed value against another NCU

      E.g., DM 1 = FF 3.35386

2) A NCU had a fixed value against the euro

      E.g., DM 1 = Euro 0.51129

3) The euro floats (managed) against other currencies such as the dollar and yen

Exchange Rate Mechanism II

- In the run up to the creation of the Euro, in 1979 EU countries joined an Exchange Rate Mechanism (ERM I) where they fixed their currencies to each other, through a series of bilateral rates, permitting their currencies to fluctuate against each other within bands of 2.25% plus or minus (Italian lira 6%)

- ERM II, exchange rate of non-Eurozone Member State fixed at a central rate to the Euro, and then can fluctuate within a band of 15% plus or minus from the central rate (States can decide to have narrower band)

- Current participants:
  - Denmark: 2.25%
  - Lithuania: 15%
  - Latvia: 1%

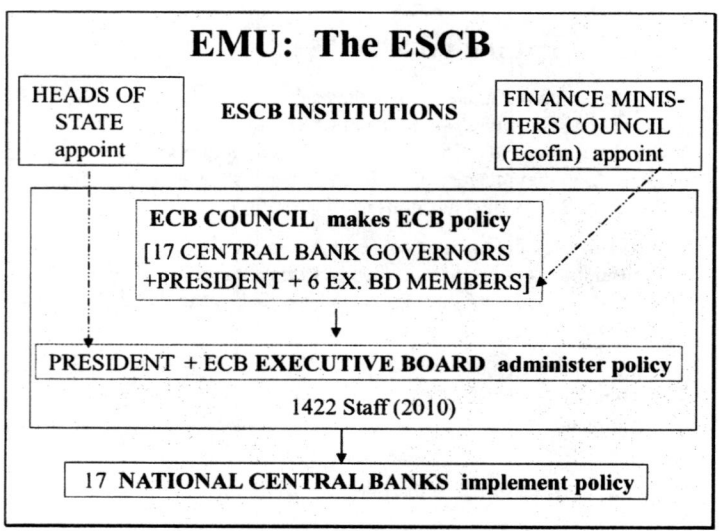

Lender of Last Resort

- Article 123 of the Treaty prohibits the ESCB from lending to any national government or buying government debt in the primary market: different than lending to a bank against government debt collateral or buying government debt in secondary market, but same effect—note ECB does not buy and sell government debt as part of monetary policy

- Until 2005, government debt traded at small yields despite significant differences in credit risk, e.g. Finland and Italy in 2004 with debt/ GDP of 45 and 106 respectively had 11 basis point spread from Germany on two year bonds

- Suggests narrow spreads are artificial (trading platform) and/or that a way would be found to bail out a government. ECB traditionally did not discriminate among different government bonds as to collateral. But Trichet set minimum credit rating of A- for use as collateral; however, when Greece went junk, this requirement was rescinded

EMU

**Was it a good idea for the EU
to adopt the Euro?**

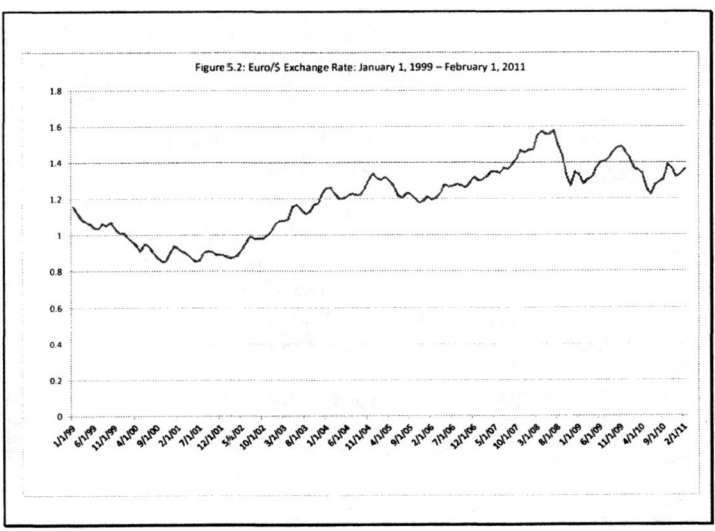

Figure 5.2: Euro/$ Exchange Rate: January 1, 1999 – February 1, 2011

The Stability Pact

- Member countries control their own fiscal policy (tax, spending, debt) subject to Stability Pact
- Original Pact: penalties imposed by 2/3 vote of ECOFIN:
  - If EMU country's fiscal deficit > 3% GDP for –
    10+ months: non-interest deposit with EC
    24+ months: 0.2% GDP fine (rising to 0.5%)
    Exemption if GDP decline >2% for 1 year
  - 60% limit on public debt/GDP (no explicit sanctions)

Was this pact effective?

Stability Pact Reform 2005

- Retains deficit limit of 3% GDP and debt limit of 60% GDP
- Creates multiple and broad exceptions
    - negative growth rate
    - accumulated loss of output during protracted period of very low growth compared to potential growth
    - spending on desirable social projects (if breach small and temporary)
- Deadline for correction: second year after occurrence but longer period may be granted
- Sanctions not mentioned

European Sovereign Debt Crisis:
Elements of Response

- Massive increase of liquidity provision by ECB through loans to banks against sovereign debt collateral and purchase of sovereign debt in secondary market: ECB balance sheet now over $3 trillion, reduces yields and stabilizes banks

- Loans by Eurozone countries through ESM ($146 billion) and then EFSF (max $957 billion, less really) to needy countries, so far Greece, Ireland and Portugal, plus IMF, with stiff austerity conditions

- Recapitalization of banks (in line with EBA stress tests) of $150 billion

- Restructuring of Greek debt, with private sector involvement, net present value haircut of over 60%, no losses for ECB

- National brakes on debt and economic sanctions for future debt issuance

IMF's Lagarde, Whistleblower in August 2011

Widely criticized for saying banks could be in trouble due to debt crisis

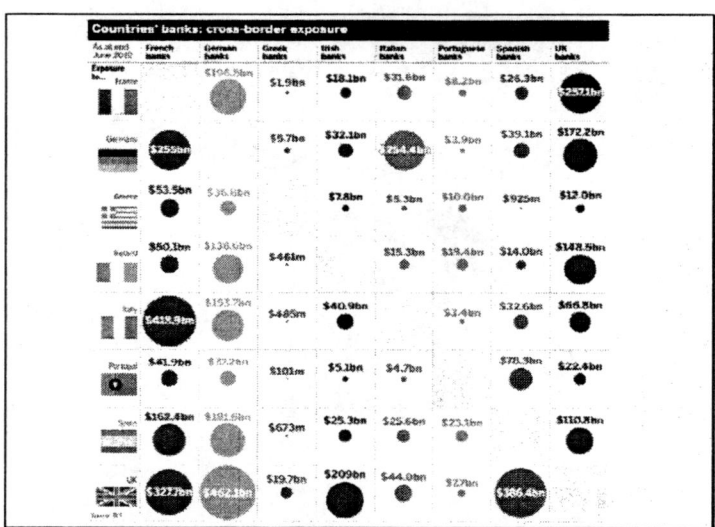

Take Greek and Irish lines end of year, note UK has largest exposure with Ireland, France to Greece.

Really want to know bank exposures as percentage of capital:

2012, German banks had 4.10% of Tier I capital exposed to Greece (not just Greek sovereign debt), Deutsche Bank 1.84, Commerzbank 11.12. To Italy, Germany had 19.38% of capital exposed, DB 6.6, CZB 35.0.

France had 3.55% of capital exposed to Greece, BNP Parisbas 5.96, Credit Agricole, .28; to Italy, France had 19.38 of Tier I capital exposed, with BNP Parisbas 32, Credit Agricole, 12.5. Roubini, Supp. Capital impact of 280-470 billion euros, depending on scenario (September 2011), p. 4.

Widely believed banks have not written down debt adequately but in position to survive Greece. However, these numbers do not take into account hedges or CDSs to mitigate impact. Also losses would be stretched over time and would not be entire exposure.

But if banks wrote CDSs on net could have CDS exposure—overall $3.2 billion, quite small (ISDA).

Recapitalization required $150 billion, stress tests

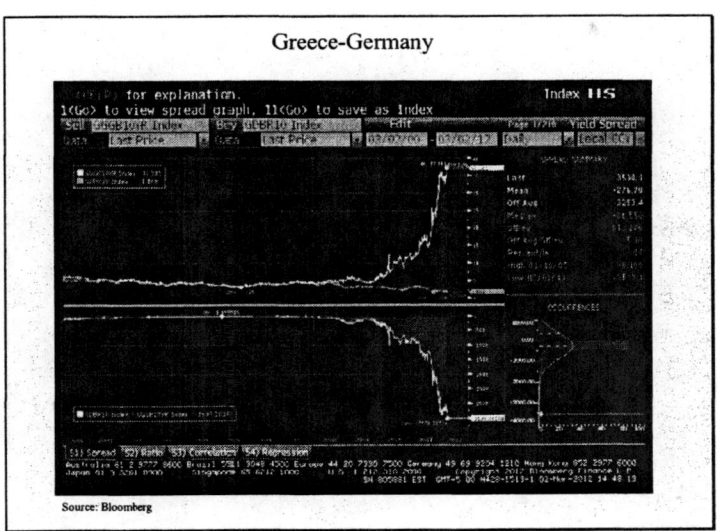

Greece-Germany

Source: Bloomberg

Note Greek spreads spiked when clear there would be private sector restructuring

Greek Crisis - 1

- March 2010 Greek public debt 115% of GDP (60% limit under Stability Pact), fiscal deficit of around 5% (3% limit under Stability Pact), 836 BP spread with German debt in April 2010

- Over 90% Greek debt issued under domestic law (not eurobonds as with developing countries)

- Interconnected to other countries through banking system: banks major beneficiaries of EZ bailouts

- April 28, 2010, Europe and the IMF formed a $146 billion rescue package, European Stability Mechanism (ESM) designed to prevent Greece from defaulting. The then 16-nation Eurozone bloc contributed $106 billion (excluding Greece) and the IMF $40 billion, for three years (may be extended), rates 5%, below 7% then demanded in market

Greek Crisis -2

- Greece forced to adopt austerity measures, public wage and military cuts and pension freezes. Will austerity stifle growth (PIMCO), is it politically sustainable (Den Plirono movement; 14.8% jobless rate)?

- May 2010, Eurozone establishes European Financial Stability Facility (EFSF) with total funding of $957 billion (IMF one-third), amounts to 7% Eurozone GDP. By comparison, PIIGS (Portugal, Ireland, Italy, Greece and Spain) account for 27% of Eurozone GDP)

  EFSF will raise funds, if necessary, through bonds issued by an SPV, collectively guaranteed by EZ countries. No direct contributions by UK (although indirect through IMF and $60 billion contribution from EU Commission); EU lending is effectively limited to about $300 billion due to too low credit ratings of all but six countries

Greek Crisis -3

- May 2010, role of ECB: buys government bonds in secondary market and accepts government debt (even Greek junk) as collateral, effectively lending to Greece

- Compare Greek debt situation to Argentina: Argentine debt held significantly by local institutions in foreign currency (dollar), while Greek debt in local currency held by foreign institutions; Greek debt issued under Greek law, Argentine debt under US/UK law; Greece not a serial defaulter and part of EU; Greece cannot adjust by devaluing currency

- October 2011, second bailout package for Greece of €130 billion (funded through EFSF and IMF-€30 billion). March 3, 2012, EZ disburses half, €71.5 billion, to facilitate restructuring of €206 billion (53.5% haircut) of private debt but withholds half for further austerity measures over which there have been riots

Balance Sheet of European Central Bank (billion Euros)

Period	Loans to Credit Institutions	Long-Term Refinancing Ops.	Securities Held	Total Assets
2012W6	820	652	283	2,593 ($3,556)
2011W52	864	704	274	2,736
2011W39	589	379	220	2,289
2011W26	455	313	134	1,944
2011W13	424	323	137	1,858
2011W1	494	298	135	1,966
2010W26	681	406	120	2,050
2010W1	724	669	28	1,880
2009W1	856	617	0	2,089
2008W1	398	268	0	1,286
2008W1	406	90	0	1,039

Source: European Central Bank

ECB becomes LLR to countries and banks: First two columns loans to banks, third purchases of government securities in secondary market—loans secured by government securities. Impact of this liquidity allows banks to fund their operations at favorable rates, and decreases yields on government debt because can be used as collateral for loans and is bought in secondary market by ECB.

$3.5T, compare March 1 balance sheet of Fed at $2.9T

Central banks cannot become insolvent, Roubini-Hart, Supp. materials because can print money but losses can impact taxpayers, through lower remittance of profits to national governments and tax impact of inflation. Dollar swap lines from U.S. to ECB, so can loan dollars without printing more euros—increases liquidity capacity without euro inflationary impact. Shows up as liability on ECB balance sheet. February 2012 Fed swap lines about $107 billion (to all central banks not just ECB, do not know maximum)

3 year cheap 1% LTROs: 12-21-2011, €489B; 2-29-2012, €529.5B (800 banks). Combined with wider acceptability of collateral. LTOs replace bond buying. What will they do with money? Carry trade, e.g. banks borrow at 1% and get 5% on Italian government bonds.

Germany has long standing concern with inflationary effects even though there is sterilization, Stark resigns from ECB, Weber resigns as Bundesbank President (Merkel supports policy).

February 28, 2012 Balance Sheet of European Central Bank

Source: European Central Bank

See 819B total loans to credit institutions and 283B of securities for monetary policy, ties into prior chart.

Irish Crisis

- Property bubble like the U.S.

- September 2010 Irish government injections in Irish banks amount to €45 billion, plus large Irish bank borrowings from ECB, €130 billion in October 2010, saddles Ireland with huge public debt

- Anglo Irish and Irish Nationwide in restructuring, liquidating bad assets, selling deposits and winding down other business—amounts to liquidation

- November 2010, EFSF lends $90 billion (€67.5 billion) to Ireland, may not be enough: some of funds to be used for further capital injections into banks (contemplates additional €8 billion injection with additional €25 billion set aside for future injections), austerity measures (difficult to sustain Irish political support), rates 5.8%, like Greece better than market (but funding cost 2.9%)

- Ruling party routed in 2011 elections on bank bailout issues (like US); "Burn the bondholders" of banks election theme; junior (non-deposit) debt of Anglo-Irish and Irish Nationwide to receive only 20% of par obligations; argument now over non-guaranteed senior debt (trading at 64% of face)—haircuts opposed by EU/IMF because of fear of contagion

- Interconnectedness with German and UK banks, Germany $138 billion, UK $148.5 billion

Source: Bloomberg

Revisions of Crisis Resolution Mechanism
(after Meeting of March 11, 2011 building on October 2010)

- New permanent Bailout Fund (European Stability Mechanism, ESM) (same size as present EFSF) to be created in 2013 (done previously); current EFSF brought up to full capacity (full €500 billion)

- Better terms on loans: 100 bp decrease for Greece to 4% with longer period to repay (market demands 18% for two years); Ireland rate remains at 5.8% because of failure to raise corporate tax rate

- Funds can buy government bonds in primary but not secondary market (only ECB does so in secondary market)

- Revitalized Stability and Growth Pact: failure to close gap between EU debt/GDP of 60% by 5% per year, results in fine of .2 percent GDP (agreed by Finance Ministers on March 14), with reverse majority vote to overrule; increased surveillance of economic and budgetary policies (excessive macroeconomic imbalance procedure, with sanctions, details to be determined)

- Possible private creditor losses (done previously for Greece) on case-by-case basis (fear that may intensify current crisis, or at last increase borrowing costs)

- CACs in bonds (with aggregation) going forward from 2013

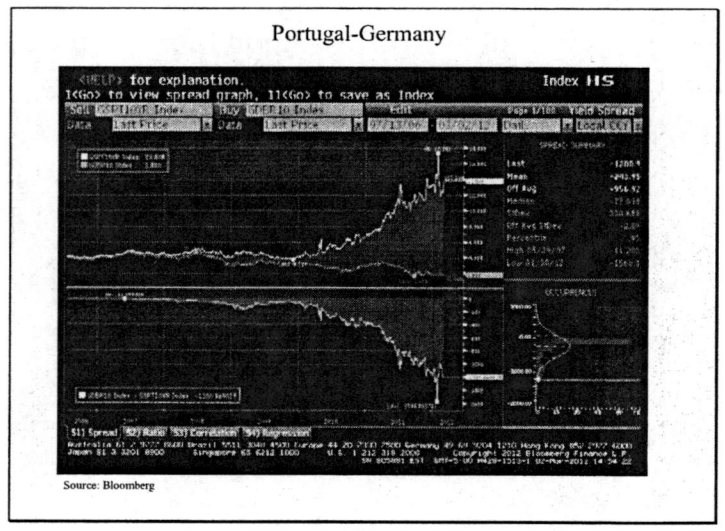

Portugal-Germany

Source: Bloomberg

Agreement of December 2011

- Second restructuring of Greece involves 50 percent private sector haircut with retroactive CACs– will not have private sector involvement (PSI) for other restructurings (sought to avoid contagion)

- EZ increases IMF contribution by €200 billion (which IMF can lend back to EZ countries with seniority and conditions)

- Enact local laws limiting debt to 60% of GDP, with automatic sanctions unless qualified majority (population weighted) opposes. UK opposition forces separate agreement and not Treaty Amendment, Hollande French socialist candidate says he will not accept sanctions (3-4-12)

- No increase in ERM €500 billion fund (but continuing pressure on Germany, including from US, to increase), but comes on board in 2012 rather than 2013

Terms of Greek Debt Restructuring-1

- Old bonds exchanged for (1) new 30 year bonds issued by Greece with a face amount of 31.5% of the exchanged bonds (68.5% haircut); (2) EFSF notes of face amount of 15% of old bonds with two years maturity from the exchange date; and (3) detachable GDP linked securities (nominal haircut of 53.5%). Also, exchanging bondholders will get EFSF notes for unpaid interest up to February 24, 2012 on old debt.

- The new Greek bonds have a step-up coupon: 2% through 2015, then 3% through 2020, then 3.65% in 2021, and then 4.3% from 2022 through 2042 (compare to yields in market before exchange of about 37%, but this reflects default).

- Unclear what net present value haircut will be on package, around 75% (reported write down of BNP Paribas)

- To be finalized by March 12, 2012.

Terms of Greek Debt Restructuring-2

- Aims for debt/GDP ratio of 120.5% by 2020 (IMF determined sustainability), still extremely burdensome, and does little to make economy more (need exchange rate depreciation)

- Retroactive CACs with 2/3 majority of the quorum vote, quorum of at least 2/3 of bond holders; Greece says wants 75% participation to go ahead (otherwise would have to use CACs, which could trigger CDSs, and if less than 66.6%, CACs do not work). No institutional exclusions from CAC voting . Will courts outside Greece accept this?

- ECB does not participate in bond exchange—so will get full payment (gets new bonds at same terms as old bonds that are part of exchange)

- March 2, ISDA says exchange terms do not constitute a "Restructuring Credit Event" so that CDSs on Greece are not triggered—could/should be different outcome if CACs are used

Restructuring and Holdouts

- Possibility of sovereign debt enforcement may make default (at least without a very attractive restructuring) more difficult

    (1)   Of the approximately €319 billion, 90 percent under Greek law

    (2)   Domestic assets like municipal tax revenues could be attachable (shaped by compliance with European Human Rights Convention), although could be changed by constitutional amendments, plus state-owned enterprises with assets outside Greece, plus threat to flows (payments to new bondholders on pari passu theory)

    (3)   Greek law does not permit amendments to bonds after issue (exit consent amendment problematic) and does not contain CACs making exchange offers more difficult--retroactive CACs may not be upheld by courts on public policy grounds—particularly a problem in UK under public policy doctrine

Update on Greek Restructuring

- Exchange offer imposes very high losses on bondholders, estimated 75% in net present value (face value 69.5%); trading at 16% of par before exchange; yields on new Greek bonds about 18.6%, indicating market expects re-restructuring, debt still expected to be 120% of GDP in 2020

- 85.8 % tender or €152 billion for €177 billion Greek law bonds outstanding, up to 95% (€25 billion additional) after triggering of CACs (assume additional 5% is held officially)

- 65.5% tender or €19 billion for €29 billion of foreign law bonds outstanding (€10 billion did not tender)

- Triggering of CACs is "credit event" triggering net payment of $3.2 billion payments on Greek CDSs (not clear extent to which tenders motivated by prospective "insurance")

- Possible lawsuits for €35 billion in CAC compelled and untendered foreign bonds

1. Given retroactive CACs, who will buy local bonds in future?—bonds can be changed completely, unless court strikes this technique down.

Scott Plan in "Sequel": Tighter Fiscal Control with Eurobonds

- Revised SGP not enough (local limits can be evaded and sanctions may not be imposed, just more of same), most countries exceed two limits

- All debt of Eurozone members—Eurobonds—issued with cross-guarantees. Subject to Eurozone approval (qualified majority) if member state debt exceeds 60% of GDP or what is otherwise thought to be a sustainable level—better than national brakes with sanctions

- Would make strong states' debt more expensive (due to guarantee obligations) but give them more control and lower future need for bailouts

- Transition rules permitting an increase of 10% over current levels without Eurozone approval for a set period of time, say 3 years

Next chart shows situation of countries
Treaty change which requires domestic limit of debt/GDP of 60% and allows qualified majority sanctions may be in trouble in France, Ireland and the Netherlands (EZ officials say will still go into effect if 12/17 favor)

Scott Plan in "Sequel": Tighter Fiscal Control with Eurobonds

- All debt of Eurozone members—Eurobonds—issued with cross-guarantees. Subject to Eurozone approval (qualified majority) if member state debt exceeds 60% of GDP or what is otherwise thought to be a sustainable level—better than national brakes with sanctions

- Would make strong states' debt more expensive (due to guarantee obligations) but give them more control and lower future need for bailouts

- Transition rules permitting an increase of 10% over current levels without Eurozone approval for a set period of time, say 3 years

Article 3 of the 235 Regulation

The introduction of the euro shall not have the effect of altering any term of a legal instrument or of discharging or excusing performance under any legal instrument, nor give a party the right unilaterally to alter or terminate such an instrument. This provision is subject to anything which parties may have agreed.

Reference

Section 5-1602 (2) of the New York General Obligations Law

None of

(a) the introduction of the euro; ...

(d) the calculating or determining of the subject of the medium of payment of a contract, security or instrument with reference to interest rate or other basis that has been substituted or replaced due to the introduction of the euro and that is a commercially reasonable substitute and substantial equivalent,

shall either have the effect of discharging or excusing performance under any contract, security or instrument, or give a party the right to unilaterally alter or terminate any contract, security or instrument.

Reference

EU Selected Countries (Eurostat, October 2011, February 2012)

Country	2010 Deficit/GDP	2010 Debt/GDP	2011 Debt/GDP
EZ Limit	**3.0**	**60.0**	
Belgium	4.1	96.2	98.5
Germany	4.3	83.2	81.8
Ireland	31.3	94.9	104.9
Greece	10.6	144.9	159.1
Spain	9.3	61.0	66.0
France	7.1	82.3	85.2
Italy	4.6	118.4 (€1.8T)	119.6
Netherlands	5.1	62.9	64.5
Austria	4.4	71.8	71.6
Portugal	9.8	93.3	110.1
Sweden	**+0.2**	**39.7**	37.0
U.K.	10.3	79.9	85.2

Only one country observed 3% deficit limit and 60% debt limit, Sweden and it was not in Eurozone.

Spanish Situation

- High budget deficit, 11.1%, but low public debt to GDP, 60%, lowered by over 2% through austerity measures in first 10 months of 2010, imposes own austerity measures

- Has created restructuring fund for banks, Fund for Orderly Bank Restructuring, which has injected capital of €11 billion into its banks, particularly the Cajas, savings banks exposed to deflation of real estate bubble—Spanish government says ailing Cajas, sare holding $136.8 billion in problem assets, estimated capital shortfall, under new capital requirements of €23-46 billion

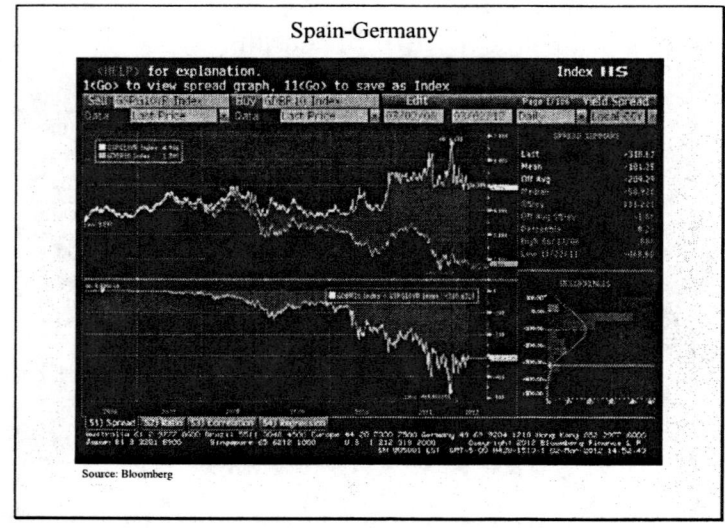

Spain-Germany

Source: Bloomberg

Italian Situation

- Third largest debtor in world, after U.S. and Japan, €1.8 trillion. Low budget deficit, 4.6%, but very high public debt to GDP, 118.4% (just the opposite of Spain). 2.2% negative growth

- Mario Monti reforms passed by legislature. The package includes spending cuts, tax rises and pension reforms. Are these real? Are they enough?

Italy-Germany

Source: Bloomberg

TEACHING PLAN FOR

CHAPTER SIX
JAPANESE FINANCIAL MARKETS

POWERPOINT SCREENS FOR NINETEENTH EDITION

Japanese Financial System

Brief Modern History of Japanese Financial System

- Post-World War I: creation of modern economy and financial system (free market period)
- 1940s centralized economic control for total war
- 1946-1980s: post-war reconstruction (managed high growth)
- 1980s: bubble economy and bank expansion
- 1992-2005: lost "decade"
- 2005-present, muddling through

Japanese Financial Markets

- 1992-2005: The Lost "Decade"—poor economy and NPLs

- Regulatory Structure: breakup of MOF and creation of Financial Services Agency (FSA)

- Changes in bank ownership from bailouts, mergers and sales to foreign investors

- Deposit insurance reforms: decrease in moral hazard by making bailouts less certain

- The failure of Big Bang to stimulate capital market

- Koizumi Postal Savings Reform in 2004 and its undoing due to NDP Election in 2009

How would you compare Japanese banking crisis with U.S. financial system crisis? Next slide.

Japan and U.S. Crises Compared

	Japan	U.S.
Period	1995-2005	2007-2010
Gross Cost	Banks (20% GDP)	Range of Financial Firms (4% GDP)
Economy	Too controlled	Too uncontrolled
Capital Markets	Weak-distrusted	Strong-but securitization fall off
Techniques	Gov. Capital	Gov. Capital/Massive Fed lending
Big Bank Mergers	Prevalent	Limited
Public Sector	P. Savings (Refuge)	GSEs ($200 billion injection)
Reg. Structure	FSA (gov) for MOF	Fragmented
Deposit Insurance	Create-limit	Increase-unlimited (during crisis, still trans)
Major Reg. Issue	Control NPLs (denial)	Dodd-Frank, total revision
Internationalized	Securities	Securities and banking
Recession	Prolonged	Limited
Unemployment	Moderate	High
Political Change	Radical DPJ (2009)	Moderate Obama (2008)
Structure	Cross-shares, G-S	Volcker Rules
Major Cause	Bad loans and stock bubble	Bad loans

- Japan NPL problem (two slides)
- MOJ Reorg (one slide)

Market share of foreign banks

The Lost Decade: NPLs (FSA)
(¥ trillion)

	1999/3	2000/3	2001/3	2002/3	2003/3	2004/3	2004
	33.9	31.8	33.6	43.2	35.3**	26.5	30.0***
Analysts			150.0*				
			($1.2T)				

*   25% GDP

**   Fukao (2003): Bank capital 2% of risk-adjusted assets; Hoshi and Kashyap (2004) negative net worth of ¥15T-20T

***   7% GDP

<u>Reference</u>
Why couldn't Japan get a handle on NPLs?   Next slide

The NPL Problem: The Delay in Response (Inaccurate Numbers)

- Cover up with foreign "technology" as in CSFB case—probably with knowledge and perhaps acquiescence of MOF—removed bad loans for cash during inspection, then returned to bank

- If the banks were acknowledged to be bankrupt much more public money would have to be spent, which would be hugely unpopular for LDP (typical problem in bad bank crises)

- Senior management of bankrupt banks would be fired, and perhaps prosecuted (happened later than sooner)

- MOF would be blamed and held accountable (happened later than sooner with breakup)

- If the banks were bankrupt, zombie companies could not be kept afloat (no bank money): estimated that if all bad loans in 2002 had been written off, unemployment would rise by 143,000 and 72,000 would drop out of work force—loss of votes, and high cost of unemployment compensation, estimated at ¥860 billion per year ($8.6 billion)

How did Japan deal with its failing banks, compared to us?

Bank Bailouts and Mergers in 1990s

- Appropriation of new public funds: ¥ 90T (20% GDP)
  - Capital injections ¥11.26T: ¥685B for Jusens (housing loan companies); ¥9.3T general; Resona ¥1.6T
  - Special DIC account for NPLs, ¥17T
  - Fund for disposal of bankrupt banks, ¥17T
  - Fund to purchase bad debts of banks under temporary public control, ¥18T
- Government owned 90% of bank shares (preferred stock convertible into common), later reprivatized
- Weakest banks merged into less weak banks
  - Mizuho
  - SMFG (Sumitomo-Mitsui financial group) acquired Daiwa Securities, 2nd largest securities firm
  - MTFG (Bank of Tokyo-Mitsubishi) acquired UFJ
- Sales and Nationalizations
  - Nippon Credit and LTCB sold to western investors (Aozora and Shinsei)
  - Resona and Ashikaga nationalized

U.S. Parallels

- Public funds: TARP $700 billion, GSEs $400 billion (w/Obama plan), $75 billion for mortgage modification (8% GDP); if count all of $1.9T of Fed lending, then 21% GDP.
- Government ownership: less of a position in
- Mergers: BofA-Merrill and Countrywide; JP-Bear; Wells-Wachovia
- Takeover and sale, IndyMac; many smaller banks

Bankruptcy Lehman, Japan did not do this

Deposit Insurance

- Idea of limited deposit insurance protection is more market discipline—depositors over ceilings are at risk

- Unlimited time deposit guarantee removed in April 2002

- Planned April 2003 removal of unlimited guarantee of demand deposit accounts and substitution of ¥10 million ceiling ($84k) was deferred until April 2005

- Reason for deferral: threat of run on banks, capital flight or vast expansion of postal savings system which is backed by complete government guarantee

<u>U.S. Parallel</u>

U.S. increases DI to $250,000 and then unlimited; FDIC guarantees senior debt

Regulatory Structure

- MOF mismanagement in 1990s (bad policy and wining and dining scandals) leads to breakup of authority: creation of FSA and independence of BOJ

- FSA: more politically responsible than MOF but continues concentration of regulatory authority

- FSA more transparent and rule-based than MOF

Is this a good solution?

U.S. parallel: Japan goes from a completely consolidated structure controlled by MOF to BOJ (more independent) and FSA. U.S. has to deal with fragmentation. UK reorganization by contrast: FSA under BOJ plus new market conduct agency, coordinated by Treasury. Treasury/MOF role in Japan minimized.

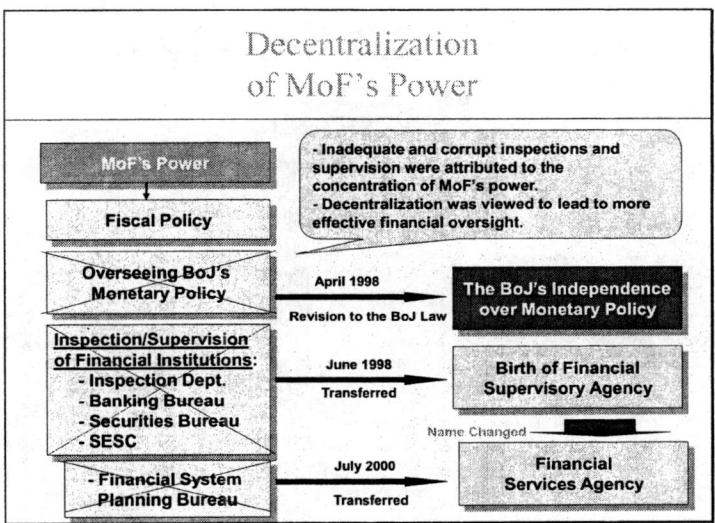

Reference

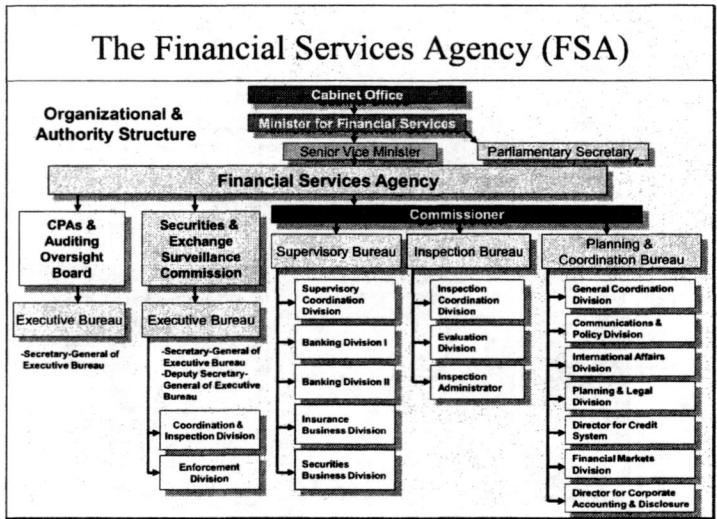

Note that Japan structure is plugged into government, FSA reports to cabinet. U.S. structure has more independent agencies (Fed and SEC). FSA style reflects MOF history: bureaucratic, technical, arms length—to avoid problems MOF had in past—now becoming more industry friendly.

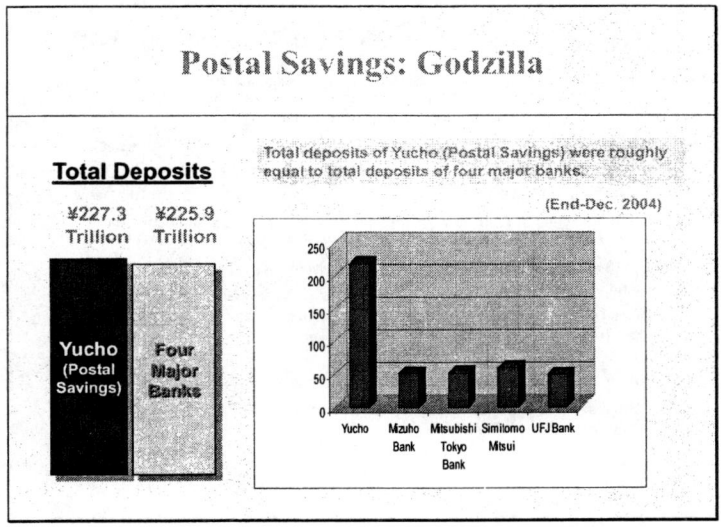

- Takes deposits through 24,000 postal offices
- Major investor in JGBs

Employs about 226,000 people and, with assets today of more than ¥300 trillion, sits at the heart of a system of public institutions that own almost half of Japan's national debt.

Privatization of Postal Savings System

- Four postal businesses—over-the-counter services, postal delivery, *Yucho* (postal savings) and *Kampo* (postal life insurance) became separate subsidiaries of a holding company, wholly owned by the government, in 2007

- Each subsidiary to be 2/3rd privatized by 2017 (state share remains 1/3rd), guarantees removed, employees lose civil servant status

- Reasons for privatization
  - Halt allocation of funds to FILP program (investment in non-productive "political" assets like wasteful construction projects) which are about ¥78T (16% GDP)
  - Shift use of personal savings to productive assets such as business loans or private equity business
  - Create even playing field with banks for attraction of deposits (postal savings has complete guarantee, and no cost of capital, taxes or deposit insurance premium obligations)
  - Avoid potential losses from guarantee
  - Eliminate source of political patronage for postal lobby of LDP (as well as Amikaduri for MOF and FSA bureaucrats)

Would this reform improve the financial system? How should it be changed?

GSE counterpart in U.S.

Privatization Problems

- Will create a huge new competitor for banks on the asset side, e.g. loans

- Formal removal of guarantees will be meaningless because the privatized *Yucho* will be too-big-to fail

- Less demand for JGBs

- A better plan would be to put declining caps on liabilities, thus forcing new deposits to go to private sector and lead to long-term phase out of postal savings system (but are deposits running off anyway?); like GSEs

DPJ Approach to Privatization of Postal Savings

- Reverses privatization. Old LDP members who opposed Koizumi and Takenaka's initiative now part of DPJ
- PS exempt from normal bank regulation and market discipline
- Continued tax exemptions
- Possible revival of bridges to nowhere—pork on grand scale, use low rates paid to depositors as funding source for projects and demand for government bonds used to finance projects
- Doubles cap on deposits from 10 to 20 million yen ($220,000)
- No sale of Japan Post shares—government will hold 1/3 of holding company shares, enough to control
- Concerns lodged by U.S. Trade Representative

The Failure of Big Bang

- Big Bang, announced on November 11, 1996, was trumpeted by the then Hashimoto government as a sweeping reform of the financial markets, particularly the capital markets (at first just a concept)

- Measures: liberalize foreign exchange, break down structural barriers between different financial institutions, free up prices (e.g. abolish fixed brokerage commissions), open up to foreign firms and products, easy market entry to firms and issues, lower taxes on financial transactions (lower capital gain rate, abolish transaction taxes); mark-to-market accounting; reorganize regulatory structure

- Mostly done but:

Capital markets are still underdeveloped, why?

Falling equity markets are unattractive to investors; no trust in disclosure, minimum enforcement
Lack of investor initiative for returns given defined benefit pensions
Local corporate bond markets are less attractive than international markets
Markets are viewed as rigged (Livedoor) and subject to government intervention and interference (attack on derivatives)
Perceived hostility to foreign banks: nit picking inspections and business suspensions (same for domestic and has improved)
Banking system doldrums had triple effect: banks do not pursue opportunities in capital markets when worried about survival, banks continue to promote banking at expense of capital markets.

Shift to Direct Finance

- Ratio of loans to shares and other equity has improved from 6x in 1980 to 2x in 2009 but still low compared to US in 2008 where bank deposits are 23% compared to equity of 21%

- More telling is what amount of debt is intermediated. In Japan, bank deposits to private debt securities is 44 to 9% compared to U.S. where it is 23 to 41%

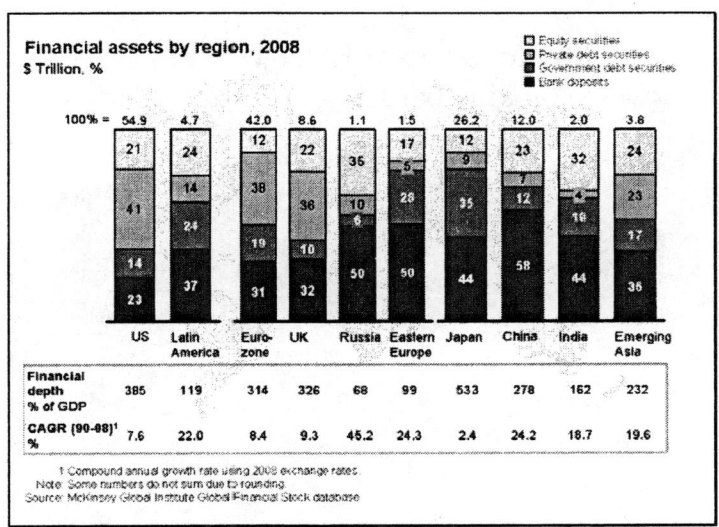

Financial assets by region, 2008
$ Trillion, %

Equity securities
Private debt securities
Government debt securities
Bank deposits

100% =	54.9	4.7	42.0	8.6	1.1	1.5	26.2	12.0	2.0	3.8
	21	24	12	22	36	17	12	23	32	24
	41	14	38	36	10	5	9	7	4	23
	14	24	19	10	6	28	35	12	16	17
	23	37	31	32	50	50	44	58	44	36
	US	Latin America	Euro-zone	UK	Russia	Eastern Europe	Japan	China	India	Emerging Asia
Financial depth % of GDP	385	119	314	326	68	99	533	278	162	232
CAGR (90-08)¹ %	7.6	22.0	8.4	9.3	45.2	24.3	2.4	24.2	18.7	19.6

1 Compound annual growth rate using 2008 exchange rates.
Note: Some numbers do not sum due to rounding.
Source: McKinsey Global Institute Global Financial Stock database

Japan much more bank centric than U.S.

Market Share of Foreign Banks: Low in Banking but High in Capital Markets

Activity	Share	Year
Lending	13.7	12-2004
Foreign Exchange Trading	71.1	04-2004
Japanese Public Equity	21.8	03-2004
Brokerage	39.9	2004
Japanese Cos. equity deals	36.9	2004
IPOs of Japanese Cos.	38.7	2004
M&A with Japanese Co.	65.6	2004

TEACHING PLAN FOR

CHAPTER TWENTY-ONE
CHINESE
FINANCIAL SYSTEM

POWERPOINT SCREENS FOR NINETEENTH EDITION

Chinese Financial System

Major Issues for Chinese Financial System

- State run economy: capitalism and the state
- State ownership of banks, advantage or problem—regulation or control
- No bank deposit insurance, parallel with Japan
- Accurate reporting of bank NPLs, p. 1207, % lower but absolute big
- Mixture of banking and securities, like Japan bank-dominated
- Restriction on foreign ownership of Chinese banks (total 25p/individual 20p, and Chinese companies (share classes, and QFII investment in RMB A-shares)
- Forcing foreign banks to operate through subs (while seeking branches in US)
- Restrictions on Chinese investment abroad
- Relationship of Hong Kong and Shanghai capital markets
- Glass-Steagall separation between banks and securities firms (historically different in 1980s but banks got into trouble)
- Chinese-dollar exchange rate, 6.32 compared to 8.28 to 1 dollar in 2005, but still undervalued
- Internationalization of RMB
- Use of foreign exchange reserves: dollar or euro

China and U.S. Compared		
	China	U.S.
Economy	Public (?)	Private
State Role	Ownership/regulation	Regulation
Bank Role	Dominant	Subsidiary to capital markets
Exchange Rate	Pegged to basket	Floating
Deposit Insurance	None	Limited to $250,000 (trans, unlimited 2012)
Political System	Non-democratic	Democratic
GDP	Second (not p.c)	First
Regulatory Structure	State/Commissions	Fragmented
Capital controls	In/out	None
Stock Market cap	China $4T; HK $2.7T (mainland second)	$17T (first)
Extent of regulation	weak to moderate	heavy
Private enforcement	none (like Japan)	heavy
Public enforcement	moderate	heavy

- Japan NPL problem (two slides)
- MOJ Reorg (one slide)
- Market share of foreign banks

TEACHING PLAN FOR

CHAPTER SEVEN
CAPITAL ADEQUACY

POWERPOINT SCREENS FOR NINETEENTH EDITION

Capital Requirements

Capital Adequacy: The Basics

- Why do governments regulate bank capital? Why internationally?
- What is capital economically? Is it correctly defined by Basel I?
- How can a bank increase capital?

Start here with why regulate capital? See next slide

Why Do Governments Regulate Bank Capital Adequacy?

#1 Prevent bank failure, due to systemic risk concern, by providing a cushion for losses

and therefore:

#2 Reduce moral hazard for owners by making sure they have substantial capital at risk and thus reduce bailout costs.

and also

#3 Attempt to insure fair competition

Why internationally? cross-border impact, systemic risk, fair competition (slides)

Impact on Competition:
Leverage Increases Return on Equity

Assume $1 profit per $100 loan

Country	Capital	Loans	Leverage	% Capital	Profit	ROC
A	10	100	100/10=10	(10/100) 10%	1	(1/10) 10%
B	10	200	200/10=20	(10/200) 5%	2	(2/10) 20%

If country A set a 10% capital rule, its banks would lose in competition against those from country B that set a 5% capital rule. Country B's banks could either earn a larger profit (ROC) or reduce the cost of their loans to win a larger share of the loan market, or some of both. But B's cost of capital should be higher due to greater risk (assuming no bailouts).
Can international capital regulation level the competitive playing field? Other factors like bailouts, accounting (revaluation reserves versus mark-to-market), uneven implementation (partially dependent on allowed discretion). Indeed, A may have to have even more capital than 10% to compete for funds with B at 5% if there is a big enough bailout differential between B and A (Scott and Iwahara). B could have higher leverage and lower cost of capital.

Capital Adequacy

- What is capital economically? Is it correctly defined by Basel I?

What is capital economically? Fair/market value of assets – fair/market value of liabilities.

What is economic capital?

Assets - Liabilities = Capital

100 - 90 = 10

How can a failed bank have capital that is
10% of assets moments before it fails?

How can a bank fail when it seems to have substantial capital?
Capital and assets are overvalued. Regulators need to know real capital,
which is real assets less real liabilities. A $100 loan may only be worth
$70 because default is likely. But they cannot accurately determine these
because loans do not lend themselves to market valuation. Next slide
However, under US accounting rules, known losses on loans should be
taken account of by treating the loan as impaired and reducing its value
and other assets would be marked-to market, e.g. mortgage-related
securities, so under accounting rules this discrepancy should be narrowed.
However, if RAP departs from GAAP, as was the case before the US thrift
crisis, there can be a difference (still a difference though narrower).
It is also the case that the bank can have adequate accounting capital
which is not sufficient to withstand a liquidity crisis, withdrawal of funds
that requires "fire sale" of assets. Cox said Bear had enough capital the
week before it failed.

What is capital?

Assets - Liabilities = Capital

100 - 90 = 10

70 - 90 = -20

What Went Wrong?

Institution	Last reported assets ($BN)	Last reported capital ratio
Bear Stearns	399	14.4%
Merrill Lynch	966	12.3%
Lehman Brothers	639	16.1%
WaMu	310	13.9%
Wachovia	764	12.4%

Source: SNL, Company 10-K and 10-Q filings. Bear Stearns data as of Q1 2008 (assets) and 1/31/08 (capital ratio); Merrill Lynch, Lehman Brothers, and WaMu as of 2Q 2008; Wachovia as of 3Q 2008, Kuritzkes, Harvard 2012

Liquidity Problem: Loss of Funding

Assets - Liabilities = Capital

$100 - 90 = 10$

$40 - 60 = -20$

- Funding of 30 suddenly withdrawn
- Only get 30 for fire sale of assets with accounting value of 60
- Left with 40 in assets and 60 of liabilities

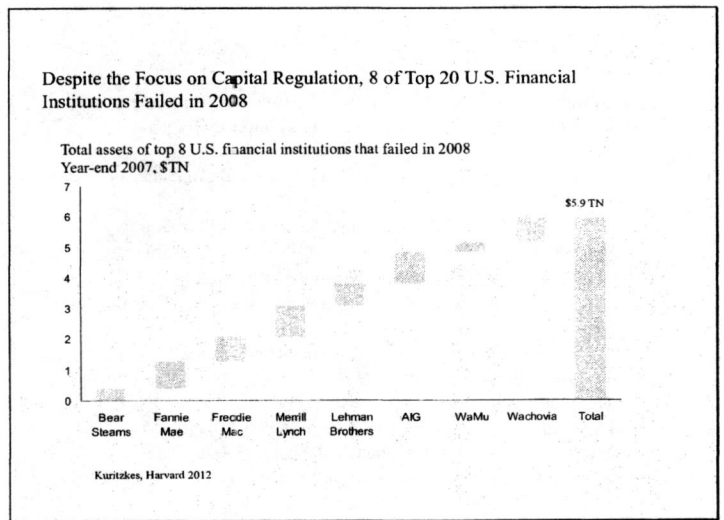

Despite the Focus on Capital Regulation, 8 of Top 20 U.S. Financial Institutions Failed in 2008

Total assets of top 8 U.S. financial institutions that failed in 2008
Year-end 2007, $TN

Kuritzkes, Harvard 2012

Some Basics on Basel Accord

- Began with U.S.-U.K. coordinated efforts in 1986 (US had leverage ratio, UK had risk-weight approach, Japan had lower leverage ratio than US)
- Promulgated in 1988 by G-10 countries through Basel Committee on Banking Regulation and Supervisory Practices

  Belgium, Canada, France, Germany, Italy, Japan, Luxembourg, the Netherlands, Spain, Sweden, Switzerland, UK, and US (13)

- EU adopts as Capital Adequacy Directive. Extends to:

  Austria, Denmark, Finland, Greece, Ireland and Portugal (non G-10 members)

- Many other countries adopt: de facto international standard for respectability and condition for entry into other countries
- Agreement of central bankers--not a treaty
- Minimum standards for **international** banks but scope extended in some countries: U.S. and EU applied to all banks; U.S. to holding companies (does not apply to investment banks, insurance companies nor GSEs until recently)

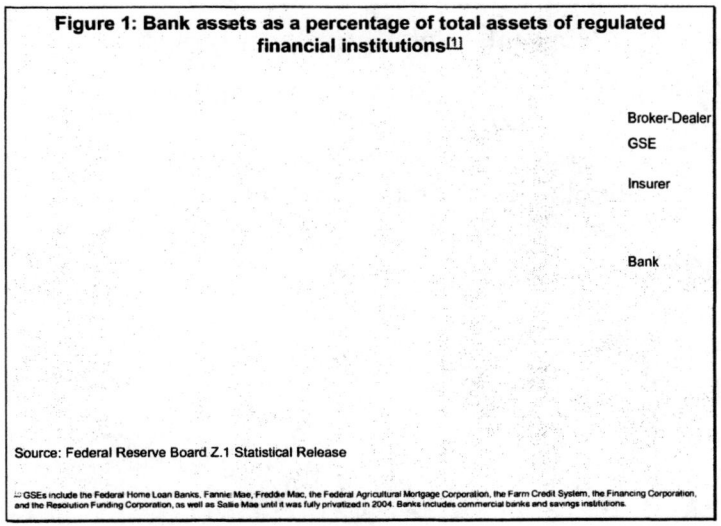

Figure 1: Bank assets as a percentage of total assets of regulated financial institutions[1]

Broker-Dealer

GSE

Insurer

Bank

Source: Federal Reserve Board Z.1 Statistical Release

[1] GSEs include the Federal Home Loan Banks, Fannie Mae, Freddie Mac, the Federal Agricultural Mortgage Corporation, the Farm Credit System, the Financing Corporation, and the Resolution Funding Corporation, as well as Sallie Mae until it was fully privatized in 2004. Banks includes commercial banks and savings institutions.

Note, that bank assets subject to capital only cover about one-half the financial system, reflection of US capital markets importance, coverage would be higher in Europe and Japan.

Capital Adequacy: Basel Issues

- Do the Basel I bank capital standards adequately deal with credit risk?
- Basel II: Is it an improvement over Basel I?
- Implications of financial crisis for Basel II
- Basel III and its general impact

Bank Capital Adequacy Rules for Banks–
Basel I Definition of Capital

What is capital under the Basel Accord? Is
it correctly defined?

Note: Basel also set capital rules for off balance sheet operations, like swaps, which we will not discuss here.
See next slide for accounting capital, Basel adjusts from there.

Accounting Capital

Assets	Liabilities and Capital
80 Loans	40 Deposits (20 insured)
20 Other	50 Debt
	10 Equity

1. Equity is accounting value of assets minus accounting value of debt, so-called book value.
- Earnings increase capital by generating cash (addition to assets) and corresponding increase in value of equity.
- Might then adjust for regulation, e.g. not count goodwill as an asset, or count revaluation reserves (value of securities over cost if use cost accounting, see Japan when Basel adopted)

Might also regard some forms of debt, e.g. subordinated debt, or contingent debt as capital.

Basel I Rules as Implemented in U.S.: Types of Capital

- Tier I capital (equity and near equity) = 4% of risk-weighted assets—6% for well-capitalized
  - Trust preferred and other hybrid instruments maximum of 15% of Tier I
  - Does not include goodwill
  - Adds back losses on available for sale assets in "Other Comprehensive Income" (divergence with normal accounting rule)
- Tier II capital: Limited to 100% of Tier I
  - includes loan loss reserves (U.S. accounting just "known") limited to 1.25% of risk-weighted assets
  - includes revaluation reserves of 45% of gains on equities (get 100% in earnings from mark-to-market of trading book)
- Total capital = 8% of risk-weighted assets
    (if Tier I is 4%, Tier II must be 4%, and total is 8%)
    10% for well-capitalized
- Capital requirements apply to banks and holding company
- Overall leverage ratio (capital to total assets) of at least 3%, 5% for well capitalized

---

Tier I is basically common stock: total residual resources available to meet current claims on the bank and ultimate claims in bankruptcy. (Non-cumulative perpetual preferred stock is very like common stock: missed dividends are not made up later). Hybrids? Qualify as debt for tax purposes (deduct interest) and as capital for Basel, like equity. Disturbing departure on AFS assets, lessened cushion in credit crisis

Tier II is a potpourri of capital that is not quite as permanent, reliable or residual as Tier I. It can be capital instruments such as subordinated debt which are almost as residual as common stock. Sub debt would rank below the deposit insurer in bankruptcy. Risky to allow revaluation reserves or to use mark-to-market due to volatility of stock/real estate (Japanese experience). LLR limits are artificial (but known loss problem). Gimmicky sources: tax deferred assets in Japan (50% of Tier II that banks might never use).

What are the major issues with this approach?

Issues on Definition of Capital

- Determination of overall percentage—may be too low
- Use of "capital" versus "equity (inclusion of loan provisions), TCE the narrowest
- Departure of RAP from GAAP, treatment of AFS losses
- Retention of leverage ratio
- Application to holding company (systemic risk; source of strength)
- Consolidation of off-balance sheet entities (was more liberal on consolidation than Fin46 for conduits (Fin46 itself too liberal and now revised with Basel tracking)
- Cyclicality, need to raise capital in credit crunch: could have higher requirements in good times (dynamic provisioning is one approach) or contingent capital (claim for capital, a capital derivative)
- Higher loan loss reserves (expected not just known)

See next chart to see how much "capital" banks were said to have in 2007, mis-measured or insufficient.

See second chart on difference between Tier I and TCE

The 4% + 4% and 8% ratios are a compromise from common experience in the 1980s and a study in 1987 that looked at existing levels of capital. The regulators had to start somewhere and did not want to raise capital requirements substantially above then current levels.

Note: higher levels of capital in real world, business risk; competitive issue

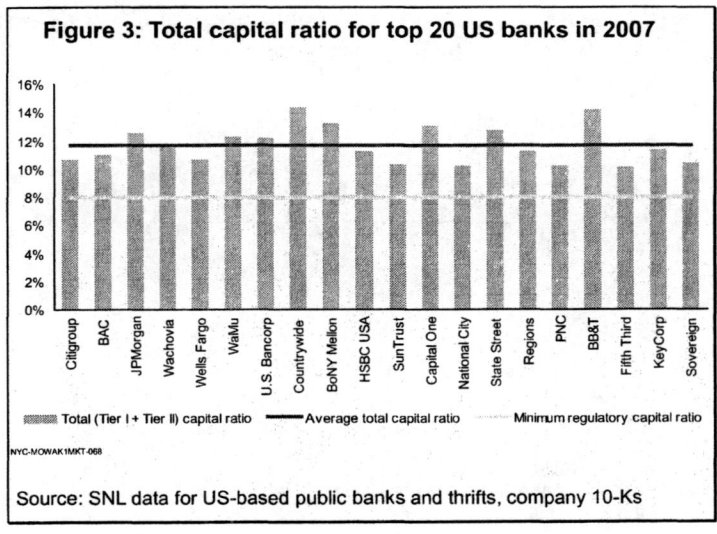

Figure 3: Total capital ratio for top 20 US banks in 2007

Total (Tier I + Tier II) capital ratio   Average total capital ratio   Minimum regulatory capital ratio

NYC-MOWAK1MKT-068

Source: SNL data for US-based public banks and thrifts, company 10-Ks

Higher than required for large banks—well capitalized 10%, average 12%, note Countrywide among top but fails. Why more than required? Ratings, business risks.

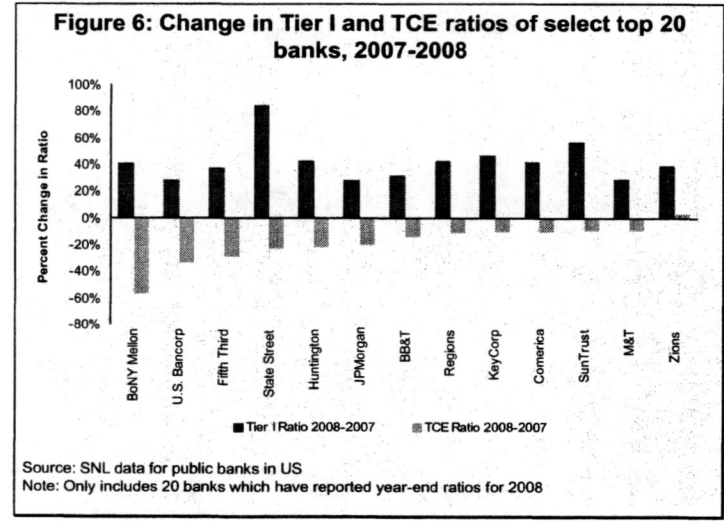

Figure 6: Change in Tier I and TCE ratios of select top 20 banks, 2007-2008

Source: SNL data for public banks in US
Note: Only includes 20 banks which have reported year-end ratios for 2008

Mellon's TCE decreased dramatically by almost 60% while Tier I capital increased by 40%. So may have had enough of Basel but not equity

If bank needs more capital what can it do?

Impact on Bank Operations:
If Bank's Capital Nears 8% Minimum, What Can It Do?

- Increase retained earnings (reduce dividends)
- Issue equity (expensive)
- Issue debt (e.g. sub debt up to 2%, ½ of Tier II)
- Reduce loans and/or securitize
- Issue hybrid instruments, e.g. trust preferred (15% Tier I)
- Shift loan portfolio to low-risk weighted assets (regulatory arbitrage) or shift risky loans/activities to affiliate with lower capital requirements (somewhat limited by U.S. holding company capital requirements)
- Merge with bank with more capital

```
Credit Risk Standards under Basel I
          Risk Weighted Assets


Weight        Description of Assets (includes)
  0%          Cash and loans to OECD governments
 20%          Short-term claims on non-OECD banks
 50%          Residential mortgage loans (secured)
100%          All other loans (including all private
              borrowers)
```

Before Basel there was just an overall leverage ratio so this was thought to be an improvement, but there were significant problems in the risk-weighting approach.

Why treat loans to all OECD governments as carrying the same risk? Both Greece and Germany are members of the OECD and the risk of lending to them differs a lot. The G-10 regulators wrote these rules and they could not, politically, distinguish among themselves. They may also have wanted to encourage investment in assets of OECD governments, like US treasuries.

Why treat residential mortgage loans as half as risky as all other loans? All residential mortgages cannot be less risky than fully collateralized loans to, say, major corporations like IBM. This was a political decision that is a form of credit allocation, encouraging loans to home owners. **How does this stand up with subprime?**

How can all other loans have the same risk-weight?
This deficiency was well recognized and generated pressure for more refinements leading to Basel II

Basel II: Overview

Pillar 1. Minimum regulatory capital charge

    a. Standardized approach

    b. Internal Ratings-Based (IRB) approach
- Foundation, F-IRB
- Advanced, A-IRB

Pillar 2. Supervisory review (stress tests)

Pillar 3. Market discipline (disclosure)

> **Basel II: Standardized Approach**
> **for Most Banks (not adopted in U.S.)**
>
> – Banks use rating agencies to classify borrowers, then Basel
>   specifies risk weights that correspond to rating categories
>
>   • for Sovereigns: 0% [AAA to AA-], 20%, 50%, 100%, 150%
>   • for Banks, Parastatals: rated as above or unrated one bucket
>   below sovereign rating
>   • for Corporates: 20%, 50%, 100%, 150%
>
> – Unrated borrowers: 100%
> – Loans with mortgage: residential, 35% (even lower!);
>   commercial, 100%
> – Capital reduced by credit mitigation techniques: collateral,
>   guarantees, derivatives, insurance and netting
> – Extremely detailed rules
>
> **Does this significantly improve on Basel I?**

Most banks in the world (but none of the really big and important ones) would follow the standardized approach. If the borrower has a credit rating, that would determine the weight, e.g., a loan to a sovereign borrower rated by S&P as AAA to AA- is weighted zero, A+ to A- is 20%, BBB+ to BBB- is 50%, B+ to B- is 100%, below B- is 150%.

Does this solve the problems of the original Accord?

Yes: distinctions among borrowers are finer and use private assessments
No: rating agencies are not necessarily qualified to judge smaller individual loans—   they have conflicts of interest because they work for issuers, see subprime, plus very wrong in financial crisis

  1. historical differences in credit performance between AA- and A+ are minimal
  2. rating only individual loans misses portfolio risk
  3. still use very rough weights (0/20/50/100/150)
  4. unrated borrowers are all weighted 100%, even those riskier than B- rated companies which have a 150% risk-weight
  5. residential mortgages still get preferential weights, see subprime
  6. does not end "regulatory arbitrage": if require too little capital for risky loans, make more of those loans (banks only worried about overall capital); plus arbitrage among institutions: if capital requirements for bank guarantees too high, some other firm, e.g. insurance company, will do); high capital requirements for credit derivatives drove business to AIG (see next two charts)

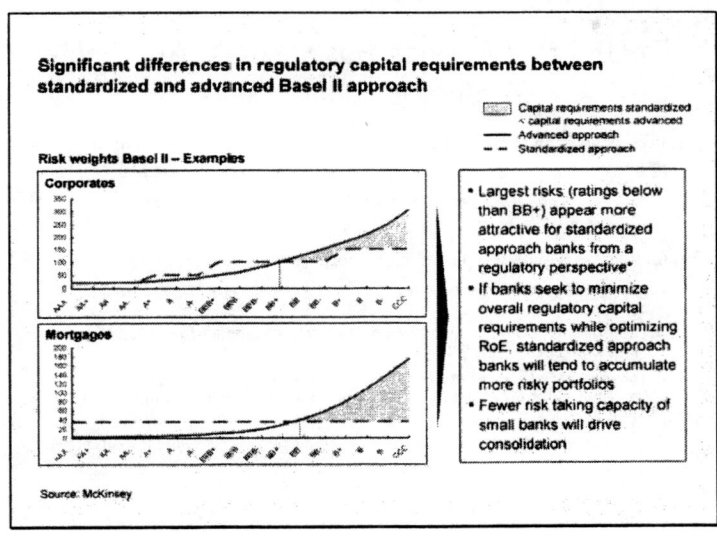

This is really an intra-bank issue, since some banks will be standardized (or something close as in US) whereas others will be using advanced approach

The Internal Ratings-Based (IRB) Approach for Sophisticated Banks

Regulators let sophisticated banks use models ("internal ratings") to rate risk

    Foundation Approach: Basel sets components of many parameters

    Advanced Approach: banks set more components

Parameters: vary with 6 types of loans (corporate, retail, bank . . .)

    a. borrower: probability of default (PD), based on internal ratings, over 1 year

    b. transaction: extent of loss given default, takes account of terms and collateral (LGD)

    c. amount at risk: exposure at default—how much would be owed, takes account of set-offs (netting of deposits against loans) and commitments (EAD)

    d. maturity: assume at least 2.5 years for all corporate credit under F-IRB (M)

    Bank ratings "map on" to risk-weights

    Capital requirements increased if credit is concentrated (granularity)

Comparison of Basel Approach to
Models for Credit, Market and
Operational Risk?

Models for
Credit, Market and Operational Risk

- Credit Risk: IRB models have regulatory parameters which do not generally take into account diversification of risk (granularity is rough adjustment)

- Market Risk: models with strict paramaters but can take account of diversification

- Operational Risk: AMA permits full use of models (insurance mitigation limited to 20% of the operational risk charge)

Why the difference?

Criticism of credit risk models on next page.
AMA = Advanced Management Approach

Criticism of Credit Risk Models

Fed: Internal models have many problems, more serious than for market risk models (bigger volumes, longer periods)

- **Not yet analytically sound** (designed for product profitability)
  - Simple default/no definition of risk misses extent of actual loss
  - 1 year time horizon to reduce exposure often too short
  - For same loan type, one bank estimated risk 10x more than another because of different modeling assumptions
- **Limited market data force many assumptions, estimates**
- **Hard to test after-the-fact**

Old criticisms, models may have improved

A Key Failure of Basel II was Over-Reliance on Complex Risk Models

Examples of Pillar I pitfalls

	Risk estimate	Reality
Market risk	Merrill Lynch's reported average 95% daily VaR from Q4 2007 through Q3 2008: $57 MM	Merrill Lynch's cumulative trading losses from Q4 2007 through Q3 2008: >$20 BN
Credit risk	Moody's estimated lifetime losses on 2006 Alt-A mortgages in May 2008: 5.5%	Moody's estimated lifetime losses on 2006 Alt--A mortgages in January 2009: 19.8%
Operational risk	Operational risk models based on historical events not including extreme market stresses caused by crisis	Many latent risks relating to market disruption, e.g. fiduciary risks on money market funds, lender liability relating to loan securitizations

Sources: Moody's Investor Service, (2009). "Alt-A RMBS Loss Projection Update", Structured Finance Rating Methodology, January 22
Merrill Lynch 10-Q from Q1, Q2, and Q32008 and 10-K from 2007

Basel II Approach to Operational Risk

- Includes All Non-Business Loss Risk, e.g. mistakes, external disasters (business risk is why most firms hold capital)
- Basic Indicator Approach: 12% of gross Income
- Standardized Approach: 12 % of gross income of 8 business lines weighted for different risk.
- Advanced Measurement Approach: internal models with parameters
- Credit for risk mitigation through insurance limited to 20%

Basel II: U.S. Implementation

- Only advanced IRB (mandatory for 10 largest internationally active banks and their holding companies, 10 more can qualify)—EU applies three levels of Basel II to all banks
- Large U.S. banks will have minimum capital floors higher than Basel during transition (congressional and FDIC pressure), new statutory floors set by Dodd-Frank, "Collins Amendment")
- Implementation delayed until April 2011—EU implemented in 2008, with revisions in 2010 (U.S. banks had Basel I during financial crisis)
- Other U.S. banks will be subject to some version of the standardized approach, for the time being Basel I (but Dodd-Frank ratings purge problem); no Foundation-IRB
- Retention of leverage ratio
- Complicated further by Basel III and Dodd-Frank

Collins Amendment:
Dodd-Frank Section 171(b)(2)

(2) MINIMUM RISK-BASED CAPITAL REQUIREMENTS.—The appropriate Federal banking agencies shall establish minimum risk-based capital requirements on a consolidated basis for insured depository institutions, depository institution holding companies, and nonbank financial companies supervised by the Board of Governors. The minimum risk-based capital requirements established under this paragraph shall not be less than the generally applicable risk-based capital requirements, which shall serve as a floor for any capital requirements that the agency may require, nor quantitatively lower than the generally applicable risk-based capital requirements that were in effect for insured depository institutions as of the date of enactment of this Act.

Investment Banks and Capital

- Prior to 2004, only had required capital (SEC net capital rule) for broker-dealer subsidiaries to protect customer accounts (securities in custody)
- EU Conglomerate Directive required that U.S. banks operating in EU have a holding company regulator, and a key part of this regulation was capital.
- SEC responded by becoming regulator (CSE program); U.S. banks avoid having European regulator. Imposes lite form of Basel II to investment bank holding companies; no leverage ratio (group of 28 mostly lawyers, supervise major investment banks)
- Investment banks had a higher leverage than commercial banks subject to leverage ratio (next slide)
- Major investment banks fail or are acquired (Bear, Merrill, Lehman) or become thrift/bank holding companies subject to normal bank capital requirements (Goldman, Morgan Stanley)— CSE program abolished by Dodd-Frank

See next chart for differences of bank and investment bank leverage ratios. CSE is consolidated supervised entity program.

Table 1: Leverage ratios of top five commercial and investment banks					
Investment Banks			**Commercial Banks**		
Bank Name	**Gross Leverage**			**Bank Name**	**Gross Leverage**
Goldman Sachs	26			Citigroup	19
Morgan Stanley	33			Bank of America	12
Merrill Lynch	32			JPMorgan Chase	13
Lehman Bros	31			Wachovia	10
Bear Stearns	34			Wells Fargo	12
Average	**31**			**Average**	**13**

Source: SNL. Gross Leverage is defined as total assets divided by total equity

Basel III is Intended to Address the Perceived Shortcomings of Basel II

Basel II

- Market and counterparty credit risks vastly underestimated

- Regulatory capital definition distorted by accounting conventions

- High failure rate at prevailing capital levels

- Moral hazard from bailouts of TBTF banks

- Liquidity risk as the ultimate killer

Basel III

- Stringent requirements for "stress VaR"

- Renewed emphasis on Tier I common capital (equity)

- Increase in overall capital requirements

- Additional surcharge for the largest global banks (G-SIBS)

- Extensive new liquidity rules

Kuritzkes, Harvard 2012

Basel III Capital Rules

Earlier 2.5 increased capital required for securitizations and trading book
- New Common Equity (includes mark-to-market losses on available for sale assets) to RWA Ratios (Pillar I implementation date)
  - 4.5% baseline (2015)
  - 2.5% conservation buffer (2016-2019)
  - Discretionary (up to 2.5%) countercyclical buffer (high growth response)
- Higher Tier I capital to RWA Ratio
  - Increased from 4% to 6% (2015), total capital remains at 8% (Tier II decreased to 2%)
- Minimum Leverage ratio of 3% of all assets (U.S. now 5% for well capitalized banks) (2018)
- Higher capital requirements for G-SIBs
  - Basel identifies 29 G-SIBs which will have to hold 1-2.5% additional capital depending on their systemic importance, also required by DFA
  - Swiss finishes, EU sovereign risk stress tests also increase
- Operates in context of tougher accounting consolidation rules
- Basel 3.5 to focus on risk weight revisions

Basel III Risk-Weight Changes

- New higher risk-weights for securitizations and resecuritizations based on credit ratings (problem that Dodd-Frank precludes reliance on credit ratings in government regulations, including capital requirements)
- Higher risk weights for bilaterally cleared than centrally cleared derivatives

Basel III Liquidity Requirements

- Basel Committee Liquidity Coverage Requirement (LCR): High quality of liquid assets = 100% of expected net outflow of liabilities in 30 calendar days under specified stress scenario (2015)
  - specifies what are high quality liquid assets
  - calculates outflows for different liabilities, e.g. from 5% on retail deposits to 100% on certain wholesale deposits
  - currently 83% for Group I (large internationally active) banks
- Net Stable Funding Ratio (NSFR): Available amount of stable funding must be at least equal to required amount of stable funding under specified stress scenario, less liquid assets (harder to sell) require more stable funding (2018), currently 93% for Group I banks

Basel Committee, Basel III: International framework for liquidity risk measurement, standards and monitoring (December 2010).
•Where do central banks as LLRs fit into these liquidity requirements? How can you really determine this with any degree of accuracy?

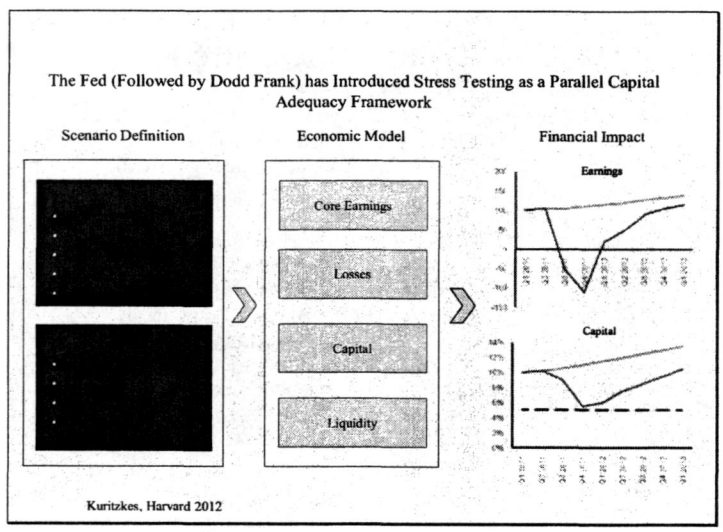

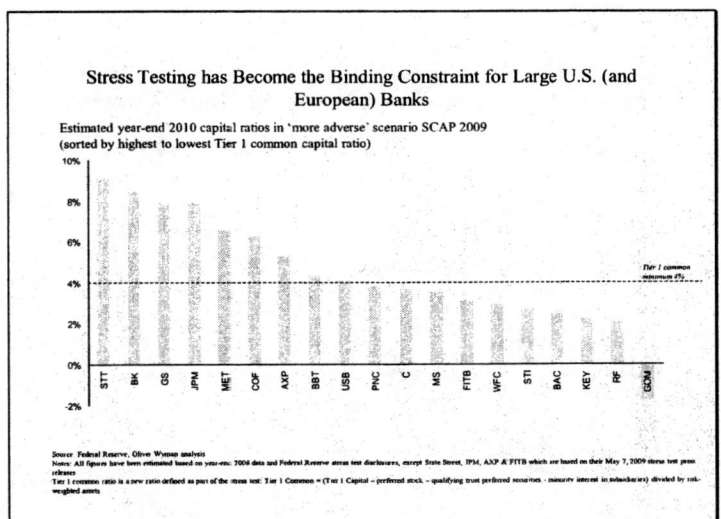

Stress Testing has Become the Binding Constraint for Large U.S. (and European) Banks

Estimated year-end 2010 capital ratios in 'more adverse' scenario SCAP 2009
(sorted by highest to lowest Tier 1 common capital ratio)

Source: Federal Reserve, Oliver Wyman analysis
Notes: All figures have been estimated based on year-end 2008 data and Federal Reserve stress test disclosures, except State Street, JPM, AXP & FITB which are based on their May 7, 2009 stress test press releases
Tier 1 common ratio is a new ratio defined as part of the stress test: Tier 1 Common = (Tier 1 Capital – preferred stock – qualifying trust preferred securities – minority interest in subsidiaries) divided by risk-weighted assets

Stress Testing has Introduced a New Set of Capital Standards

Outcome is dependent on the definition of the economic scenario – how severe is the stress?

Fed has discretion to determine the level of post-stress capital required

Fed restricted the ability of all banks in 2011 from distributing capital in excess of 60% of earnings

Reconciliation between Basel III capital rules and stress testing is unclear

Kuritzkes, Harvard 2012

Basel III Economic Impact

- Basel Committee, An Assessment of the Long-Term Economic Impact of Stronger Capital and Liquidity Requirements (August 2010): At range of common equity/RWA from 8-16% net positive impact of about 2% increase in steady state GDP
  - due to high cost of banking crises, with median cumulative losses of $158 billion (compared to somewhat less lending in short term)
  - depends on economic scenario and assumption that higher capital requirements would make banking crisis less likely
  - G-SIB buffer causes an additional loss of GDP of less than 1 basis point per year over 8 years
- Federal Reserve Board of New York. Staff Report No. 485, P. Angelini et. al., "Basel III: Long-Term Impact on Economic Performance and Fluctuations (February 2011): 0.09% loss in steady state GDP per year in U.S.-Europe from capital requirements and additional 0.08% loss from liquidity requirements, total of 17 basis points
- OECD: 5 to 15 basis points loss in steady state GDP per year
- Institute of International Finance (December 2010): Loss of steady state GDP of US-Europe would be 3.2% over 5 yrs. 300 basis points
- Elliott (Brookings 2010) thinks economic impact minimal because would only increase lending costs by around 2 basis points

Who knows? IIF (2011) on all regulatory changes, mostly result of capital increases:
- Increased capital requirements of $1.3T and long-term debt issuance of $0.3T by 2015.
- Increase in bank lending rates of 3.64% over next 5 years
- Higher lending rates will reduce real GDP by about 3.2 percent over next 5 years; 7.5 million fewer jobs

McKinsey (2011) on impact on bank ROE
- Tog global firms will have ROE reduced from average of 20% to 7% by new capital rules, before mitigation, could get back to 14% with mitigation in some cases. Mitigation: repricing of lending

Will further promote capital markets (shadow banking) at expense of banks

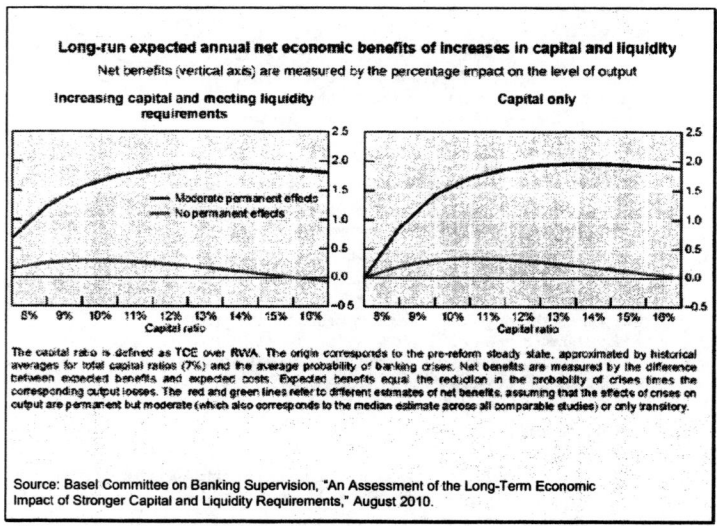

Long-run expected annual net economic benefits of increases in capital and liquidity

Net benefits (vertical axis) are measured by the percentage impact on the level of output

The capital ratio is defined as TCE over RWA. The origin corresponds to the pre-reform steady state, approximated by historical averages for total capital ratios (7%) and the average probability of banking crises. Net benefits are measured by the difference between expected benefits and expected costs. Expected benefits equal the reduction in the probability of crises times the corresponding output losses. The red and green lines refer to different estimates of net benefits, assuming that the effects of crises on output are permanent but moderate (which also corresponds to the median estimate across all comparable studies) or only transitory.

Source: Basel Committee on Banking Supervision, "An Assessment of the Long-Term Economic Impact of Stronger Capital and Liquidity Requirements," August 2010.

Stress net benefits line: benefits equal the reduction in the probability of a crisis x out put losses. The red line assumes crisis effects are permanent, therefore more benefit, the green line says only immediate and wear off over time.

Capital Adequacy: Other Issues

- Capital Surcharges
- Should CoCos count as capital?
- Market discipline: stress tests and instruments

Surcharges

- Basel: GSIBs, 1-2.5% (Tier I common equity, no mark-to-market on available for sale assets), phased in 2016-2019
- European Bank Authority (EBA): raise Core Tier I capital to 9% to deal with sovereign debt crisis following stress test, by June 2012
- Swiss Finish (to deal with too big to save), only UBS and Credit Suisse: by 2019, core Tier 1 capital ratio of 19%, of which at least 10% must be common equity and up to 9% can be CoCos

Contingent Convertible Bonds: CoCos

- Contractual arrangements with defined trigger (market price, capital ratio) to convert debt to equity, different than bail-ins where regulatory discretion

- Basel does not allow CoCos to satisfy capital requirements, cf. Switzerland

- EBA allows to satisfy stress test requirements if trigger when common equity falls below 7% (trigger in some Credit Suisse bonds)

- Would fall in share price (compared to book) or CDS spreads (from treasuries—US or EU) be a better basis for trigger?

- Market is not embracing these instruments, expensive if buy at all

Shadow Committee Proposal (2000)

- **End risk weights:** require 10% leverage (unweighted assets + OBS commitments)—currently 5% for well-capitalized (minimum 3%)

- **End 2 capital tiers:** let market set qualified debt/equity/other mix

- **End use of book capital:** use market values for assets and liabilities (MTM accounting brings closer on assets)

- **Require large banks to regularly issue subordinated debt.**

  - At least 2% of assets (including OBS), and require regulatory action if rate hits junk levels.

  - Must be in minimum $100,000 denominations (not insured, now $250,000)

  - Not protected in bailouts

  - At least one year remaining maturity

I was then member

Simple leverage? Simple, no worse competitively, does not misallocate lending, but 10% is still arbitrary. Ignores that assets are not all same and one level of capital does not fit all. But really relies on market discipline.

Is is it safe to let the market set the debt/equity mix? 4+4 was arbitrary but subordinated debt is not as permanent. Can make permanent by regular issue requirement.

Reliance on sub debt. Will it cost too much, especially in tight markets, why not look to other instruments for market signals (equity methodology), small banks can't issue? Can we be sure of no bailout? See Hal S. Scott, ed., Beyond Basel (Oxford University Press 2005): hierarchy of markets, models, rules.

Stress Test Approach: SCAP

- April 2009 Fed conducts stress tests on 19 largest banks that received TARP money to determine feasibility of repayment of TARP funds
- Postulates consensus and more extreme economic scenarios for 2009 and 2010 (in 2009 reality was generally more benign than scenario)
- Capital requirements: 6% Tier I and 4% Tier I common (a new measure)
- Bottom up approach: predict earnings (and losses) and capital against scenarios. Says $75 billion in more capital needed
- Standardized approach detects outliers
- Finds nine banks could repay TARP, many others quite close (all but one of the largest has now repaid)
- Disclosed basic results to market (some think because good)—a first, examination results never previously disclosed on grounds could create panic and interfere with bank-central bank frank communication.

  If market had adequate knowledge through disclosures of repeated stress tests could it better discipline bank capital? Should we have regular stress tests?

Requires real market discipline, no bailouts of failure and whether this is useful information—not complete disclosure of details of methodology. EU stress test shows danger of bad stress test (do not assume there can be a default, only losses on trading book), could discredit entire process.

Table 2: Supervisory Capital Assessment Program
Aggregate Results for 19 Participating Bank Holding Companies for the More Adverse Scenario

Gives you starting capital and losses, resources other than capital to absorb losses, but does not tell you how to get from there to $185 billion needed buffer (capital of 412.5 + earnings and reserves of 362.9 – losses of 600 = 175.4 in capital, not 185) which is then reduced to $75 billion for capital already raised (including through earnings) after starting capital date of December 2008. Need more complete disclosure.

Comprehensive Capital Analysis and Review (CCAR): Stress Tests 2012

- Forward looking capital planning process for supervisory assessment (Basel pillar 2), first CCAR was in 2011
- Same 19 largest banks: projections of losses, revenues, expenses, and capital ratios under severe macroeconomic scenario (deep recession in US, significant declines in asset values, increases in risk premia
- Assume banks make planned dividends and other capital distributions (buybacks, debt retirement etc.)
- Ratios used: Tier 1/RWA; Tier 1=2/RWA; Tier 1/average assets (leverage ratio); common equity component of Tier 1/RWA
- Aggregate results: -$222 net income before taxes; aggregate Tier I common falls from 10.1 in Q3 2011 to 6.3 in Q4 2013, but higher than 2009 SCAP ratio
- 4 of 19 BHCs (Cit, Ally Financial, Sun Trust and MetLife bank) have one or more projected regulatory capital ratios below the minimum, with 3 having tier I common below 5 percent target (Citi ok if changes buybacks/ does not raise dividends)
- Use data from banks and Federal Reserve models
- March 13, 20102, disclosed stress test results (at high level) of each bank—for markets and analysts

SCAP, one off, this is now permanent approach, mandated by DFA.

CCAR Stress Test 2012: Critiques

- Selection of capital standard, why 5% common equity, other standards are current requirements
- Bank and Fed models—required by DFA, but why both—perhaps Fed can refine based on bank results
- Fed scenarios, extreme, should there be some "economic consensus"
- Fed does not release its models—is gaming concern valid?
- Lack of granularity of exposure of bank results

Stress Testing has Introduced a New Set of Capital Standards

Outcome is dependent on the definition of the economic scenario – how severe is the stress?

Fed has discretion to determine the level of post-stress capital required

Fed restricted the ability of all banks in 2011 from distributing capital in excess of 60% of earnings

Reconciliation between Basel III capital rules and stress testing is unclear

Kuritzkes, Harvard 2012

We Now Live in a State of Capital Confusion

Conflicting Guidance

TCE	Common equity adjusted for goodwill, unrealized losses	Predominant market metric during crisis
SR 99-18	Economic capital	Internal risk models
Basel I	Tier I plus Tier II capital	Simple risk-weights
Basel II	Tier I plus Tier II capital	Three pillars; internal models for credit, ops, market risks
Basel III	Tier I TCE	Revised Basel II models G-SIB surcharge Leverage ratio
Stress Tests (SCAP, CCAR)	Tier I Common	Stress test of losses, earnings, market values under adverse macro scenarios

Kuritzkes, Harvard 2012

Some Lessons on Capital from Financial Crisis

- Basel methodology discredited (bureaucratic dictates and review of models does not work)—move to Pillar 2 and 3; consider just higher leverage requirement with more market discipline

- Widen federal capital requirements to other institutions, e.g. hedge funds and insurance companies—content may have to be different

- Need to address liquidity, different than capital

- Pro-cyclicality problem: expected loss reserve requirements (accounting and disclosure issue) or contingent capital arrangement

- More capital for systemically important institutions—but costs in tiering financial system: moral hazard and cost of funds

- Definition of capital, same or different than accounting? Use of mark-to-market?

- Economic impact hard to determine

TEACHING PLAN FOR

CHAPTER NINE
THE PAYMENT SYSTEM

POWERPOINT SCREENS FOR NINETEENTH EDITION

Large Value Dollar Payment System

Payment System

- International Importance of U.S. Payment System
- Operation of Fedwire and CHIPS
- Risks and Risk Reduction in Fedwire and CHIPS
- Herstatt Risk amd CLS Bank

The focus is on dollar payment systems. **What is their international importance?** While these systems are obviously important to the United States, they are also important to the world because of the dollar's importance as a transaction and reserve currency. Also, many of the players in the dollar systems are foreign banks. In addition, many of the features of the U.S. systems, including the risk issues, are shared by the payment systems of other countries.

Fedwire Transfer

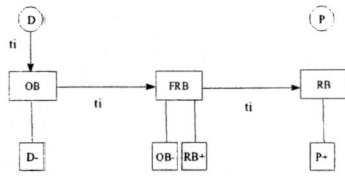

- Owned and operated by 12 Federal Reserve Banks
- 8323 bank participants (2010); 23 account for 80% of value
- Real Time
- Gross Settlement
- Transfers $2.4 trillion per business day (2010), average transaction $4.86 million [US GDP 2010, $14.8 trillion]
- Average daylight funds overdrafts (2008) about $62 billion per day (almost doubled since 2005) but down to $9.8 billion per day in 2009; total daily "peak" overdrafts $169 billion in 2008, down to $55 billion 2009
- "Good" funds

Start with hypothetical $1 million transaction.

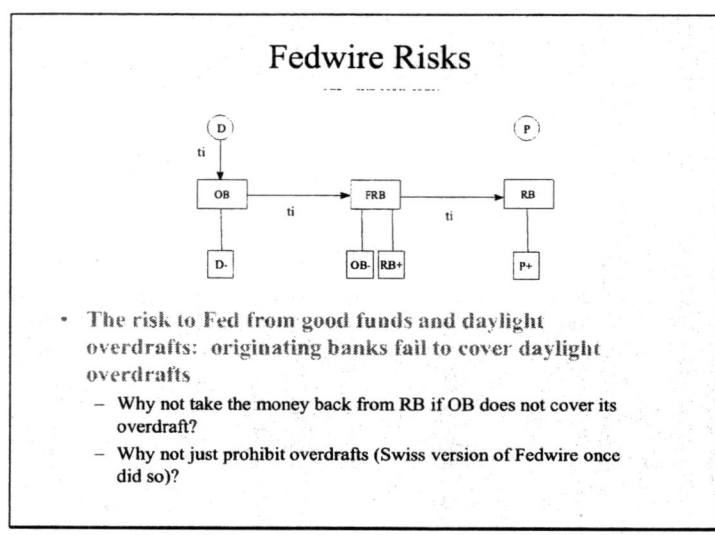

Fedwire Risks

- The risk to Fed from good funds and daylight overdrafts: originating banks fail to cover daylight overdrafts
  - Why not take the money back from RB if OB does not cover its overdraft?
  - Why not just prohibit overdrafts (Swiss version of Fedwire once did so)?

Why not take the money back?

Reason given is that Fedwire relies on finality, receiving banks need to know that the funds are good so they can allow the receivers to use them. Finality supports the high velocity of money in the economy, particularly in the financial system. So Fed absorbs risk, and loans the money to OB overnight or longer. If loan not repaid, Fed loses, and Treasury receipts decrease (Fed gives Treasury its earnings). Competition with CHIPS.

Why doesn't Fed just prohibit overdrafts?

This risks slowdown and gridlock. OB can't send funds to RB until RB sends them to OB. This used to be a problem in SIC, the Swiss version of Fedwire. Lack of overdrafts would also prompt users to go to CHIPS, a competitive system with its own set of risks. As we shall see, Fed limits level of overdrafts and also now charges for them.

Fedwire Risk Reduction
Daylight Overdraft Ceilings-Pre 2008

- Maximum is 2.25 x capital per day and 1.50 x capital as a two week average, no collateral required but caps can be increased with collateral
- Self-assessment of (1) bank credit worthiness; (2) operational controls to control risk in payment systems and from customers; (3) credit policies and procedures; and (4) systems/contingency procedure (SOSA)
- Ex-post monitoring (no automatic cutoff if exceed cap)
- Special rules for branches of foreign banks (FBOs)
  - Capital base is a specified percentage of worldwide capital: 35% for FHCs, and 25% or 10% for other banks based on SOSA, strength of support assessment (1 or 2 respectively). 5% of net liabilities to other depository institutions for banks with a SOSA 3
  - SOSA factors for foreign banks: financial condition, supervisory system of home country, support by government of banking system, ability to access and trasmit U.S. dollars
  - Higher if collateralized

What do you think of these special rules for branches of foreign banks? Are they discriminatory or justified?
Fed is worried about having a large credit exposure to a foreign bank, when it can only grab its U.S. assets (including perhaps its clearing accounts). On the other hand, restricting the capital base is artificial and may violate national treatment standards (the EU has complained).

FedWire Risk Reduction: Daylight Overdraft Pricing (pre-2008)

- Price was 36 BP (.0036) annual rate for a 24 hour operating day (actually 21.5 hours)—with a deduction of 10% of capital
- Assume a U.S. bank has $10 billion in capital and $6 billion in daily average overdrafts over a 24 hour operating day. Price per day will be:

.0036/360 x {6 - (.10 x 10 billion dollars)} = $50,000

Banks and customers (to the extent pricing fees are passed on to them) will only change their transaction patterns, or borrow private funds (in an intraday funds market), to reduce overdrafts when it is efficient to do so. If the cost of these adjustments exceeds the achievable reduction in price, there will be no adjustments. To some extent whether pricing is a good idea depends on getting the price right. If it is too low it will fail to induce efficient changes; if it is too high it will only impose additional cost on the system with no adjustment and thus no resulting benefit of risk reduction. Note that the ability of banks to pass on the costs of overdrafts to their customers will be subject to competitive constraints. Banks with more capital or low overdraft generating payment patterns will have lower overdraft fees which result in lower prices to customers.

Changes in Daylight Overdraft Policy
December 24, 2008 (effective March 2011)

- Collateralized daylight overdrafts for healthy depository institutions (CAMELS-3 supervisory rating or higher) at zero fee (15 of 20 largest users banks had sufficient unencumbered collateral pledged for discount window borrowings to cover average daily overdrafts at time of proposal)—may have changed
- Uncollateralized daylight overdrafts at 50 BP annual rate (old rate was 36 BP)
- Only single day ceiling for healthy depository institutions (same 2.25 capital) (effectively raises ceiling since 2 week ceiling was 1.50)
- FBOs—FHC or SOSA 1-rated gets a ceiling based on 35 percent of worldwide capital uncollateralized, plus an additional 65 percent collateralized (no fee)

What will be the impact on risk for Fed from Fedwire? No risk because collateralized but depends on what collateral is and how it is valued. But before almost everything was uncollateralized, so net less risk? But now much less restraint on growth. Fed says more need in system to get smoother transfers—another way to look at it is that the costs of adjustment to price (delaying transfers) are inefficient.

Why did Fed do it? System needs or CHIPS competition. Pressure from EU on treatment of FBOs.

SOSA=Strength of Support Assessment.

Changes for FBO? Get more overdraft capacity but still not as good as US, e.g. US gets 100% collateralized at zero prices, FBOs only get 65%

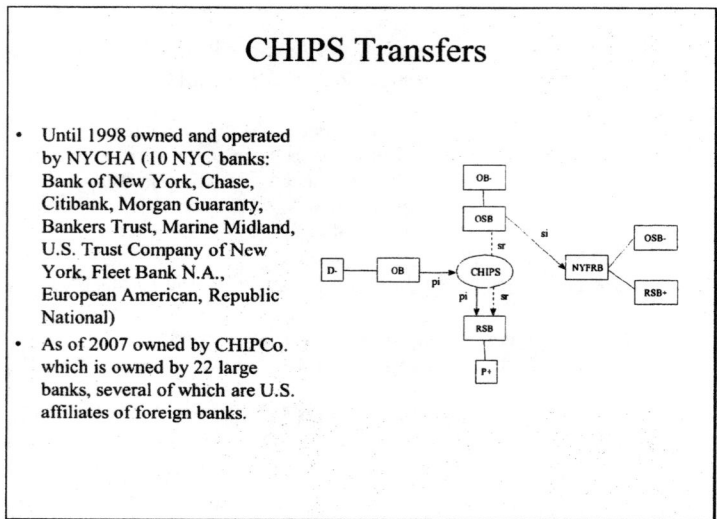

CHIPS used to be a Net End of Day Settlement System (DNS). Banks sent funds to each other during the day, allowed customers to use these funds immediately, and settled their net positions through Fedwires at the NY Fed at 4:30 p.m. each day. Today, CHIPS payments are now settled continuously during the day, and unsettled transfers are returned to the originators.

Reorganization reflects user base. International. NYCH is an operator. **What are main differences between Fedwire and CHIPs?** Public versus private, net settlement versus gross settlement.

CHIPS Transfers: Basic Facts

- 50 participants (majority foreign from 21 countries) (2010)
- Intra-day continuous bilateral and multilateral net settlement (2001)
- End of day net settlement
- Transfers about $1.4 trillion per business day (2010), average transfer about $4.0 million (2010) (compared with $4.86 million average on Fedwire)
- More international than Fedwire (95% market share of foreign bank transfers)

Net Settlement Risk

- Bank A's Overall Position
  - Funds owed to others (sends): 25 to B and 50 to C = 75
  - Funds owed to it (receives): 50 from B and 100 from C = 150
  - Net: net claim (creditor) for 75 (150 receives - 75 sends)
- Bilateral Positions with A
  - B: net debtor for 25 (sent 50 - received 25)
  - D: no position (no sends or receives)

Transactions among Four Participants in a Funds Transfer Clearinghouse

I. Gross payments among banks before netting

Bank receiving payment	Bank originating payment				Sum of claims
	A	B	C	D	
A	...	50	100	...	150
B	25	...	125	100	250
C	50	150	...	125	325
D	...	25	50	...	75
Sum of obligations	75	225	275	225	800

II. Net claim or obligation of each bank with the clearinghouse

	A	B	C	D	Net
Total	75	25	50	-150	0

Used to be net settlement at end of day for entire amount settled. Now continuous net settlement and whatever is unsettled at end of day is just not processed.

Why was CHIPS such a potential source of major systemic risk?

What Happens if D Fails? Delete and Unwind

	A	B	C	D	Net
Pre-Failure	75	25	50	-150	0
Post-Failure	75	-50	-25	xx	0

- Is A Unaffected?
- What can A do if B and C do not come up with 75?
- What will the Fed do?

See next **Is A unaffected?** Was owed 75 before and still owed 75? Not really. The problem is whether B and C are going to be able to come up with the 75. B is suffering a 75 loss: unpaid receives from D (100) - unpaid for sends to D (25). C is also out 75, 125 receives - 50 sends.

What can A do if B and C do not come up with the 75? Has right to take funds back from its customers under normal contracts, but there is a question of whether it can get the funds. If not it will fail. We are looking at the essence of systemic risk, a chain reaction of bank failures triggered through the payment system.

What will the Fed do?

The Fed will not allow a chain reaction of bank failures, it will cover D's 150 obligation and absorb D's credit risk--in a sense the Fed is liable for the net debit positions of the CHIPS banks. No matter how many times they say they are not responsible (so that banks will limit risks) everyone knows they are. So Fed has credit risk in both Fedwire and CHIPS.

CHIPS Delete and Unwind Calculation

I. Gross payments among banks before netting

Bank receiving payment	Bank originating payment				Sum of claims
	A	B	C	D	
A	...	50	100	...	150
B	25	...	125	~~100~~	150
C	50	150	...	~~25~~	200
D	...	~~25~~	~~50~~	...	~~75~~
Sum of obligations	75	200	225	~~125~~	500

II. Net claim or obligation of each bank with the clearinghouse

	A	B	C	D	Net
Total	75	-50	-25	xx	0

Delete all of D's transactions and recalculate. A unchanged because of no transactions with D. B sent D 25 and received 100, so net loss of 75. Net position goes from +25 to -50. C also has net loss of 75.

Pre 2001: CHIPS Risk Reduction Measures

- Bilateral Credit Limits: Set by each participant on each other participant (net of receives - sends)

  > Example: X sets 1000 limit on Y, so that receives from Y - sends to Y cannot exceed 1000

- Net debit caps: 4% of the sum of all bilateral credit limits extended to participants
- Collateralized Additional Settlement Obligations (ASO)—loss sharing

---

Did these measures greatly curtail systemic risk?
How effective are bilateral credit limits?
In principle, bilateral credit limits can be effective in limiting risk. With respect to hypo, if B had been stricter in setting its bilateral limit, then the consequence to it of D's hypothetical default would have been less.
The problem is that if B knows the Fed is going to bail out D or any other bank that fails why should it set realistic bilateral credit limits. One might impose ceilings on these limits, like we do with daylight overdrafts but no one proposed this. CHIPS required banks to set bilateral credit limits on other banks but put no limits on them.
How effective is the net debit cap?
In principle, a net debit cap also reduces risk because it sets a limit on the losses that can be imposed by the failure of any participant. In CHIPS, they were not a real constraint; a bank's net debit position limit was 4% of the sum of bilateral credit limits set by other banks on the participant in question, which as we have seen were unconstrained due to bailout expectation
ASO System
After 1991 banks were required to collateralize ASOs, about $3 billion. Since ASO's increased with one's bilateral credit risk to the largest net debtor, discipline on bilateral positions was introduced. The cost of the collateral is the opportunity cost on the collateral, i.e. banks hold more T bills than they otherwise would (estimated to be 25 basis points on an

annual basis). Note that this cost (estimated at $6-8 million per year) also limited the ability of banks to avoid daylight overdraft limits and prices on Fedwire by shifting transactions to CHIPS.

The New CHIPS Arrangements (2001)

- Prefunded Balances based on past activity, can be increased during day (average $2.8 billion per day, 2007—compared to $1.4 trillion total transfers at time of measurement)

- Balances cannot go below zero or over two times initial balance

- Payments settled during day by bilateral or multilateral netting against balances by a balance release algorithm designed to get the most settlement out of the available balances

- End of day net settlement: unsettled messages returned to sender (if largest two banks did not settle, would have to unwind $2.8 billion)

Cost Comparison with Fedwire?
Value of interest on $2.8 billion. 1-2007 fed funds rate was 5.25%, $147 million per year. Note with lower fed funds rate in 2009, .25%, much lower cost, $7 million. Fedwire now provides you can collateralize daylight overdrafts and avoid caps and fees, so need to compare collateral cost in both systems

Elimination of Systemic Risk?
Implication: no systemic risk in wholesale payment system? CHIPS better than Fedwire, abolish Fedwire? Still netting exposure, next slide

Discuss

Practice in other countries? Ask class

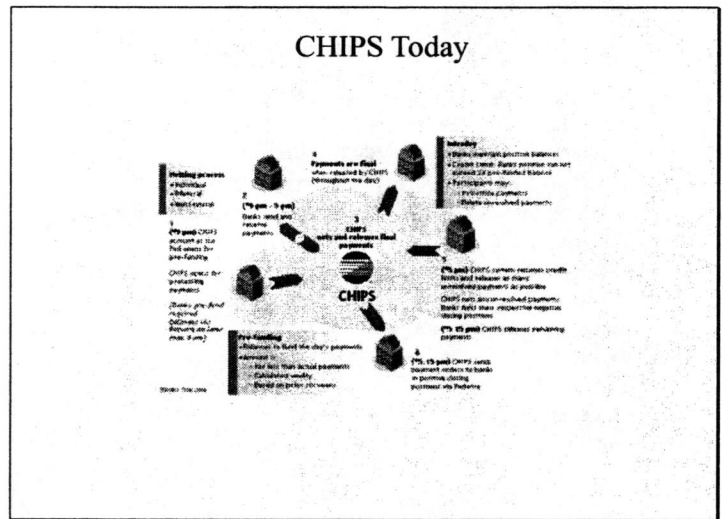

Reference

Netting: Issues for CHIPS

- Suppose Bank F, a CHIPS participant, fails at the end of the day.
- Suppose Bank A has sent $7 billion to Bank F (the failed bank) during the day and received $6 billion (the difference funded by A's pre-funded balance)
- If netting respected by F's bankruptcy trustee, no claims either way (paid for excess in sends with $1 billion)
- If netting not respected by F's bankruptcy trustee, A might have to pay $7B (sends) and claim $6B (receives) in B's bankruptcy
- U.S. banks still have a significant risk that netting would not be respected by a foreign bank's bankruptcy trustee

---

U.S. has passed legislation insuring that netting is valid. But this does not completely solve the problem?

Most participants are foreign and will, like BCCI, be subject to foreign bankruptcy proceedings which may or may not respect the CHIPS netting. Need international agreement in this area, or exclude banks from jurisdictions with unclear netting rules from CHIPS settlement (but latter approach might exclude Japan).

Foreign trustee could unravel intraday netting under new CHIPS system.

CHIPS requires legal opinions that netting is valid in foreign jurisdictions but unclear how reliable such opinions are when foreign law is unclear.

Herstatt Risk

- What is it?
- Will CLS Bank eliminate it?

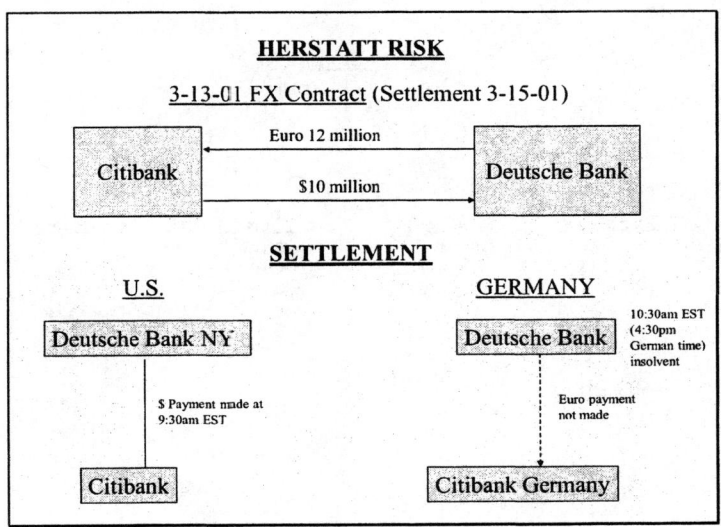

So, Citibank will be out $10 million, due to the use of the different payment systems in different time zones.

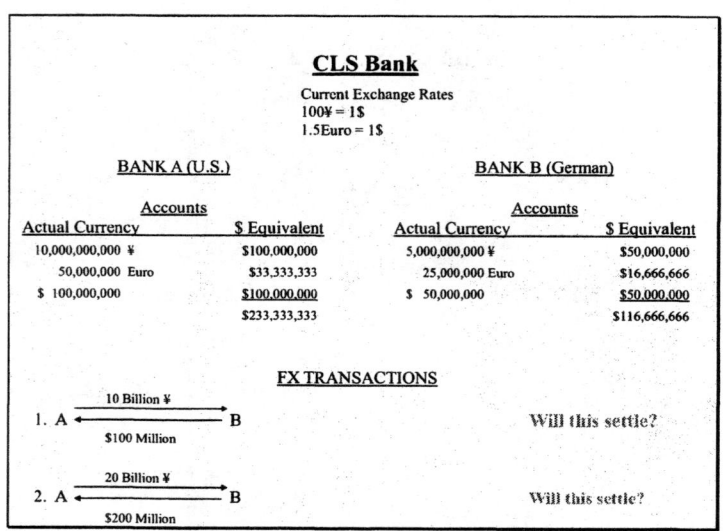

The first transaction will settle. Although B does not have $100,000,000 (only $50,000,000) could convert other currencies to dollars. Would convert at then current rates. Second, will not settle because B does not have enough funds (even after transaction 1 settles, total dollars are $116 million). This transaction will be put into queue until B has enough funds.

Will CLS completely eliminate Herstatt Risk?

No transaction will be processed unless both sides pay at same time. But what if CLS bank fails? Lose balances, could be worse. Not all FX through CLS (2007 only had 55% of deals). Rest like Herstatt, correspondent settlement.

TEACHING PLAN FOR

CHAPTER FIFTEEN
SWAPS

POWERPOINT SCREENS FOR NINETEENTH EDITION

Swaps (OTC Derivatives)

Swaps

- Basics of Interest Rate Swaps
- Basics of Currency Swaps
- Credit and Market Risks
- Credit Derivatives—Credit Default Swaps (CDSs)
- Dodd-Frank requirements for central clearing
- EU versus US approach to derivatives regulation

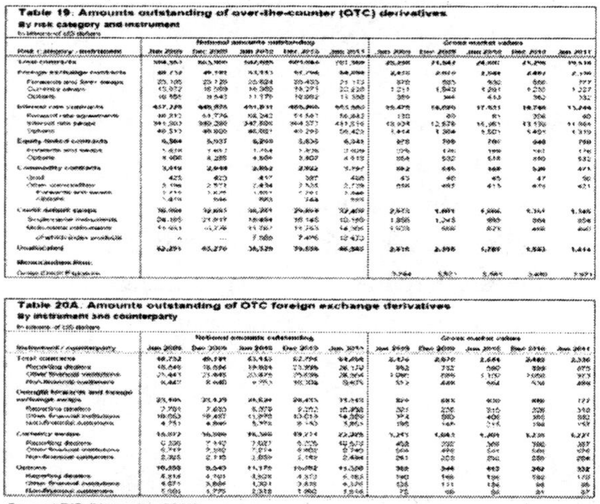
Table 19: Amounts outstanding of over-the-counter (OTC) derivatives
By risk category and instrument
Table 20A. Amounts outstanding of OTC foreign exchange derivatives
By instrument and counterparty

Source: BIS (November 2011)

Global OTC Derivatives Market is huge. June 2011, \$707.5T (total assets in financial system around \$200T--(\$19.5T market value), gross-credit exposure (\$2.9T), netting and collateral.

Is this a legitimate comparison? Gross market value of swaps, amount by which in/out of money, is abut \$20 trillion, much less. For plain vanilla interest rate risk and currency swaps, the actual risk to the parties is a small fraction of the notional amounts as discussed in the reading. The risk depends on the volatility of the rates, interest or currency, over the life of the swap. Risk can be limited at any time by taking an offsetting position, just as with exchange-traded futures and options. In June 2011, gmv/notional was 19.5/707.5 = 2.8%

Swaps currently can be traded anywhere and everywhere where you can hook up a computer and telephone. They are predominantly traded in London. This may change with heavier British regulation and taxes.

CDS get all the press but notional amount is 32/707 = 4.5%%, of OTC and market value, CDS gmv/otc gmv is 1.4/19.5 = 7%.

This still overstates because does not take account of netting and collateral, this brings down the market to \$2.9T overall of which CDS, \$1.3T or 45%

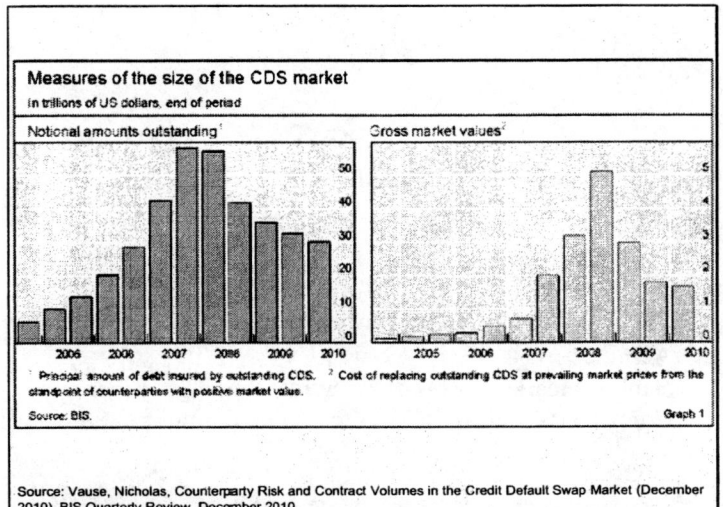

Measures of the size of the CDS market

In trillions of US dollars, end of period

Notional amounts outstanding[1]   Gross market values[2]

[1] Principal amount of debt insured by outstanding CDS. [2] Cost of replacing outstanding CDS at prevailing market prices from the standpoint of counterparties with positive market value.

Source: BIS.   Graph 1

Source: Vause, Nicholas, Counterparty Risk and Contract Volumes in the Credit Default Swap Market (December 2010). BIS Quarterly Review, December 2010.

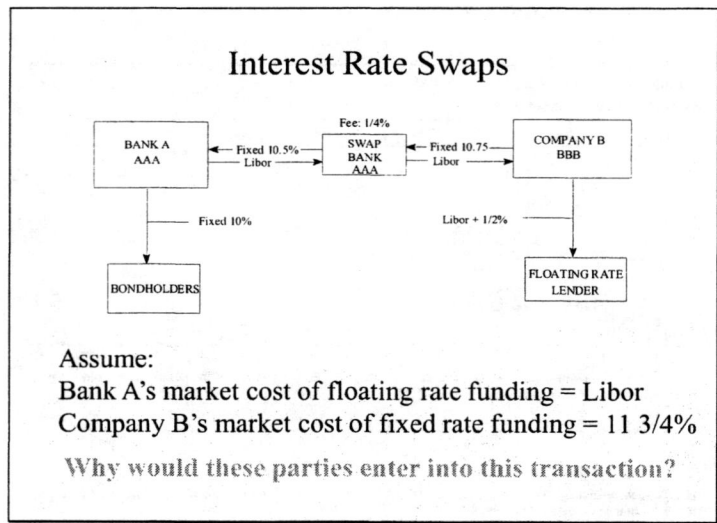

Get general reasons of hedging, speculation and reducing funding costs on next chart, then will examine each rationale individually.

In explaining transaction, stress fact of independence of swap contracts from each other and from bond/lending transactions.

Reasons for Entering into Swaps

- Hedging
- Speculation
- Reduce Funding Costs

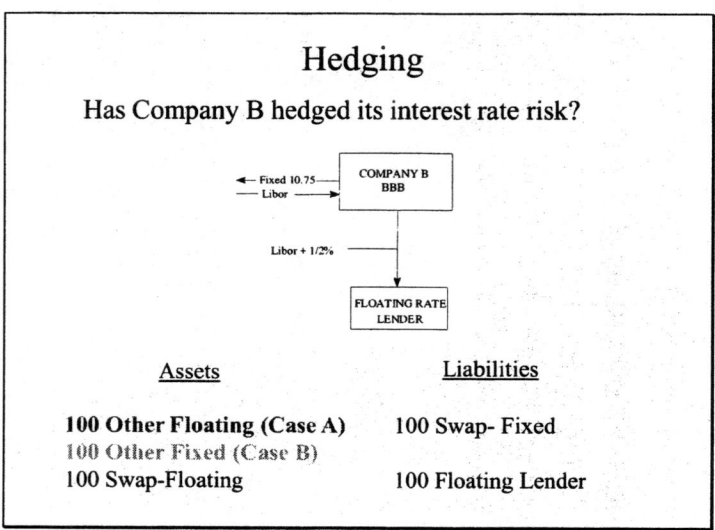

Hedging

Has Company B hedged its interest rate risk?

Assets	Liabilities
100 Other Floating (Case A)	100 Swap- Fixed
100 Other Fixed (Case B)	
100 Swap-Floating	100 Floating Lender

It has hedged its floating rate liabilities to the floating lender with floating rate swap revenues, but this is not a complete hedge because must pay fixed rates of interest and we do not know that it has fixed rate revenue to cover this obligation. If it's a manufacturing company it probably doesn't. There is also a possibility of basis risk on floating, e.g. different reset periods for Libor.
There are two possibilities here:

If non-swap assets are floating (Case A), then Company B is not completely hedged. If rates go down, its non-swap floating assets may not generate enough revenue to service its fixed rate swap liability. If rates go up, its floating rate assets revenue may exceed its fixed rate liability.

If, on the other hand, non-swap assets are fixed (Case B), Company A is hedged.

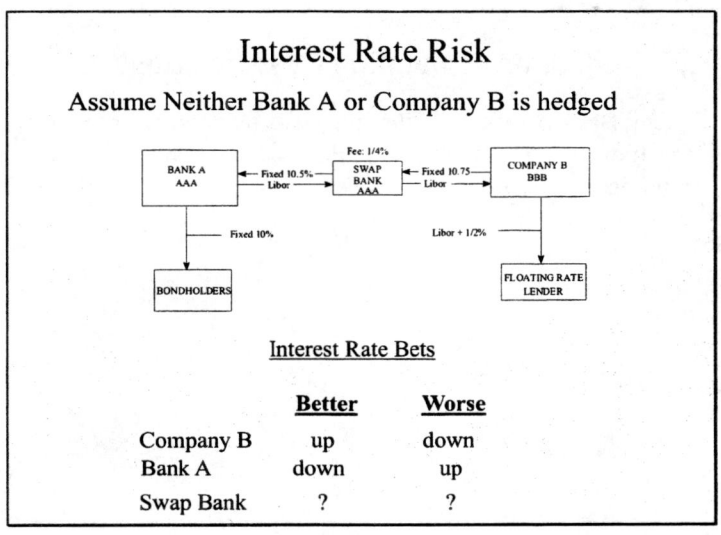

Company B is better off if rates go up because gets more in Libor. Bank A is better off if rates go down because pays less in Libor.

Better   Worse

Swap Bank   up   down

What's good for B, the poorer credit, is good for Swap Bank because B more likely to default.

Reduction of Funding Costs for Bank A

Did Bank A reduce its funding costs by entering into this transaction? (Bank A's market cost of floating rate funding is assumed to be Libor)

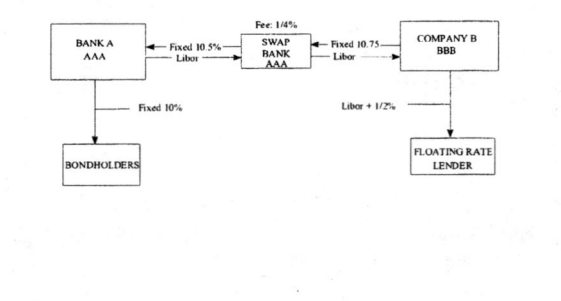

Calculation on next page, do on blackboard

Reduction of Funding Costs for Bank A

Did Bank A reduce its funding costs by entering into this transaction? (Bank A's market cost of floating rate funding is assumed to be Libor)

<u>Analysis of Bank A's Savings</u>

1. Direct Cost (to bondholders):	(10)
2. Swap Cost (to Swap Bank):	(Libor)
3. Swap Revenue (from Swap Bank):	10 1/2%
4. Net Cost:	Libor - 1/2%
5. Cost Savings:	Libor - (Libor - 1/2) = 1/2%

Hide slide

If Bank A wanted to fund at floating rates, it would have had to pay Libor, now it pays Libor -½. <u>But Bank A has also acquired some risk it might not have had if it went directly to the market for Libor funding. Here its funding advantage depends on Swap Bank making good on the 10.5%.</u> This risk might be small, Swap Bank is assumed to be AAA credit, but there is some risk. Also, typically collateralized, but not as efficient as exchange mark system (intermediated through clearing and settlement system of exchange).

Futures/Options v. Swaps

If Bank A wants to hedge or speculate on interest rates. Should A use swaps or futures/options?

- *Liquidity:* You get liquidity in swaps market in the same way as in futures/options market--you get out of your position by entering into an offsetting position, but this is more difficult off an exchange, thus less liquidity. You could not trade your swap position (without consent of counterparty) because of credit risk consideration. For example, if after entering our paradigm interest rate swap, Bank A thinks rates will go up (Libor payments will increase for same amount of fixed), it will swap fixed for floating. This offset can be with original or new counterparty. Alternatively it could terminate original swap for a payment
- *Maturities:* Most interest rate swaps are over two years, whereas most options/futures are under two years.
- *Credit Risk:* Much less with futures/options because of margining and collective responsibility of exchange's clearinghouse for fulfillment of contracts; but reduced credit risk generates unpredictable cash flows due to margin requirements, and margin requirements impose significant costs. On the other hand, collateral requirements, are de rigeur for swaps, play a similar role to margin requirements and can be more fine tuned, plus get swap bank with AAA credit rating in middle. Transaction costs may, however, be more expensive for swaps. Plus, some parties may take less collateral than should exposing system to systemic risk

- *Participants:* Swaps are largely done by financial institutions, mainly banks. Wider group of participants in futures/options markets.
5. *Customization:* with swaps and not with futures/options. Important especially to commercial end-users

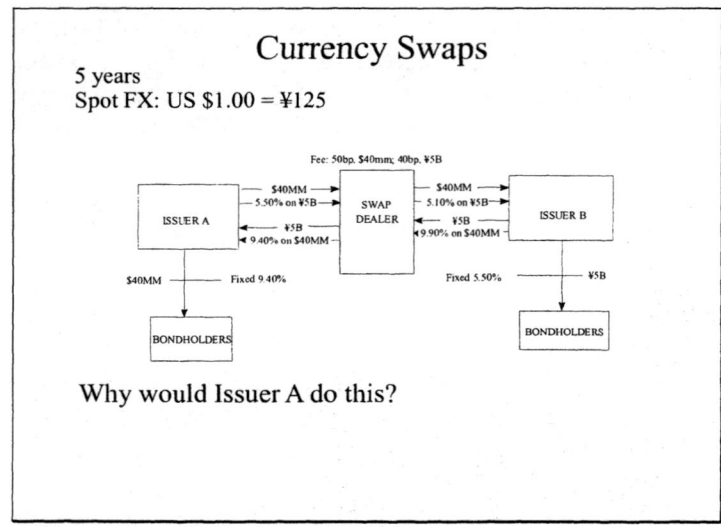

Currency Swaps

5 years
Spot FX: US $1.00 = ¥125

Why would Issuer A do this?

What is going on here? Hedging with foreign currency derivatives, swaps or exchange traded instruments increases firm value on average by 4.87%. G. Allayanis and J. Eston, The Use of Foreign Currency Derivatives and Firm Market Value, 14 Review of Financial Studies 244 (2001)

Issuer A has raised $40mm by issuing bonds paying 9.40% and swapped the dollars for 5yrs for ¥5 billion, at the current spot FX rate (¥ 5B = 40mm x 125), paying 5.50% interest on the yen and receiving 9.40% on the dollars. At the end of the term, Issuer A must return the ¥5 billion for $40mm.

Issuer B has done the reverse, raised Yen and swapped into dollars.

The Swap Dealer is the counterparty to both issuers, perhaps reducing credit risk, making spreads on both interest rates.

Why would Issuer A do this? Discuss

The simple answer is that it needs yen not dollars (for example, a U.S. company with Japanese operations), but if this is so why doesn't it go directly to the market to raise Yen? Again, might have cheaper funding cost story, i.e., it would get a worse exchange rate or pay a higher interest rate if it raised Yen directly, but this might ignore added risk on the swap.

Perhaps issuer A is a U.S. company that is unable to issue Yen bonds in Japan (in past MOF excluded issues because of credit rating) and is not a high enough rated credit to issue in Euroyen market. Thus, it raises dollars and swaps for yen; its Eurodollar bond issue is swap driven. Domestic Regulation may create demand for swaps.

FX Risk on Currency Swaps

Assume that $1 = ¥100 now (1 year into swap)

Exchange Rates and Swap Amounts for B

	At Swap Inception	Now
FX Rate	$1.00 = ¥125	$1.00 = ¥100
Swap Rate	B received $40MM for ¥5B	B to pay $40MM for ¥5B (at maturity)
Swap Market Rate		B would pay $50MM for ¥5B

Right now, does B have a FX market risk or credit risk on this transaction?

Yen has appreciated—at inception took 125 Yen to buy a $1.00, now only takes 100 Yen

B has a credit risk now. If rates stay the same and if A defaults at maturity B will never get ¥5B for $40mm in the marketplace. Instead will have to pay $50mm (plus given dealer spread) to get ¥5B, given appreciation of Yen. The swap is in the money, B made a good deal. B has a risk if A defaults; will have to pay more to get the same deal. B has no current market loss, since B is in the money—a party has either market risk or credit risk at a particular point in time. Once you go out of the money because of market risk you no longer have credit risk.

B has experienced no market losses right now but could have market risk going forward. Exchange rates could change in other direction, e.g. at time of swap's termination they could be $1.00 = ¥150. Yen could depreciate. B would then have incurred market risk since could get more Yen in market than on swap. This is estimated future exposure.

Note that the amount of credit risk is related to the market value of the position. Here we assume that the market value of the position is $10 million, the difference between $40MM and $50MM—the more that B is in the money, say the position is worth $20 million, the more credit risk. In crisis, on some swaps, these values were uncertain.

OTC Derivatives Issues

- CDS
  - Purpose and Transaction Basics
  - Reference Entity Risk
  - Counterparty Risk (Systemic Risk)
  - Capital Requirements
- Liability to counterparty, *Dharmala*
- Dodd-Frank and Implementation
- EU Proposed Reforms

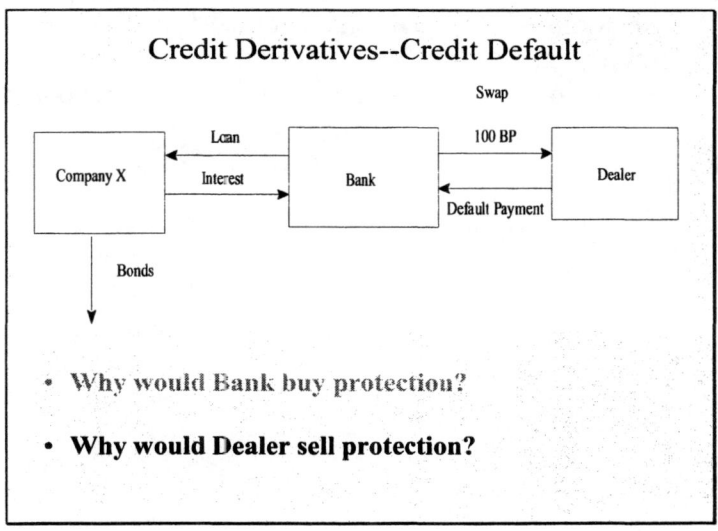

Bank

The obvious reason is to reduce its credit risk on the loan.

Might the Bank enter into the swap without having made a loan (a naked swap)? It may want to short Company X's credit, get paid if Company X defaults. Allows diversification of portfolio or just speculation. Way to avoid short sale restrictions.

Dealer

Like an insurer, just sell insurance for a price, and then make a spread on another hedging swap. Suppose Dealer held bonds issued by Company X, returning 5%. It could increase its yield on these bonds by selling protection to Bank, get 6% for added risk. Also, an unhedged seller of protection has in effect made a synthetic loan to the Company X (profits if a good loan).

Note: A credit default swap may provide for a basket of reference entities, e.g. Bank buys protection on loans made to Companies X,Y and Z. Suppose these loans were $10 million each, or a total of $30 million. Bank might buy protection for $30 million if any one of the loans defaulted. The transaction is leveraged because the chances of default by any one of several entities triggers full settlement, thereby increasing the risk to the seller of protection, presumably for an increased return.

One could also provide that if a credit event occurs for any of the companies, there is a payoff of just $10 million, only on the defaulted loans, and the total value of the swap is reduced to $20 million. Here the seller of protection is acquiring the risk of a diversified loan portfolio (if the default correlations of the three companies are low) through making a proportional settlement.

Many CDSs are sold on indexes that track credit of multiple companies.

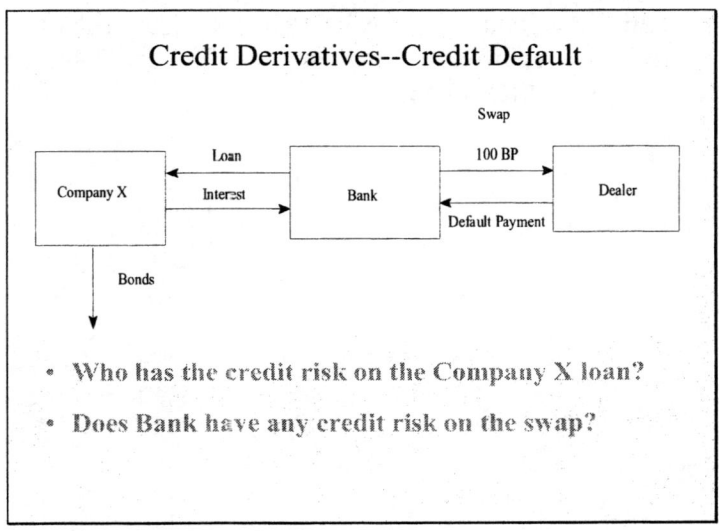

Credit Derivatives--Credit Default

- Who has the credit risk on the Company X loan?
- Does Bank have any credit risk on the swap?

Credit Risk on Loan
Bank
The degree to which the Bank has credit risk on the loan is determined by the extent of protection against the deterioration in value or default of the loan. For example, if Credit Event did not include a credit rating downgrade, Bank may have to write down loan with no compensating payment. There may also be deductible (seller of protection/insurer wants bank to have incentive to monitor), so bank's protection may be less than the total amount of loan. Regulators want to know what exposure bank has because its capital requirements should depend on this.
Dealer
The Dealer may have the exposure. The amount of its exposure depends on what its obligation is at default (to be discussed later). It also depends on whether the dealer is hedged. If the dealer has bought protection, then the last man standing (whose identity may be unknown, e.g. Landesbanks or union pension funds) have the exposure. Are we concerned that we do not know who this is? Is there a systemic risk issue here? Perhaps if banks wind up as ultimate sellers of protection but bank regulators should monitor. Trade repositories will help on this

Credit Risk on Swap
Bank does have credit risk on the swap if it goes into the money (e.g the loan has decrease in value), which means that it has converted credit risk on Company to credit risk on Dealer. How might the Bank reduce this

risk? Get another party to guarantee the dealer's obligation, e.g. write a CDS on its swap party, require the dealer to post collateral if swap goes in the money. Collateral requirements typical. This is what Goldman was doing with AIG before AIG failed, more later.

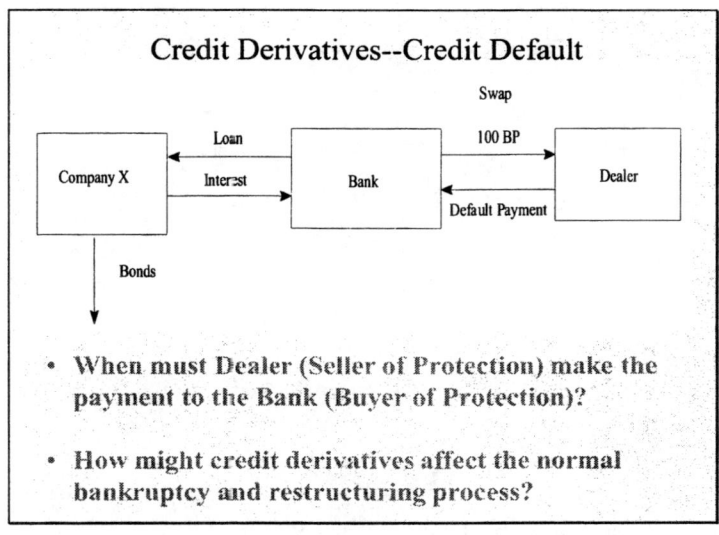

Credit Derivatives--Credit Default

- When must Dealer (Seller of Protection) make the payment to the Bank (Buyer of Protection)?

- How might credit derivatives affect the normal bankruptcy and restructuring process?

When the Dealer must make a payment is determined by the definition of Credit Events in the swap contract. For example, when Company X defaults on loan, or misses payments, or its bonds decline by 50% (is likely to default). The definition of a credit event is crucial since it triggers the obligation. Governed by ISDA documentation. As in Greece, a committee of ISDA makes this determination? **Is customization good?** Serves interests of parties, creates less liquidity.

How might the existence of credit derivatives change the bankruptcy process? Lenders or Bondholders, who have bought protection from dealers, may want a clear default to get the derivatives' payoffs, changing normal incentives to restructure. Restructuring may not be an event of default—and even if it were, why waste the time and money on restructuring? The real parties in interest, the sellers of protection, would not be involved in the decision of default even if they had status in a later bankruptcy.

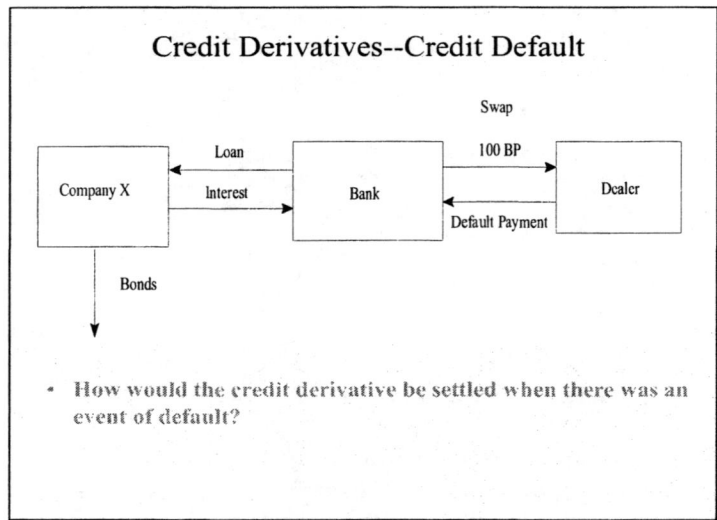

What was the problem in Delphi? Deliverable obligations, bonds, a tenth of the credit derivatives outstanding and a physical settlement required. Short squeeze (someone buys all of the bonds) and then sells them off to buyers of protection, price increase of bonds from 58 to 72 cents (Air France proposed retirement of bonds an extreme case).

What is the solution? A cash settlement with an ISDA auction of the bonds determining the cash settlement (amount of protection – price of bonds). Can also have cash and physical settlement. Process is on next slide.

Lehman Senior Bond Auction			
Securities dealer	Bid	Offer	Physical settlement request ($ millions)
Barclays Bank PLC	8	10	buy: 130
Credit Suisse Securities (USA) LLC	8	10	sell: 755
Deutsche Bank AG	8	10	sell: 870
Merrill Lynch, Pierce, Fenner & Smith Inc.	8	10	sell: 141
Morgan Stanley & Co. Inc.	8.25	10.25	sell: 480
UBS Securities LLC	8.75	10.75	sell: 464
Goldman Sachs & Co	8.875	10.875	sell: 1470
BNP Paribas	9	11	sell: 390
JPMorgan Chase Bank, N.A.	9	11	buy: 612
Citigroup Global Markets Inc.	9.25	11	sell: 574
The Royal Bank of Scotland PLC	9.25	11.25	sell: 191
Banc of America Securities LLC	9.5	11.5	sell: 170
Dresdner Bank AG	9.5	11.5	buy: 30
HSBC Bank USA, N.A.	10	12	sell: 187

Source: Jean Helwege, Samuel Maurer, Asani Sarkar, Yuan Wang, "Credit Default Swap Auctions," Federal Reserve Bank of New York Staff Report No. 372, May 2009.

Bids and offers are in percentages of the par value of the bonds rather than actual prices. This is because pool of senior bonds on auciton may have a mix of bonds with different par values.

The shaded bids and offers, which represent 50% of highest of bids and offers, are used to calculate the midpoint between these bids and offers, here 9.75. This is just the initial price (Stage 1). There is a Stage 2 if the terms of the CDSs also permit physical settlement, as was the case with Lehman. The actual price is determined in Stage 2 by an auction of the "open interest," the net of all bids and offers for actual bonds (last column), if there are such bids or offers. In Lehman there was a negative open interest of $4.92 billion in senior bonds (negative meaning more sells than buys), and a second round of limit orders (orders at a particular price) were submitted. The price of trades where bid exceeded or was equal to offer was $8.625 and this was the final cash settlement price, $1.125 lower than the Stage 1 price. So buyers of protection got better deal from Stage 2.

Lehman Senior Bond Auction			
Securities dealer	Bid	Offer	Physical settlement request ($ millions)
Barclays Bank PLC	8	10	buy: 130
Credit Suisse Securities (USA) LLC	8	10	sell: 755
Deutsche Bank AG	8	10	sell: 870
Merrill Lynch, Pierce, Fenner & Smith Inc.	8	10	sell: 141
Morgan Stanley & Co. Inc.	8.25	10.25	sell: 480
UBS Securities LLC	8.75	10.75	sell: 464
Goldman Sachs & Co	8.875	10.875	sell: 1470
BNP Paribas	9	11	sell: 390
JPMorgan Chase Bank, N.A.	9	11	buy: 612
Citigroup Global Markets Inc.	9.25	11	sell: 574
The Royal Bank of Scotland PLC	9.25	11.25	sell: 191
Banc of America Securities LLC	9.5	11.5	sell: 170
Dresdner Bank AG	9.5	11.5	buy: 30
HSBC Bank USA, N.A.	10	12	sell: 187

Source: Jean Helwege, Samuel Maurer, Asani Sarkar, Yuan Wang. "Credit Default Swap Auctions." Federal Reserve Bank of New York Staff Report No. 372, May 2009.

But buyers of protection will want low price, so get more from insurance—can they rig the auction by bidding low, by bribing others not to bid? Can sellers of protection bid up the bonds? In the auction procedure high offers of CDS sellers (trying to force price up) and low bids of CDS buyers (trying to force price down) are penalized by standardized quotation size ($5 million) x the difference between their offer and bid and the midpoint price determined in Lehman (presumably the fairer price). HSBC was penalized $12,500 in the Lehman offer, $5 million x .0025. Big whoop.

Authors believe the prices from the 43 auctions that they looked at (prior to May 2009) were "reasonable." **Why do they believe this?** First, the price seems to move in the direction of the open interest, here more sells than buys drives price down in Stage 2—so what? (2) bond prices on the day before the auction and the day of the auction are essentially the same as the final recovery price—what is driving what? Thin corporate bond market. But only 4 of the 43 auctions they looked at also permitted physical settlement. So without physical settlement how do they know the cash prices were reasonable?

CPSS (BIS) and IOSCO Key Proposals for Standards -1

Organization
Principle 1: Legal basis

Principle 2: Governance

An FMI (financial market infrastructure) should have governance arrangements that are clear and transparent, promote the safety and efficiency of the FMI, and support the stability of the broader financial system, other relevant public interest considerations, and the objectives of relevant stakeholders.

Principle 3: Framework for the comprehensive management of risks

Credit and liquidity risk management
Principle 4: Credit risk

An FMI should effectively measure, monitor, and manage its credit risk from participants and from its payment, clearing, and settlement processes. An FMI should maintain sufficient financial resources to cover its credit exposure to each participant fully with a high degree of confidence. A CCP should also maintain additional financial resources to cover a wide range of potential stress scenarios that should include, but not be limited to, the default of the [one/ two] participant[s] and [its/their] affiliates that would potentially cause the largest aggregate credit exposure[s] in extreme but plausible market conditions.

CPSS (BIS) and IOSCO Proposal for Standards - 2

Principle 5: Collateral
An FMI that requires collateral to manage its or its participants' credit risk should accept collateral with low credit, liquidity, and market risk. An FMI should also set and enforce appropriately conservative haircuts and concentration limits.

Principle 6: Margin
A CCP should cover its credit exposures to its participants for all products through an effective margin system that is risk-based and regularly reviewed.

Principle 7: Liquidity risk
An FMI should effectively measure, monitor, and manage its liquidity risk. An FMI should maintain sufficient liquid resources to effect same-day and, where appropriate, intraday settlement of payment obligations with a high degree of confidence under a wide range of potential stress scenarios that should include, but not be limited to, the default of [one/two] participant[s] and [its/their] affiliates that would generate the largest aggregate liquidity need in extreme but plausible market conditions.

CPSS (BIS) and IOSCO Proposal for Standards - 3

Settlement
Principle 8: Settlement finality
Principle 9: Money settlements
Principle 10: Physical deliveries
Central securities depositories and exchange-of-value settlement systems
Principle 11: Central securities depositories
Principle 12: Exchange-of-value settlement systems
Default management
Principle 13: Participant-default rules and procedures
An FMI should have effective and clearly defined rules and procedures to manage a
    participant default that ensure that the FMI can take timely action to contain losses
    and liquidity pressures, and continue to meet its obligations.
Principle 14: Segregation and portability
A CCP should have rules and procedures that enable the segregation and portability of
    positions and collateral belonging to customers of a participant.

CPSS (BIS) and IOSCO Proposal for Standards - 4

General business and operational risk management
Principle 15: General business risk
Principle 16: Custody and investment risk
Principle 17: Operational risk
An FMI should identify all plausible sources of operational risk, both internal and external, and minimise their impact through the deployment of appropriate systems, controls, and procedures. Systems should ensure a high degree of security and operational reliability, and have adequate, scalable capacity. Business continuity plans should aim for timely recovery of operations and fulfilment of the FMI's obligations, including in the event of a wide-scale disruption.

Transparency
Principle 23: Disclosure of rules and procedures
An FMI should have clear and comprehensive rules and procedures and should provide sufficient information to enable participants to have an accurate understanding of the risks they incur by participating in the FMI. All relevant rules and key procedures should be publicly disclosed.
Principle 24: Disclosure of market data
A TR should provide timely and accurate data to relevant authorities and the public in line with their respective needs

---

Proposal for a Regulation of the European Parliament and of the Council on OTC Derivatives, Central Counterparties and Trade Repositories, 2010/0250 (September 15, 2010)

CPSS (BIS) and IOSCO Proposal for Standards - 5

Access

Principle 18: Access and participation requirements

An FMI should have objective, risk-based, and publicly disclosed criteria for
participation, which permit fair and open access.

Principle 19: Tiered participation arrangements

An FMI should, to the extent practicable, identify, understand, and manage the risks to
it arising from tiered participation arrangements.

Principle 20: FMI links

An FMI that establishes a link with one or more FMIs should identify, monitor, and
manage link-related risks.

Efficiency

Principle 21: Efficiency and effectiveness

Principle 22: Communication procedures and standards

Counterparty Risk

- How do you reduce counterparty risk?
- Can counterparty risk be systemic risk? Was it in AIG?

- Counterparty Risk: First, deal with highly rated entity (AIG was AAA). Second, take collateral. Collateral comes in two forms initial and variation margin. Variation covers the change in the value of the position, initial margin is a buffer to cover interim exposure through new transfers of variation margin or the close out of the position if the counterparty fails. Collateral is determined by ISDA procedures and is usually cash but can be other securities. Note whether you are adequately collateralized depends on correctly valuing the amount you are in the money which requires knowing what a replacement contract would cost and what the value of your collateral is, values that may be difficult to know. Asking for more collateral from AIG is what triggered its downfall. In the case of Bear Stearns, counterparties in the money, fearing Bear would default, closed out their position. This entitled them to ask for their intial margin back which was an important source of funding for Bear, and would have cause their demise but for the JP Morgan acquisition. Of course, central clearing mutualizes risk.

Systemic Risk: Counterparty exposures can cause systemic risk if the losses of the in-the money party wipe out its capital. The failure of the in-the-money counterparty may trigger another party's loss and this could initiate a chain reaction of failures—this is what connectedness systemic risk is all about. Was this a problem in AIG? Is that why the Fed rescued it with an investment of $85 billion? But Goldman, which had bought protection on a CDO portfolio from AIG, has said repeatedly that it had excess cash collateral. Of course, to know this is true we need to know how much more Goldman would pay for a replacement contract—what its position was worth, a value very hard to determine at the time.

AIG-Goldman Sachs $12.9B Cash Flows, Post AIG Takeover
(GS 2009 Annual Report, Letter to Shareholders)

**AIG had borrowed $4.8 billion in loans from GS and sold
GS $14B in CDS protection on CDO portfolio**
- AIG repays GS $4.8B for loan fully collateralized by Treasuries
- AIG gives GS $2.5B in additional variation margin on CDSs
- AIG gives GS (Fed Maiden Lane) $5.6 billion to settle existing CDS
  contracts and avoid further collateral calls (face value of protection on
  CDO portfolio of $14B - $8.4B in previously received collateral)
  - GS gives portfolio of CDOs to AIG/Fed
  - GS uses "the vast majority" of this payment to buy portfolio (and end hedges
    from other counterparties) whom had sold protection to GS (GS had hedged
    possibility of AIG default)
  - SIGTARP (TARP auditor) thinks Fed should have paid less by not valuing
    protection at contact price.

The exposure of GS was the cost of replacing the CDS protection – value
of the collateral plus the value of the other hedges. Would now cost more
in premiums to obtain the same protection given the downward movement
in CDO prices making it more likely that a CDS seller would have to pay.

Counterparty Risk

- Does counterparty risk generally differ for deals with banks as compared to other institutions, like hedge funds and bank holding companies? Should it?

- <u>Bank and Non-Bank Counterparty Risk</u>: Banks that fail are resolved by the FDIC (and now under Dodd-Frank systemically important non-banks, including bank holding companies). Under normal FDIC practice counterparty positions are transferred to solvent third parties (FDIC will have to pay them to take over their out of the money position), so in the money parties suffer no losses. In AIG, which was a one-off situation, rather than transfer the book, AIG bought back the in-the money positions from its counterparties like Goldman.

  Absent a bank bankruptcy or a special bailout, a bankrupt firm is dealt with in bankruptcy, including bank holding companies—this was the case with Lehman. Bankruptcy provides that, unlike other secured creditors, in the money counterparties can terminate their positions and keep their collateral. To the extent collateral is not sufficient, they will have losses which will be filed as unsecured claims against the bankrupt (given valuation difficulties claims could be vastly inflated).

    So if your counterparty is a bank (or SIFI) or is bailed out you will lose nothing even if you have no collateral because a solvent third party will honor the contracts, whereas if your counterparty is not a bank or SIFI, you can have big losses on your unsecured positions. Interestingly, this triggered no systemic risk in Lehman (Lehman was in the money)—

but is this difference in treatment justified? Don't the FDIC rules create severe moral hazard problems? Mark Roe believes bankruptcy counterparties are even too favorably treated because they are immune from the automatic stay and preference attack for initial collateral increases taken within 90 days of bankruptcy.

Bank Capital Requirements: Buyers of Protection

- Special Rules for Credit Derivatives
  - **Substitution Approach** (Basel I and standardized Basel II) : take lower risk-weight of the seller of protection or underlying obligor, e.g. debtor on loan (lower will usually be seller of protection)
  - **Split Approach** (Original Basel II standardized proposal): risk weight is the weighted average of the obligor's risk weight and the protection seller's risk weight.
  - **Double Default Approach** (Basel II IRB):

$$K_{DD} = K_U \cdot (0.15 + 160 \cdot PD_g)$$

K_{DD} =	Total capital required
K_U =	Capital required under substitution approach
Parenthesis =	Reduction factor based on empirical studies
Assume:	Seller of protection has at least A- credit rating

Basel III Capital Requirements (December 2009)

- Must stress test positive exposure—expected in the money position since counterparty risk may be positively correlated with market risk—the more you are in the money, the more likely counterparty default may be.
- Calculate capital needed to cover counterparty exposure based on default probabilities of counterparty bonds at a 99.9% confidence level
- More capital for higher asset correlations on swap portfolio (take diversification into account)
- Longer horizon on close-out exposure (time needed to take new position to replace old one or to terminate exposure by hedging)
- Bigger haircuts when use securitized collateral (usually collateral is cash)—amount of capital generally depends on adequacy of collateral
- Require adequate collateral management—amounts and management
- Less capital (2% risk weight) for exposures to central counterparties than on bilateral swaps (December 2010 proposal)

Capital Arbitrage among Sellers of Protection on Credit Derivatives	
SofP	**Capital**
Bank	Basel
Insurance Company (AIG)	Insurance Regulation Rules

Insurance regulation did not extend to holding company where AIG did business (compare to investment banks before CSEs).

Liability for Dealers: Dharmala (I)

Swap One: 2 years for notional $50 million, starts 1-19-94

- Dharmala pays BT 5% interest - 1.25% interest - N/183 x 5% where N = number of days in 6 month period ("look period") beginning 8-15-94 in which Libor is <u>less than</u> 4.125%
- So if Libor under 4.125% during entire "look period", **Dharmala gets** 1.25% x $50 million per year ($625,000), or **$1.25 million** for 2 years ($625,000 x 2)

  5% - 1.25% - 5% = -1.25% (BT pays)
- So if Libor over 4.125% during entire "look period", **Dharmala pays** 3.75% x $50 million per year ($1,875,000) or **$3.75 million** for 2 years (1.875 x 2)

  5% - 1.25% - 0% = 3.75% (Dharmala pays)

Explain Slide: Barrier Swaps

The basic deal is that Dharmala is betting that interest rates never go over 4.125% for most or all of the look period. Maximum gain in two years (not PV) is $1.25 million, maximum loss is $3.75 million.

Why did Dharmala do this do you think? Hedging or speculation.

After, Dharmala was losing on Swap 1, parties agreed to replace it with Swap 2.

Liability for Dealers: Dharmala (II)

Swap Two (replaces One): 2 years for notional $50 million, starts 2-16-1994

- Dharmala pays BT: (Spread x $50MM) – (350 basis points x $50MM), per year
- Spread
    - 0 if 6 month Libor <u>never</u> goes over 5.25% during first year (2-16-94 to 2-16-95) ("look period")
    - If 6 month Libor <u>ever</u> goes over 5.25% during "look period", spread for both years is (6 month Libor on 2-15-95/4.50%)-1
        - So **if Libor on 2-15-95 were 6%**, the Spread would be .33, [(.06/.0450)-1], a decimal not a percentage
        - **Dharmala pays** BT per year (.33 x $50MM) - (.0350 x $50MM) $16.5MM - $1.75MM = **$14.75MM**
    - If Libor never goes over 5.25% during "look period", **Dharmala gets paid $1.75MM** per year

        0 spread - (.0350 x $50MM) = $1.75MM

    In fact, Dharmala owed BT $65MM on Swap Two (interest rates rose substantially)

Explain slide

Now Dharmala is betting that interest rates never go over 5.25% in the look period. Dharmala's maximum gain is $1.75 million, with losses if Libor ever goes over 5.25% during look period. Losses could be unlimited. Note would still have losses if Libor goes over barrier during look period but below barrier on 2-15-95.

Losses would be $14.75 million per year if interest rates were 6% on 2-15-95; in fact, interest rates were a lot higher, so losses were $65 million (include interest owed on unpaid amounts at swap end).

Dharmala's Claims (Swap Two)

- Misrepresentation/Duty of Care

Would this be actionable under U.S. law? (No liability under English law)

U.S. legal standard on next slide.

U.S. Legal Standards

- Liability under P&G: BT had duty to disclose "material information to plaintiff both before the parties entered into the swap transactions and in their performance, and also a duty to deal fairly and in good faith during the performance of swap transactions."
- **Would there be liability under *P&G* standard?**
- **Is this the right standard?**

---

1. *P&G* Standard: Did BT disclose all material information? Did not disclose Swap Two formula, not full presentation of interest rate scenario. Here one would argue that the failure to disclose was not material because Dharmala had access to this information, interest rates, or could have figured it out, formula. Dharmala's people, e.g. Thio (Cal. State MBA), were sophisticated, even if not as much as BT's people, e.g. Hyun (Yale, East Asian Studies, master of derivatives).

However, it is very disturbing, that Swap One had a negative value to Dharmala of $2 million at its inception, and Swap Two a negative value of $8 million. The Swap Two negative value might reflect BT's willingness to abandon a contract with positive value, but the Swap One negative is difficult to explain. Should there be mandatory disclosure of the market value of the swap? Would this be information that only a dealer is likely to have? Was this bad faith? See next slide on German case.

Another question is whether Dharmala actually understood the crucial difference between whether the Spread formula produced a decimal or a percentage. In the example of 6 month LIBOR being 6% on February 15, 1995, the Spread calculation date, Spread is the decimal .33. However, if the product of the formula was to have been a percentage, .33%, this would be .0033 as a decimal. At .33 Spread was $16.5 million per year on the $50 million swap; at .0033 it would have been $165,000.

2. <u>Correct Standard</u>? Does not directly take into account sophistication of parties like, for example, the Voluntary Framework (six securities firms), have obligation of "good faith" if counterparty is not a "professional intermediary" which Dharmala was not, or could argue buyer beware like the Principles formulated by ISDA and some other trade groups coordinated by the New York Fed (pro bank for safety and soundness reasons).

Negative Value at Inception: Deutsche Bank Swaps Case
(German Supreme Court, March 2011)

- Obligation to disclose initial negative value
  (amounting to 4% of the reference amount) to
  German mid-size customer
- Could initial negative value just be reflection of
  bank's fee for arranging transaction

Dodd-Frank: Derivatives - 1

- Central clearing and reporting of OTC standardized and liquid derivative contracts (issue of exclusion of foreign exchange swaps). Trading of these derivatives on an exchange or SEF (swap execution facility). Intended to diminish the connectedness problem by collectivizing the impact of a participant failure

- Fed can extend access to discount window in unusual or exigent circumstances, §806(b)

- Limited exclusion for commercial companies using derivatives to hedge and not having a substantial net exposure

- Enhanced regulation of risk management by the clearinghouses (mainly through margin requirements and backup funding of members)

- Extensive regulation of ownership and governance of clearinghouses (CCPs), e.g. see CFTC proposal that restricts dealer ownership, maximum $50 million capital for membership

EU Approach to Derivatives
(European Market Infrastructure Regulation, EMIR)

- Regulators: European Securities and Market Authority and European Systemic Risk Board

- Like US requires central clearing of liquid standardized derivatives but does not focus on non-discriminatory access to membership and access

- Does not like US require exchange trading or price transparency

- No requirement of access to ECB discount window (provided by US)

- Broader exemption for end-users, only covered if their positions exceed a specified threshold with less strict margin requirements (US, covered if substantial net position)

- Like US, allows cross-border clearing by recognizing equivalent non-domestic CCPs

- Need for exchange trading of OTC derivatives to be addressed by MiFID

- No push out of derivatives trading into affiliates as in US

Proposal for a Regulation of the European Parliament and of the Council on OTC Derivatives, Central Counterparties and Trade Repositories, 2010/0250 (September 15, 2010)
Also, new international standards consistent with US and EU approach set forth by Committee on Payment and Settlement Systems, Technical Committee of the International Organization of Securities Commissions, **Principles for financial market infrastructures, Consultative Report** (March 2011).

TEACHING PLAN FOR

CHAPTER TEN

CLEARANCE AND SETTLEMENT

POWERPOINT SCREENS FOR NINETEENTH EDITION

Clearing and Settlement

The General Nature of Clearance and
Settlement: Clearance (NSCC)

• Matching Trades (capture trade facts)

• Net Position Calculation and Multilateral Netting

Lecture: What is involved in the clearing of securities?

1. *Matching Trades*: confirming the identity and quantity of the security being traded, the transaction price and date, and the identity of the buyer and seller. This is often referred to as the trade comparison process.

2. *Net Position Calculation:* calculate the net position of the participants in terms of securities that must be delivered and funds that must be paid.

How does this happen where securities are traded on an exchange?
The trade facts may be captured in two principal ways. The trade may be done on an automated system, e.g. NASDAQ or most of NYSE trades, where the relevant terms are captured by the computer system at the time of the trade. Alternatively, where there is floor trading, each side may submit their own version of the relevant terms, and a comparison must be made to determine whether each side's story matches up. The former may be a lot quicker than the latter. This function is usually performed by a clearinghouse.

Multilateral Netting: An Example

Hypo: A buys 100 IBM from B at $1, B buys 50
IBM from C at $3, and C buys 40 IBM from A at $2

	Securities				Cash		
	A	B	C		A	B	C
	+100	-100			-100	+100	
		+50	-50			-150	+150
	-40		+40		+80		-80
Net:	+60	-50	-10		-20	-50	+70

How does multilateral netting work?

Multilateral netting involves netting between more than two parties, as in
the example on the slide. It is more risky than bilateral netting because it
is difficult or impossible to unwind if one party fails to deliver securities
or pay cash. Like the problem in a multilateral payment system, old
CHIPS. Deliveries and payments depend on netting among hundreds of
participants. To reduce systemic risk, the NSCC becomes the
counterparty, and the NSCC must find ways to reduce its risk by looking
to members. In a bilateral netting, if one party does not deliver or pay, the
settlement can be undone as to those parties without necessarily creating
systemic risk, but less efficient. On the other hand if one of the parties
fails in a bilateral world it may increase systemic risk since there is no
mutualization of losses.

Note: securities are netted by securities, but can net cash across all
securities.

Settlement of Securities Trades

- DTCC Transfers Securities

-100 IBM	+100 IBM
Broker A	Broker B

- Payment for securities through payment system, e.g. FedWire
- Does it matter whether securities and funds are transferred at same time?
- Two level settlement
  - Broker level
  - Customer-broker level

The actual transfer of the securities may occur by a variety of means, physical delivery of certificates or by book entries denoting a change of ownership. Where transfer is by book entries, the securities may be held by a central depository which will make the appropriate debit or credit entries to the appropriate parties. This is what DTCC does (merger of DTC and NSCC). Payment is made separately through Fedwire.

Who has the obligation to deliver the securities and pay the funds?
As we have discussed, this is usually the clearinghouse which becomes the counterparty to each trade in order to reduce risk.
Does it matter whether delivery of securities and payments occur relatively simultaneously? Discuss
If securities are delivered before funds, and the paying party fails to pay, the party that has delivered the securities is out the cash, and is at risk for the counterparty's failure to pay during the delay period. Conversely if funds are paid out before securities are received, the party that has paid the funds is at risk for the failure of the counterparty to deliver the securities. This is why some systems have a DvP requirement.
Comment on two-level settlement
Customers must settle with brokers and brokers must settle with each other

---

Risk to DTCC in Clearing System

Hypo: A sells B 100 IBM at $100 per share for a total of $10,000. Locked in at T+1. Settlement at T+3

- What is the risk to DTCC?
  - If Failure of B to Pay? Suppose IBM shares go down $50 per share at T+3
  - If Failure of A to Deliver? Suppose IBM shares go up to $150 per share by T+3
- What factors affect the magnitude of the risk of failure to deliver securities?

  - Is the failure "routine" or a result of delivering broker (DB) insolvency?
  - If insolvency, then depends on (1) whether DB becomes insolvent on T+3 or T+4; (2) whether DB becomes insolvent before or after the market closes; and (3) whether DB becomes insolvent before or after paying its mark (if increase in stock value).

Lecture: The clearing process begins on T, the trade date, and is completed with settlement on T + 3. What is the risk to DTCC? Discuss

1. Failure to Pay: B may not pay DTCC $10K on T + 3, but DTCC must still pay A $10K on the same date. If price of IBM has gone down since T + 1, the IBM shares DTCC gets from A may be worth less than the $10K it must pay A. If they were worth only $5K, because they are now selling at $50 per share, DTCC has a $5K loss. Failure to pay case usually result of insolvency.

2. Failure to Deliver: A may not deliver the shares to DTCC on T + 3, but NSCC must still deliver the shares to B on the same date. If the price of IBM shares has gone up since T + 1, DTCC must buy the shares at a higher price than $10K, the funds it gets from B. If the shares were worth $15K, because they are now selling at $150 per share, DTCC has a $5K loss. If failure to deliver is merely operational problem, no risk.
How does DTCC protect itself from these risks? Next slide (hidden).

How Does DTCC Protect Itself Against Failure to Deliver?

- Marks at close of trading
- Clearing Fund to cover potential losses (monthly payments based on 20 day rolling average of a participants' portfolio value away from the initial stock price, measures volatility and therefore risk)
- Membership requirements
- Third Party Guarantee
- Minimum capital requirements for participants
- Assess member for shortfalls
- Monitor participants' solvency

Lecture (just go over list quickly)

Between T + 1 and T + 3, the clearing fund for each member is supposed to cover potential losses, based on a 20 day rolling average of a participants' portfolio value away from the stock price. Less risk if T+!

Does this adequately protect DTCC?

The 20 day average measures your positions and market risk in the past; this could change at any time. IBM could have remained unchanged in the last 20 days, and then may sharply rise in T + 1 to T + 3 period. Also, the money due is only actually collected once a month.

How do the risks in OTC derivatives clearing differ from those in equity clearing?

Much shorter period of exposure, more complex pricing, not on exchanges, so less liquidity.

G-30 Requirements (Generally Met by G10 Countries)

- Institutional Comparison on T+1
- Affirmation of Trades on T+2
- Rolling Settlement on T+3
- Central Securities Depository
- Securities Netting
- DvP (delivery v. payment)
- Same day funds
- Securities lending
- Technical standards for securities messages

What is the objective? To reduce settlement risk and costs

Second Round of G-30 Proposals

- Strengthened Interoperable Global Network, e.g.
  - more automation, eliminate paper
  - synchronize timing among networks, e.g. securities with payments and FX (T or T+1)
  - expand use of central counterparties
  - facilitate securities lending and borrowing to facilitate settlement
- Mitigation of Risk
  - financial integrity of providers of clearing and settlement
  - risk management of users
  - final, simultaneous transfers
  - business continuity and disaster recovery
  - plan for failure of systemically important institution
  - enforceability of contracts, legal rights to securities, cash or collateral (see Hague Convention)
  - closeout netting: validity and valuation
- Improved Corporate Governance

Lecture: Review, more technical, same objectives

G-30 Standards

- Are common private standards a good idea?
  - As opposed to no standards
  - As opposed to public standards

Discuss: Are Common standards a good idea? Short discussion

1. The G-30 (private think tank) was generally interested in increasing the efficiency and reducing the risk inherent in the clearing and settlement process. Effort greatly supported by regulators of banks and securities firms.

2. Apparently less interested in particular stock markets gaining trading advantages from more efficient systems, or independent C&S systems competing. At any rate, implementation of these recommendations would reduce the contribution of this factor to competition between clearing and settlement systems. Most of the participants trade, clear and settle across multiple country markets.

3. Investors, particularly large institutions, want standard rules to facilitate their ability to keep track of their positions and to monitor the performance of their global custodian and sub-custodians in different markets. Mastery of different rules in different markets, makes it more difficult to monitor.

4. Private standards more easily changed than public ones, but less binding. Note SEC had to force U.S. into T+3.

G-30 Standards

- Should U.S. go to T+1 (Hong Kong and some other countries have already)?

Discuss

1. *Benefit:* Reduces time in which there are unsettled positions. Already limited by contribution and mark-to-market requirements, but will further reduce risk.

2. *Cost:*

(a) Must have faster trade comparison which requires more automated capture of trade data, or faster matching of trades. Seems doable.

(b) Requires faster delivery of securities by customers or willingness to hold securities with brokers, and faster payment--no checks from California to New York. Issue for movement from T+5 to T+3, but 80% of retail money was in by T + 3, suggesting that the real issue was float. If B/d gets funds at T + 3 and does not pay until T + 5, has positive float. If B/d gets or has securities before T + 5 can lend the securities (to others who need them for settlement). Different for T+1. Less value of float, and less timely delivery by customers—requires changes in how customers hold and pay for securities.

(c) Might increase strains on liquidity or funding costs--net purchasers need funds faster to settle trades.

Originally, everyone was pressing to move to T+1, to further reduce risk, but now costs seen as major obstacle.

Cross Border Linkage: Cross-Exchange Trade

Hypo: US seller (S) sells 100 IBM shares, traded on
NYSE and cross-listed on Tokyo Stock Exchange
(TSE), to Japanese buyer. How would this
transaction be settled?

Discuss and then show next slide.

Cross Border Linkage: Cross-Exchange Trade

Hypo: US seller (S) sells 100 IBM shares cross-listed on
Tokyo Stock Exchange (TSE) to Japanese buyer. How
would this transaction be settled?

Securities Settlement

    DTCC (DTCC Rules)   → JASDEC
S's Custodian   JASDEC (link) ←   Buyer
    -100   +100   +100

Cash Settlement
Buyer pays Seller Yen through Japanese payment
system

Why are securities held and settled at DTCC?

What is the purpose of this link?

Investors typically hold securities in custody in the home country of the traded security, the U.S. in the IBM example. This is because this is where most of the trades with respect to that security occur. Otherwise, securities would constantly be moved in and out of the trading country with the attendant expense.

Note that even if securities are only transferred by book entry, still need to be all in the same place to keep track of.

A possible alternative would be to go through Euroclear or Clearstream, as discussed below.

Cross Border Linkage: Cross-Border Trade

Hypo: US investor sells 100 Mitsubishi Chemical,
       listed on TSE, to Japanese buyer. How would this
       transaction be settled?

Not handled through bilateral links between Central Securities
Depositories (CSDs) like DTCC and JASDEC, because this is a trade of a
Japanese stock on TSE (previous cross-listed example, on the other hand,
was U.S. stock traded in U.S. and on Japanese exchange). U.S. investor
goes through global custodian (State Street) which holds Japanese stock at
JASDEC through local office (State Street Trust Bank) or independent
sub-custodian (Sumitomo Trust Bank). The custodian's participation in
Japanese system is the link. Alternatively, one could use Euroclear or
Clearstream.

Cross Border Linkage: Cross-Border Trade

Hypo: US investor sells 100 Mitsubishi Chemical,
listed on TSE, to Japanese buyer

Securities settlement

JASDEC (JASDEC Rules)

Seller's Custodian Bank (**link**)   Buyer
          -100   +100

Cash Settlement

Japanese buyer pays Seller's custodian bank through
Japanese payment system

Not handled through bilateral links between Central Securities
Depositories (CSDs) like DTCC and JASDEC, because this is a trade of a
Japanese stock on TSE (previous cross-listed example, on the other hand,
was U.S. stock traded in U.S. and on Japanese exchange). U.S. investor
goes through global custodian (State Street) which holds Japanese stock at
JSCC through local office (State Street Trust Bank) or independent sub-
custodian (Sumitomo Trust Bank). The custodian's participation in
Japanese system is the link. Alternatively, one could use Euroclear or
Clearstream.

Euroclear

- System for clearing and settling securities: competes with national systems (Clearstream similar)
- Participants hold cash and securities accounts for over 33,000 different debt and equity securities in multiple currencies with JP Morgan Chase's Brussels branch which are "redeposited" by Morgan branch with designated securities depositories, in effect sub-custodians

<u>Custody Chain for U.S. corporate bonds</u>

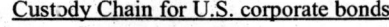
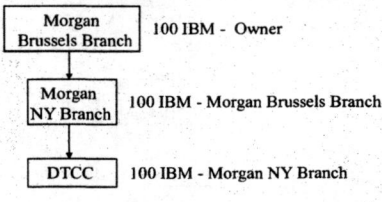

Morgan Brussels Branch	100 IBM - Owner
Morgan NY Branch	100 IBM - Morgan Brussels Branch
DTCC	100 IBM - Morgan NY Branch

Lecture

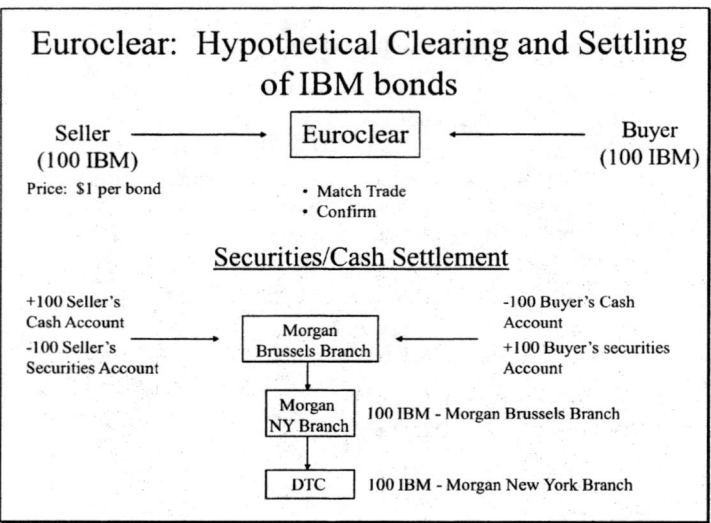

The selling and buying party report the trade to Euroclear which matches the information, just like DTCC. If the seller has the securities in the Euroclear system (held with a Euroclear sub-custodian, Morgan N.Y. which in turn will have a DTCC account), and the buyer has the cash, Euroclear debits the seller's securities account and credits its cash account for the amount of purchase, and credits the buyer's securities account and debits the buyer's cash account. Sub-custody accounts are unchanged. Settlement by algorithm to maximize value of cash balances (see CHIPS) If the seller does not have the securities in the Euroclear system, it can transfer them in, i.e. by having its U.S. custodian transfer them through DTCC (a book entry) to Morgan N.Y., the Euroclear sub-custodian for U.S. debt securities. Alternatively, it can borrow the securities from another Euroclear participant. If the buyer does not have the cash, it can transfer the cash through Fedwire from its bank to Euroclear's U.S. cash correspondent, also Morgan N.Y. Alternatively, it may borrow funds from Morgan under the preadvise procedure.

Would parties want to clear a U.S. NYSE equity trade through Euroclear rather than through DTCC? (next hidden slide)? Class discussion

---

> ## Would Parties want to clear a US Equity Trade through Euroclear rather than DTCC?
>
> - Can clear faster than T+3 (but no automatic capture)
>
> - True DvP
>
> - Centralization of Trades/Cash for different markets
>
> - No contributions to funding of clearing corporation
>
> - Chaining v. Netting
>
> - Securities lending/borrowing easier than in local markets

Are there any disadvantages in using Euroclear?

1. May require movement of securities from normal custodian to the Euroclear designated depositary.

2. No automatic capture of trade information; both the buyer and seller must input trade information to Euroclear.

3. No clearing corporation as counterparty; if your counterparty does not have the securities or cash the trade is not settled.

4. Requires Euroclear to register with SEC as clearing organization. SEC concerned that organizations clearing U.S. securities have systems to protect against systemic risk. Euroclear depends critically on solvency of JP Morgan Chase bank. Have exemptions to clear U.S. government securities and U.S. equity trades involving foreign counterparties.

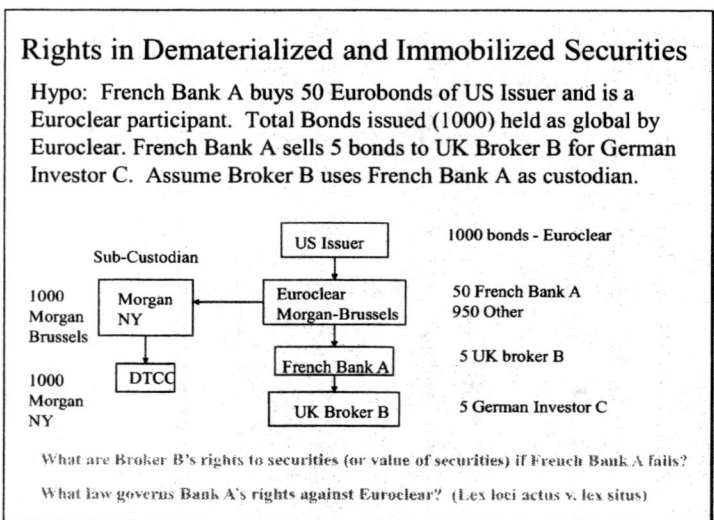

Rights in Dematerialized and Immobilized Securities

Hypo: French Bank A buys 50 Eurobonds of US Issuer and is a Euroclear participant. Total Bonds issued (1000) held as global by Euroclear. French Bank A sells 5 bonds to UK Broker B for German Investor C. Assume Broker B uses French Bank A as custodian.

Is it important whether Broker B's rights against French Bank A are contractual or proprietary?

Yes. If Broker B's rights are merely "contractual" then B is a general creditor of the Bank and is at risk for the bank's insolvency. If, however, B has proprietary rights in the securities (albeit fungible) then the securities are legally segregated from the Bank's own assets.

If French Bank A's rights against Euroclear are proprietary, does that mean Broker B's rights against Bank A are also proprietary? Are ownership interests derivative?

No. The rights of the parties are separately determined at each level. Ownership interests are, however, derivative in the sense that Broker B's rights to securities at A cannot exceed the amount of securities A actually held at Euroclear (50). This means that if A fraudulently sold all 50 for its own account, including Broker B's 5, Broker B would be at risk. Similarly B at risk if A's rights against Euroclear are only proprietary

What law governs Bank A's rights against Euroclear? Assume that Euroclear actually holds the securities through a Morgan N.Y. account at DTCC?

Belgian law says Belgian law applies under the *lex loci actus* principle, the place where the transfer is effected. The transfer to Bank A of 50 securities occurred on the books of Euroclear in Belgium. This would be the case even if the actual securities were held by Euroclear in the account of a U.S. depository, e.g. DTCC. Of course, what law is actually applied is up to the court applying it. It is possible that a non-Belgian court might apply *lex situs*, the place where the securities are held, in this case the law of New York where DTCC is located. Note that many of these issues are now dealt with in Revised Article 8 of the Uniform Commercial Code but that is only U.S. law.

What would the Hague Convention provide as to the law governing Bank A's rights against Euroclear (next hidden slide)?

Hague PRIMA Convention

- Law specified in the contract, provided intermediary has an office there, Article 4. If not applicable, then
- Location of office of intermediary which contract specifies is the office through which the intermediary entered into the agreement, Article 5(1). If not applicable, then
- Law of the place of incorporation of the relevant intermediary, Articles 5(2) and (3). Where is the "relevant intermediary"? New York or Belgium?

European Clearing Arrangements

- 20 plus clearing organizations (compare DTCC monopoly), but consolidation underway
- Vertical silos (Deutsche Borse's ownership of Eurex Clearing AG and Clearstream) versus horizontal arrangements (LCH.Clearnet and Euroclear owned by group of banks and clear and settle cross-border trades for several exchanges)
  - Vertical silo can be established by exchange rules, requiring one clearer, as well as ownership, or be compelled by economies of scale of trade capture (see DTCC)
  - Merger issue: UK Competition Commission says any acquiror of LSE would need to sever relationship with clearer—would not be required if exchanges maintained separate identity (but precludes economies of scale)
- Fragmentation: C&S costs in Europe 7-10 times those of DTCC
  - apples and oranges comparison?
  - estimated 20% savings if Euroclear and Clearstream merged
  - legal barriers, e.g. Italy and Spain provide only one organization can hold electronic shares in their countries
  - EC Commission proposes fine of Clearsteam for discriminating against Euroclear—charges it higher prices for clearing and settlement (link)

What Should be done?

What should be done?

On 11 July 2006, the industry (the Federation of European Securities Exchanges (FESE), European Association of Central Counterparty Clearing Houses (EACH) and European Central Securities Depositories Association (ECSDA)) agreed to a Code of Conduct to avoid regulation by the EU.

The measures detailed in the Code address three main issues:

(i) transparency of prices and services;

(ii) access and interoperability;

(iii) unbundling of services and accounting separation.

Initially, the Code will apply exclusively to cash equities. While the implementation of the Code is under way, the Commission expects the scope of the Code to be gradually extended to include other financial instruments, such as bonds and derivatives. The signatories may however – and the Commission encourages them to do so – apply all or some of the provisions of the Code to most or all financial instruments from early on, if they so wish.

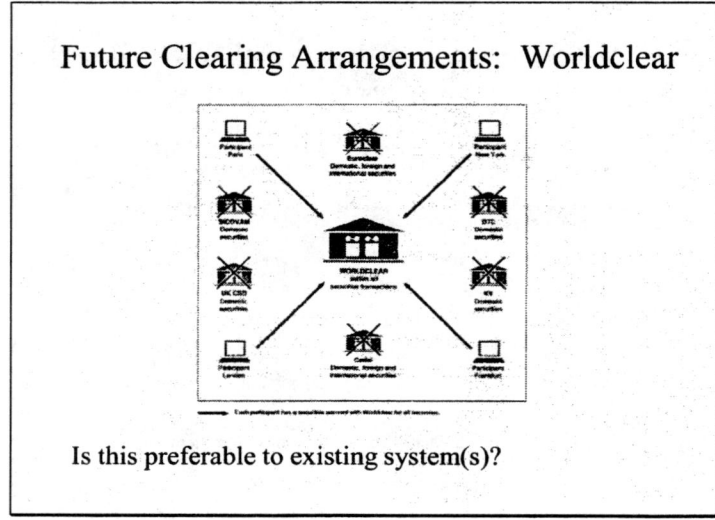

Future Clearing Arrangements: Worldclear

Is this preferable to existing system(s)?

Discuss Worldclear

Worldclear (Euroclear or other, see DTCC ambition) would clear, settle and hold in custody all securities. All participants of existing national CSDs would become participants of Worldclear. This is what some want in Europe or world. Is this a good solution?

Strengths: One set of rules; no pipeline liquidity problem, all trades could be netted out.

Weaknesses: Massive risk assumed by Worldclear; monopoly or public utility and increased operational risk. Payment split from settlement. Note that Worldclear might be closer if Euroclear and Clearstream were to merge.

Key Questions on OTC Derivatives: Clearinghouses and Exchange Trading

- Should we mandate that all credit derivatives be cleared through a clearinghouse?
- How many clearinghouses should there be?
- Should we mandate that some or all credit derivatives be traded on an exchange?
- Should we promote wide clearinghouse membership by limiting the minimum capital, e.g. $50 million, a clearinghouse can require
- In the U.S., who regulates the clearinghouses? Who should?
- What problems might be raised by the US and EU both having equivalent regulation requirements for financial institutions in their country to use foreign clearinghouses?

(see CCMR letter of March 4, 2010)

Mandated Use of Clearinghouses
- Current systemic risk problem forces bailouts for fear of consequences of defaults on swaps positions. Clearinghouse (CCPs) would collectivize risk. Note: we do not need clearinghouses to actually know the positions of parties on CDSs because all of these positions are reported to DTCC on a daily basis (but do not get data on positions in other swaps).
- Collectivization only occurs for transactions between clearinghouse members, a limited set of dealers (need to be assured of ability to support clearinghouse—could be expanded to some non-dealers). Non-members access CCP with a member guarantee, no net reduction of systemic risk.
- Problem of non-standardization would limit netting and make margining difficult, might require more standardization (industry headed that way). Interest rate and FX swaps are highly standardized (and becoming more so, big issue is inclusion of restructuring as Credit Event). Bigger standardization with CDSs, may only be 65% standardized.
- Which non-member contracts should be centrally cleared—arguably get some reduction of systemic risk if relying on regulated member guarantee than unregulated bilateral, e.g. Morgan Stanley (MS)

guarantees Citadel through clearing—MS exposed to Citadel default but margining imposed by clearinghouse and more controls on MS failure than on Citadel's.

- End user problem—we are not really worried about failure of commercial companies like Delta Airlines but sometimes commercial companies, e.g. Enron or AIG, act as financial institutions by taking speculative positions. So we say only force through CCP where large net exposure.

TEACHING PLAN FOR

CHAPTER SIXTEEN
MUTUAL AND HEDGE FUNDS

POWERPOINT SCREENS FOR NINETEENTH EDITION

Mutual Funds

Mutual Funds

- Investment Company Act of 1940 ('40 Act)
- Taxation and Adjustments
- Money Market Mutual Funds

U.S. market share fairly constant, near 50% since 2005, next slide.

Mutual Funds Worldwide
(Trillions dollars)

	2005	2006	2007	2008	2010
U.S.	8.9	10.4	12.0	9.6	11.8
World	17.8	21.9	26.1	18.9	24.7
U.S. Share	50%	47%	46%	51%	47.8%

R=Revised data; Components may not add to the total because of rounding.

Source: Investment Company Institute, 2011

Currently $11.8 trillion US, does not count $1 trillion in exchange traded funds in US, (index tracking mutual funds that trade like stocks)

Investment Company Act of 1940:
Basic Approach - Registration

- Requires registration of all funds sold to public (absent exemption); those sold to the general public must also register under '33 Act
- Disclosure of investment policies, fees and portfolio
- Rules to control pyramiding, conflicts of interest, and embezzlement
- Limit retail investor risk, e.g. leveraging restrictions and diversification requirements

---

So-called "hedge funds" are exempted from registration under '40 and '33 Act because they are sold to a limited number of persons or to certain qualified investors. Like a private placement exemption.

> ## Why Require Foreign Investment Companies to Register under '40 Act?
>
> - Foreign Law inadequate - must subject to U.S. Law (or meet the requirements of Section 7(d))
> - Enforcement is the key concern

Lecture

A foreign investment company is incorporated outside the United States. This means that it will be subject to the rules of another legal system that may not be adequate in the view of U.S. regulators and it may be difficult to enforce U.S. extraterritorial rules against such a company. Since foreign companies are almost always subject to foreign law, it will be difficult for the fund to meet U.S. registration requirements. Pursuant to Section 6(c) of the Act, a foreign company may be exempted from registration under Section 7(d) of the '40 Act if by "reason of special circumstances or arrangements, it is both legally and practically feasible effectively to enforce the provisions of [the Act] against such company and that the issuance of such order is otherwise consistent with the public interest and the protection of investors."

How does the SEC generally decide whether the 7(d) requirements are satisfied?

Rule 7d-1 sets out some key guidelines: (1) the foreign applicant's charter and by-laws must contain the substantive provisions of the 1940 Act (investor protection); (2) all parties involved with the management and investment of the funds must file an agreement stating that each will comply with the 1940 Act (enforcement); (3) at least a majority of the directors and officers of the applicant foreign fund must be U.S. citizens, and of these, a majority must reside in the United States (enforcement); (4) all of the foreign fund's assets must be maintained in a U.S. bank (anti-embezzlement); and (5) the applicant's principal underwriter and auditor must be U.S. entities (enforcement re liability of agents).

Section 7(d): Union - Investment (UI)

Under German Law,

- Mutual funds are not separately incorporated (typical still in Europe): Unifonds was a "separate estate" run by UI, a management company owned by 40 banks
- Managers of fund could not be U.S. citizens or residents
- All assets must be in custody of German bank

West German law and practices were different and inconsistent with U.S. As a result, UI was seeking to be exempted from the 7(d) requirements. UI ultimately withdrew its application after the SEC announced it would hold a hearing on its application.

Separate Incorporation

- Why does incorporation make a difference?
- In U.S., management companies, and not shareholders or Boards of a fund, actually run funds
- Management company selects Board, but usually 40% of the Board must be independent
  - In 2006, under proposed SEC rule, rejected by courts, 75% of Board had to be independent and there had to be an independent chairman
  - Not true of management companies in Germany

Probably could have exempted on this issue.

U.S. Citizens or Residents as Managers

Under German law, managers of fund could not be
U.S. citizens or residents.

Why is this a problem?

U.S. Citizens or Residents as Managers

- Enforcement problem against Europeans
- Letter of credit (5% holdings of U.S. investors) alternative?

The residence/citizenship requirement is critical for enforcement and deterrence. The application acknowledges that it would be difficult for the Commission or a shareholder to enforce an injunction or bring a criminal action against the European executives of UI. The letter of credit provides some financial protection (actually quite limited, 5% of holdings of U.S. investors), but not nearly the deterrence provided by personal civil and criminal liability.

SKIP: How do U.S. bank custodian rules protect shareholders in the Fund? It does not necessarily prevent looting by the investment management company because custody banks generally follow investment manager instructions; they are not held to a fiduciary duty to the Fund. Moreover, under U.S. law the bank custodian can be owned by the investment management company (so-called in-house arrangements). UI pointed out that West German law dealing with the duties of bank custodians was equivalent to U.S. law. Thus, (1) the custodian bank must segregate Fund assets (bankruptcy of bank protection?); (2) the BAK approves the selection of the custodian bank (3) the custodian bank keep transaction records; (4) the regulators appoint an auditor to perform a regular audit of the Unifonds account including an examination of its portfolio transactions; (5) the manager is liable to the Fund for stolen assets; and (6) Fund cash deposits are protected against a bank failure by the Deposit Protection Fund. But assets are still in German banks; harder to get.

Pattern of SEC Action on 7(d)

- 1960 - 1973: Permitted foreign funds from Canada, Australia, Bermuda, United kingdom and South Africa to register
- 1973 - No further registrations (or applications)

What explains this pattern?

Early exemptions were for countries with U.K. type legal systems. Tax consequences preclude foreign fund offerings.
Discuss before showing next slide

> ## Taxation of Offshore Funds: Why U.S. Investors Will Not Invest in Foreign Funds
>
> - U.S. anti-deferral rules, PFIC (passive foreign investment company), requires that shareholders be taxed on fund earnings even if not distributed
>   - Applies to foreign (as well as U.S.) investment company whose gross income is 75% or more passive
>   - Foreign funds usually do not distribute because foreign jurisdictions permit deferral, e.g. Luxembourg
> - If PFIC provides shareholder with report of earnings, shareholder can elect to be taxed on undistributed share of earnings (QEF-qualifying electing fund), thus mimicking U.S. tax treatment of domestic funds
>   - Many funds do not provide, for expense/disclosure reasons
> - Mark-to-Market alternative: taxpayers can pay tax on current net asset value of shares - adjusted basis, e.g. cost, but then taxed on Fund's unrealized gains, and need mark-to-market information.
> - Default Rule: When taxpayer sells Fund's shares, pays gain plus interest representing value of tax deferral, which is often excessive compared to actual economic value of deferral

Lecture

Result is U.S. investors do not generally invest in foreign funds.

Note: PFIC does not apply to partnerships—usual organization of hedge funds (wholesale mutual funds which we shall come to later today).

Public mutual funds, however, cannot be organized as partnerships. Thus, U.S. investors cannot invest in them without penalizing taxes.

Do foreigners invest in U.S. funds? Discuss before showing next slide.

Why Foreigners Do Not Invest in U.S. Funds

- U.S. funds must distribute current realized income (taxable to shareholders) to be exempt from current tax at fund level: most foreign funds (tax havens like Luxembourg and Ireland) do not have to do so, so foreigners invest only in them
- Dividends to foreign shareholders subject to 30% withholding taxes (reduced to 15% by tax treaties)

Lecture

Thus, the retail mutual fund market is completely segmented: U.S. investors invest in U.S. funds and foreign investors invest in foreign funds. Odd effect of tax laws given increasing globalization.

What can be done about this? Mirror-cloning and master-feeder.

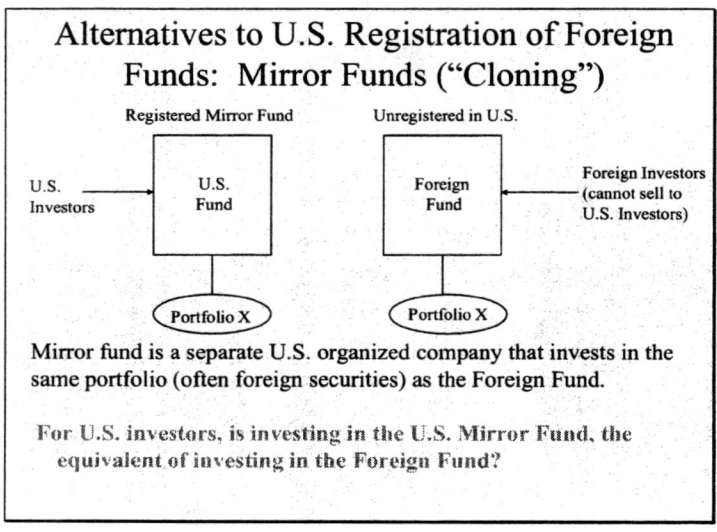

Alternatives to U.S. Registration of Foreign Funds: Mirror Funds ("Cloning")

Mirror fund is a separate U.S. organized company that invests in the same portfolio (often foreign securities) as the Foreign Fund.

For U.S. investors, is investing in the U.S. Mirror Fund, the equivalent of investing in the Foreign Fund?

Lecture
Obviously the tax treatment is different, but what about apart from that?
Try to give investors in both funds same returns.

Mirror Funds and Rebalancing

Problem: U.S. investors sell U.S. Fund, while foreign
investors increase investment in Foreign Fund

T_1 Opening Positions

U.S. Fund Portfolio			Foreign Fund Portfolio
($1)	50x	50x	($1)
($1)	50y	50y	($1)
($1)	50z	50z	($1)
$150			$150

T_2 Changes in Positions

U.S. Fund Portfolio:	Foreign Fund Portfolio:
50% redemptions	Purchases increase by 50%
What does it liquidate?	What does it buy?

The Banque Indosuez Luxembourg (BIL) decision on cloning, discusses
the problem caused by the fact that two funds will experience different
inflows and outflows of capital on any day, e.g. U.S. investors redeem
shares in U.S. fund, while foreign investors increase their investment in
the offshore fund. Absent some fix to this problem, the portfolio of stocks
in the U.S. fund would have to contract, while the portfolio of the foreign
fund would have to expand. This could make it impossible for the two
funds to have the same portfolios; indeed if one fund is larger than the
other they cannot have the same portfolios.

Couldn't you keep the same proportions of stock in each fund? But this
would require significant adjustments in the portfolios of both funds. In
our example, U.S. fund would have to sell a percentage of each of its
stocks and foreign fund would have to increase the percentage of each of
its stocks.

The BIL cloning technology tries to reduce the cost of that operation by
having the fund with net sales at the end of the day, the foreign fund in our
example, buy a "strip" of the portfolio of the U.S. fund. In effect, the
foreign fund gives the U.S. fund cash to meet its redemptions and gets a
share of the U.S. fund. No underlying securities need be bought or sold.

In addition, the cloning technology permits the "bunching" of trades.
This might occur when rebalancing won't work because there is a net
inflow/outflow of money in both funds. Suppose, for example, new
investors increase their investment in both the U.S. and foreign funds and

the investment advisor decides to buy IBM; the IBM orders for both funds would be bunched.

How about the master feeder? How does that work?

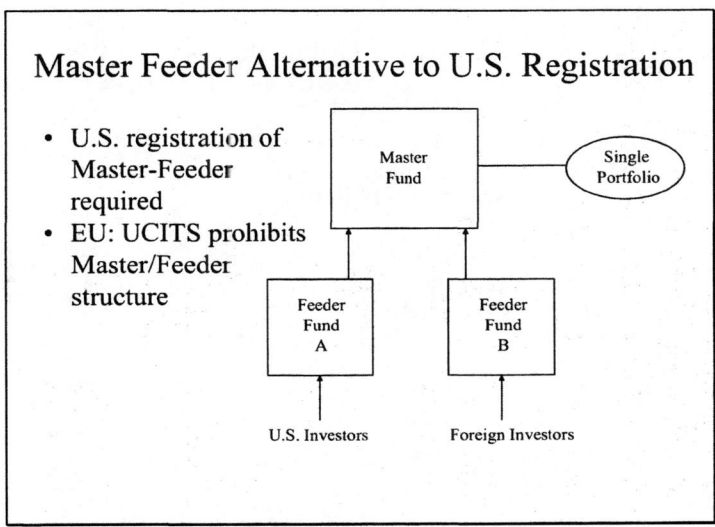

Master Feeder achieves exact duplication because each fund owns a share of the Master Fund, and only one portfolio is maintained. As a duplication technique this is cheaper and preferable to the mirror/cloning approach. However, the U.S. would require the master/feeder to be registered in the U.S. and comply with all U.S. requirements. Might be in conflict with EU rules or rules of other countries

For a long time, the EU did not permit the master/feeder under UCITS (the directive creating a single market for mutual funds). EU revised UCITS in December 2002, and after much debate decided against allowing.

However in UCITS IV, adopted by the Parliament and Council on July 13, 2009 (effective on July 1, 2011), the EU now will permit master feeders but only within EU—wants controls on what kinds of master the feeders can invest in.

So, we are left with mirror funds which are an imperfect substitute for the direct offering of foreign funds to U.S. investors in the U.S. but master feeder may well solve problem.

What are the effects of segmented markets on competition between U.S. and foreign funds? Note U.S. funds may have substantial operations abroad, e.g. investment advisers, processing. But overall U.S. funds are uncompetitive in the world with respect to foreign investors,

---

Trading Violations

- Late trading: trade after 4 p.m. (illegal)
- Market timing—in and out, day-to-day (requires disclosure of policies)
- Three Questions
  - How do you make money on market timing?
  - Who is hurt by market timers?
  - How can you control this?

See next two slides (hidden)

Making Money and Dilution

- Late trading—after 4 p.m. (illegal) and market timing—in and out, day-to-day (requires disclosure of policies)
- Both practices dilute gains of other shareholders—market timing:
  - 4 p.m. NAV is based on closing prices of stocks in the portfolio
  - Prices of foreign securities are stale, e.g. LSE has been closed for 5 hours when NAV is calculated
  - Suppose London stock X announces big deal after close of trading in London (say 11 am EDT), then NAV is too low because based on London closing price before big deal announcement
  - So I buy in at low NAV today and sell my position tomorrow at tomorrow's NAV that now reflects the big deal (all other things being equal)

Who is hurt? Other investors through dilution. Suppose the fair market value of the fund at 3pm and at close is $12 (if the London news were fully reflected in the price) but it is actually $2. Suppose the market timer buys half the fund for $2 at 3pm. He will now get 50% of the London gain when he sells tomorrow, as will the existing shareholders. If there had been no purchase, existing shareholders would have gotten 100%. But all shareholders could have done this—market timers were just smarter.
How can this be controlled? Hidden next slide

Control of Market Timing

- SEC proposed in December 2003 "hard" trade close which would prevent any trades being <u>processed</u> after 4 p.m.
  - Currently many trades, e.g. pension funds, are entered before 4 but processed after 4 (processing takes time)
  - Late traders abused late processing (entered trade before 4 but cancel after 4 if market moves against them, market timers do not do)
  - Did not adopt because of liquidity and processing concerns
- SEC adopts enhanced disclosure requirements on April 13, 2004
- SEC proposed 2% redemption fee for funds redeemed within 5 business days of investment: did not adopt because of liquidity concerns—instead gave funds the option of imposing such fees (March 2005)
- Other solutions
  - fair value pricing (update price after market close)
  - T+1 pricing (purchase on Day 1 but get closing price on Day 2)
  - Exchange-traded funds (ETFs), currently passive index, beginning to be actively-traded

Governance: Board Structure and Independence

- SEC Proposal: for each mutual fund board, 75% independent directors and independent chair—shot down twice by D.C. Circuit for inadequate cost-benefit analysis—SEC has let lie (heavily opposed by Fidelity and Ned Johnson their control shareholder)
- Reason for the proposal?
  - Management has conflict of interest between interest of fund investors and own interests, so need independent board members to represent interests of board. But dubious protection from Board.
- Costs
  - Direct: Chamber of Commerce estimates per board, $4 million over 5 years, or $800k per year; even less on per fund basis since independent directors dealt with an average of 40 portfolios (cluster) in 2005 (median 23, Fidelity has one board for all funds). Given $8 trillion in assets, this cost is really inconsequential—also in 2005, the average ratio of independent directors was 80% and 52% had independent chairs. So many have already made change. Greater impact on smaller or start-ups
  - Indirect: cost is worse investment decisions, would have to look at performance, SEC OEA memorandum of December 29, 2006: two main conclusions: (1) boards with a greater proportion of independent directors are more likely to negotiate and approve lower fees, merge poorly performing funds or provide more investor protection from late-trading and market timing; (2) no consistent evidence that more independent directors or independent chairs are related to higher returns for shareholders—but statistical techniques fall short since poor governance can lead to higher returns without adjusting for risk.

Total Net Assets of Mutual Funds
Billions of dollars

	Feb 2011	Jan 2010	% chg	Dec 2009
Stock Funds	5,960.5	4,775.2R	1.2	4,957.6
Hybrid Funds	782.3	632.8R	1.2	640.7
Taxable Bond Funds	2,181.7	1,796.2R	1.2	1,749.1
Municipal Bond Funds	456.9	463.7R	-1.0	457.1
Taxable Money Market Funds	2,417.5	2,330.4R	-1.2	2,918.8
Tax-Free Money Market Funds	323.5	385.2R	-1.2	397.4
Total	**12,122.4**	**10,883.5R**	**1.1**	**11,120.7**

R=Revised data; Components may not add to the total because of rounding.

Source: Investment Company Institute, Trends in Mutual Fund Investing, February 2011

- MMFs are about $2.7 trillion of $12.1 trillion U.S. mutual fund market, or about 22%, a big part of the industry, but down from a year ago. A money market fund generally invests in short-term high quality assets, like treasuries and commercial paper.

Stable NAV of $1 per share—cash management vehicle and marketing against bank deposits.

SEC Reforms (January 27, 2010)
Regulation of Money Market Funds (MMFs)

- Weighted average maturity decreased from 90 to 60 days
- Fewer second tier securities (rated in the second highest rating category, reduced from 5 to 3%; limit to single tier 2 issuer of .5%; longest tier 2 maturity reduced from 397 days to 45 days
- Enhanced cash reserves to increase liquidity: daily 10% in cash, weekly 30%
- Know your customer requirements—gauge potential for large redemptions
- More portfolio disclosure, including monthly disclosure of a firm's shadow NAV with a 60 day lag
- MMF Board can halt redemptions if fund breaks the buck—designed to stem motivation for runs and fire sales of assets

Could cost from 11-30 BP in yield.

Portfolio Management Changes to Rule 2a-7

	Current Rule 2a-7	Proposed SEC Rules	Final SEC Rules	Estimated Yield Impact (bps)[1]
Daily Liquidity - Taxable	None	5% - Retail 10% - Institutional	10%	0
Daily Liquidity Municipal	None	0%	0%	0
Weekly Liquidity Taxable	None	15% - Retail 30% - Institutional	30%	(9 – 12)
Weekly Liquidity Municipal	None	15% - Retail 30% - Institutional	30%	0
Weighted average maturity (WAM)	90 days	60 days	60 days	(0 – 8)
Weighted average life (WAL)	None	120 days	120 days	(1 – 3)
Illiquid securities	10%	0%	5%	(1 – 3)
Second tier securities	5% 1% per issuer 397-day limit	0%	3% 0.5% per issuer 45-day limit	(0 – 3)
Total	...ual reductions in annual fund yield in a normalized rate environment over time. Reductions show impact to fund that ...mits. Yield impacts differ among rated, institutional, and retail funds. ...rsion and Fidelity.			(11 – 29)

| Highly Confidential   22

Fidelity Analysis, total changes will impact yield from 11-29 BP, Hidden slide

---

Additional Regulation
of Money Market Funds (MMFs)

- "Break the Buck" problem in the credit crisis: the Primary Fund and the government response
- Should we mark-to-market MMFs like other mutual funds (floating NAV)?
- Should we insure MMFs like banks?

- Break the Buck problem—funds like Primary Fund invested in Lehman CP to increase yield and get competitive edge. When Lehman went into bankruptcy it defaulted on CP causing these funds losses. This triggered withdrawals that would have forced fire sale of other assets. Primary Fund suspended redemptions causing runs on other funds, only stopped when Fed supplied liquidity to funds (for orderly sale of their assets) and Treasury to guarantee their liabilities (for a fee). Investors have ultimately lost about 1 BP although at time it looked like a 3 BP loss (Primary valued Lehman CP at zero, although looks like bankruptcy recovery will be 22 cents)
- Mark-to-market interferes with cash management because do not know how much "cash" you have. Is this really serious? Real problem is hurts competition with bank deposits. Floating NAV would create tax and recordkeeping issues for investors which institutional investors say would lead them to alternatives. Also a lot of pricing discrepancy (pricing of difficult to price assets) within the usual very small NAV range variation. Continuous pricing would arguably not reduce systemic risk (any small negative variation could trigger withdrawals increasing instability).

No need for panoply of bank regulation but may require them to hold capital (see SEC increased liquidity requirements) based on risk given that government is de facto guaranteeing fund liabilities in a crisis. Even if guarantee were formally removed, it would be expected to come back in time of trouble. Should there be an insurance fund? Must be public, then how priced and what will it cover.

THAT'S ALL FOLKS!

TEACHING PLAN FOR

CHAPTER ELEVEN
EUROMARKETS

POWERPOINT SCREENS FOR SIXTEENTH EDITION

Class Outline
Euromarkets

- Eurocurrency deposits
- Eurocurrency loans
- Eurobond market
- Withholding taxes
- Future of Euromarket

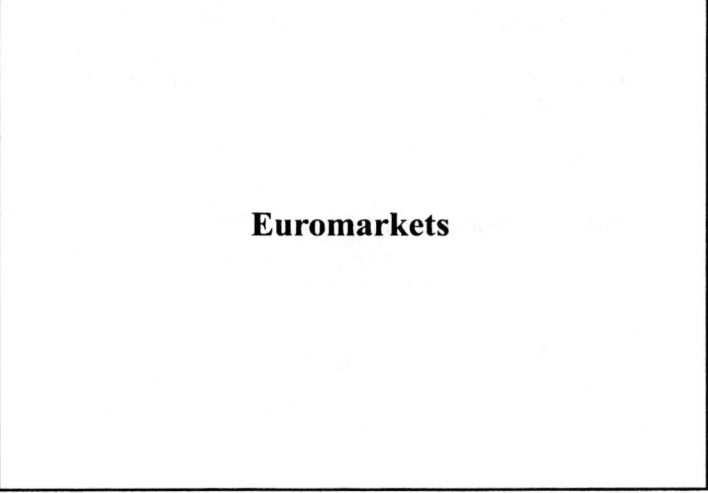

Euromarkets

Absence of home country (U.S. for dollar) regulations like reserve requirements or deposit insurance, often lower tax, no power of currency country to freeze (LAFB), higher rate on deposits, lower all-in cost of funds. Different time zones.

Less regulation means the euro-$ depositor may have higher risk than the depositor in the U.S. and wants a higher interest rate. Unclear, however that offshore funds will always be more risky. Are euroyen deposits in London less risky than yen deposits in Japan?

Less regulation also reduces the bank's costs, so its all-in costs (including cost of funds) is lower in the eurocurrency market than the home market. This permits the bank, and in a competitive environment forces the bank, to pay a higher rate of interest.

Reliability issue: possible underreporting of borrowing cost in credit crisis to disguise banks' increased riskiness.

What is a Eurocurrency deposit?

A deposit in a currency other than that of the bank's
country of residence

- e.g., a $ deposited in a London bank, a eurodollar
- Even euro deposited in a London bank, a "euro-euro"

Eurocurrency rates are offshore interbank deposit rates

- The London Interbank Offer Rate (LIBOR) is the rate a London bank offers to pay other banks for their deposits (in various currencies)
- Is LIBOR reliable?

How does a eurodollar deposit differ from a U.S. dollar deposit?

Absence of home country (U.S. for dollar) regulations like reserve requirements or deposit insurance, often lower tax, no power of currency country to freeze (LAFB), higher rate on deposits, lower all-in cost of funds. Different time zones.

Less regulation means the euro-$ depositor may have higher risk than the depositor in the U.S. and wants a higher interest rate. Unclear, however that offshore funds will always be more risky. Are euroyen deposits in London less risky than yen deposits in Japan?

Less regulation also reduces the bank's costs, so its all-in costs (including cost of funds) is lower in the eurocurrency market than the home market. This permits the bank, and in a competitive environment forces the bank, to pay a higher rate of interest.

Reliability issue: possible underreporting of borrowing cost in credit crisis to disguise banks' increased riskiness.

Syndicated Eurocurrency Loans

Banks in a syndicate lend to a borrower medium term at prevailing euromarket interest rates

The parties include:

- Borrowers: companies and governments

- Lead manager and other managing banks

- Participating banks

- Agent banks

Eurocurrency loans are loans priced off euromarket interest rates. Let's look at the role of the different parties of the syndicate. Apart from pricing, similar structure and issues in domestic syndicated loans.

The *lead manager* deals with the terms, may be an underwriter, and is the main communicator with the borrower and lenders until the agreement is signed.

The *other managers* help assemble participating banks. In a big loan, other managers may come from various countries and would organize participating banks from their country.

Participants are the banks that simply provide funds.

The *agent bank* deals with the ongoing administration of the loan, communicating between the borrower and the participants. It coordinates the payments to the borrower, the calculation of interest due, and the distribution of payments from the borrower among the participants. Note: avoid repetition with next screen

---

Special Features of Eurocredits

Special features include:

- large amounts
- smaller participations
- speed in completion
- flexible drawdown with commitment fee
- many possible currencies
- medium term maturities (e.g., 5 years) with 1, 3, 6 month rollover (and repricing) of advances
- floating interest rate, using LIBOR as the base rate plus a margin (or spread)

The special features that make syndicated eurocredits interesting to the parties

1. Large amounts: Some eurocredits are for billions of dollars; this one (example in book) is for $250
million. Syndication reduces each bank's participation to a smaller, acceptable level

2. Eurocredits can be arranged quickly. The market is organized. Banks know each other, so word of mouth deals work. The lead bank can easily learn acceptable terms by quick phone calls. Lenders can fund easily from the interbank market. No filing is required.

3. Drawdown is flexible. The borrower need not draw the funds immediately. It pays the commitment fee to ensure the banks' willingness to stand ready to lend at the agreed term.

4. Multi-currencies. The dollar is the dominant currency, but any major currency may be used: euro–Sterling, euro–yen, euro–euro

Lecture: These features help the parties: Borrowers get access to large loans quickly. Eurobonds are fast, but many borrowers do not have the reputation to issue eurobonds. Participants can diversify their portfolios, taking a small piece of many loans with almost no overhead cost. Of course, they can now do the same in the credit derivatives market, as well. Lead banks get wholesale business (a small fee on a big volume) with limited overhead costs.

A Hypothetical Eurocredit

- In mid-1996, a government-owned Korean firm negotiates a $250 million 5-year eurocredit

  - short-term loan rolled over at 1, 3, or 6 months (at borrower's choice) for 5 years

  - 1 1/8th% fixed spread over LIBOR

- Lenders include banks from Europe, Japan, and U.S.

- Citibank lead manages

Interest Payments "Float"

§4.1 [I]nterest shall accrue on each Advance during its Term...at a rate per annum equal... to the sum of the Margin and LIBOR for that Advance....

e.g.	LIBOR	+	Margin	=	Interest at Advance End
Advance #1	5 1/4	+	1 1/8	=	6 3/8 annualized rate
Advance #2	6 1/8	+	1 1/8	=	7 2/8

In a loan there may be several advances, functions of borrower's need and bank's target requirements. Each advance may be periodically repriced.

1) Payment of interest is due at the end of the term of the advance (though the excerpts from the agreement do not disclose this).
2) LIBOR is the base rate and represents the cost of funds to the lending banks. It is the rate a top quality bank will pay when it takes a deposit from other banks.
3) The margin is a fixed percentage rate (here 1-1/8th %). LIBOR changes over the life of the loan (at the end of the term of each advance), the margin does not.

Why do this? The idea is that the banks cannot know the cost of funds over the five year life of the loan so this must be adjusted periodically (e.g., every three months). The banks can estimate their other costs over the life of the loan: administration, capital, profit, and risk. Thus they can accept a fixed margin for the full term. This is efficient.

The borrower's risk that the cost of funds will increase. **How can the borrower reduce this risk?** Caps (excess goes into principal), stretch out repricing.

How did the subprime crisis affect Eurocredits? LIBOR dramatically increased thus increasing the borrowing rate.

Risk Allocation: Banks and Borrowers
Events of Default: The Cross-Default Clause

§12.1. If...the Borrower...fails to pay any...indebtedness as and
when it becomes payable...any...party [to that debt has] the right
to accelerate the maturity of any amount owing... [then]

§12.2. ...the Eurodollar agent shall, upon the request of Majority
Banks...declare the obligations of each Bank...terminated ...and
all amounts payable ... immediately

· **What is the purpose of these clauses?**

• **Should the agent (and Majority Banks) trigger 12.2 if 12.1
event occurs?**

Clause.
This guards against (a) the borrower is a deadbeat and its creditworthiness disappears and
(b) if lenders on loans (other than the syndicated credit) collect against the debtor,
syndicate banks may get nothing unless its loan is due immediately too (the pari passu
clause—not in the reading—provides for pro rata payments of money due other banks,
but only as due). But note the cross-default trigger requires request of Majority Banks
(by value).

The exercise of the cross-default clause could put all (or most) of the borrowers' loans
into default—if syndicated credit a big piece of overall debt (nuclear threat), and may
prevent anyone from being paid.. Note also, that some of the syndicate banks may have
other and bigger loans to the same borrower outside the syndicate which want paid If the
borrower was the Korean government, could cause a country and regional crisis.
Majority action is a safeguard.

Risk Allocation: Banks and Borrowers
Adverse Change

§15.4. "The Borrower shall reimburse each Bank in Dollars on demand for all costs..., as determined by that Bank, that are attributable to that Bank's Advances or the performance by that Bank of its obligations...and that occur by reason of the promulgation of any law, regulation or treaty...including the imposition...of any reserve...requirement against the assets [or] liabilities of...that Bank"　　　or

"the Borrower may terminate the Commitment of that Bank and prepay all outstanding Advances of that Bank"

Suppose in 1997, a Japanese bank, due to MOF requirements, had to increase its bad loan provisions generally. Must the Korean borrower pay the cost or terminate and payoff the loan?

Clause.

Discuss: Must the Korean borrower pay or terminate the loan?

YES: The Japanese bank has increased costs because the loan is riskier for reasons having to do with the borrower. The language arguably extends to loan loss reserves required by FSA.

NO: Reserve requirements (on deposits) are not the same as bad loan provisions (but the language says "including"). Plus there is not clearly any regulation here. The spread was supposed to be priced for the borrower's risk. This gives this Japanese lender special treatment compared to other participating banks. For other banks, there was no regulatory change so they cannot claim reimbursement from the borrower or be released from the loan. How would you price the increase?

Problem could be dealt with by better definition of reserves or generally require that the change affect all bank lenders. If going to include, should have pricing methodology to protect borrower.

Risk Allocation Between Lead Manager and Participating Banks

The lead manager's functions:

- Locates borrower

- Assembles participating banks

- Negotiates terms, contract

Lead manager's pay:

   1% of the loan ($250mm) = $2.5 mm

What does a lead manager do?   For participating banks, the lead manager locates the borrower and negotiates financial terms and the contract. The lead manager gets fees of 1% of $250 million or $2.5 million. It is unlikely the costs of doing the work came remotely close to this. The leader also gets prestige, which generates more lead management business.

Can any bank do this?   No. A lead bank must be strong, credible, and have good information about the borrower to bring other banks into the syndicate.

Hypothetical for Risk Allocation Between Lead
Manager and Participating Banks

Citibank lead managed a eurocredit in late 1996 to the
Korean state controlled firm. Citi knew, but did not tell,
small regional U.S. participating banks that the:

- economy was highly leveraged (debt/GNP)
- won was greatly overvalued
- borrower was corrupt, with many bad loans
- borrower had outstanding loans from Citi
- loan circular was inaccurate

The borrower defaulted 12 months later.

Would the other banks have recourse against Citi?

Discuss General (off syllabus)
Hard to justify regional bank not knowing about the leverage economy and overvalued
won but Citi might have exclusively known the other information and had a conflict of
interest. Move to next slide when terms of loan agreement mentioned.

Risk Allocation Between Lead Manager and Participating Banks

Contract terms for lead manager's duty to other banks (14.2):

- Gross negligence or willful misconduct
- *Not* liable for borrower's statements, performance or creditworthiness
- *Not* liable for the accuracy of the agreement or loan notes

---

The lead manager is only responsible for gross negligence or willful misconduct and specifically is not responsible for statements by, performance of, or creditworthiness of the borrower. Nothing prevents it from having other business with the borrower. No liability absent more information about Citi's knowledge, e.g. could be problem if knew loan circular was inaccurate.

But could this be overridden by case law imposing a fiduciary duty on the lead manager? This, of course, depends on choice of law. Some cases suggest a court-imposed duty of care. Is this a good idea? Arguably, the manager cannot afford a fiduciary standard; if it were applied, these loans could not take place. The manager's own share of the loan keeps it honest; participating banks should ensure the manager's share is large.

Eurobonds, International Bonds and Global Bonds:
Terminology

Eurobonds: Bonds issued, and largely sold, outside the domestic
market of the currency in which they are denominated

Example: Exxon Corporation (U.S. Company) issues and sells
dollar denominated bonds to investors in Europe.

International Bonds: Bonds issued, and largely sold, in one country
outside the domestic market of the currency in which they are
denominated

Example: Exxon Corporation (U.S. Company) issues dollar
denominated bonds and sells them to investors in Germany.

Global Bonds: Bonds issued and sold in several countries
simultaneously

Example: Exxon Corporation (U.S. Company) issues dollar
denominated bonds and sells them worldwide, including in the
United States.

Difference between eurobonds and global bonds—global bonds sold in domestic market
of the currency in which they are denominated. Terminology now collapses eurobonds
and international bonds into one category, sometimes called international and sometimes
called eurobonds.

All these definitions require at least some bonds to be sold outside country of currency.

Growth of Eurobond Market

• Original development due to 1960s U.S. interest equalization tax (IET): 15% tax on interest paid by foreign debt issuers to investors in U.S

Goal: discourage U.S. purchases of $ bonds issued by foreign companies, which was pushing the $ down (foreign issuers exchange dollar proceeds for local currency)

Response: foreign companies (including foreign subsidiaries of U.S. companies) issue dollar denominated bonds outside U.S. to U.S. and foreign purchasers who are outside the U.S.

• The market continued to grow after the tax was abolished in 1974 (once a market moves it is hard to get back)

Old example of U.S. losing a market due to regulation.

The Future of the Euromarkets

Maughan predicted that globalization will integrate domestic financial markets, removing barriers that created the euromarkets, and possibly eliminate them.

Will the euromarkets wither away?

Maughan, in the introductory class.

Discuss: Will the euromarkets wither away?

Yes: Global bonds are already reducing the distinctions between domestic and offshore bonds

         Competition will force regulation to a common denominator across countries, eliminating the differences that euromarkets exploit

No: Offshore markets have practical advantages:
- Time zones
- Lower costs: banks lack reserve requirements
- Convenience for transactions: for company in Poland, use London for $ deposits
- Tax differences will persist despite globalization
- Inertia: the office of a U.S. bank in London will be hard to close

Withholding Taxes: A Key Problem for the
Eurobond Market

- Until 1984, the United States imposed a withholding tax on interest paid by U.S. issuers on debt (bonds and loans) issued to foreigners (opposite of IET)
- Intended to make sure foreigners who were required to pay U.S. tax, did so

  Example: $100 interest payment. If withholding tax is 25%, foreigners get $75 in interest

    (foreigners can seek refund if actual tax owed is less than 25%)
- This would cause a problem for U.S. companies raising funds in the Eurobond market

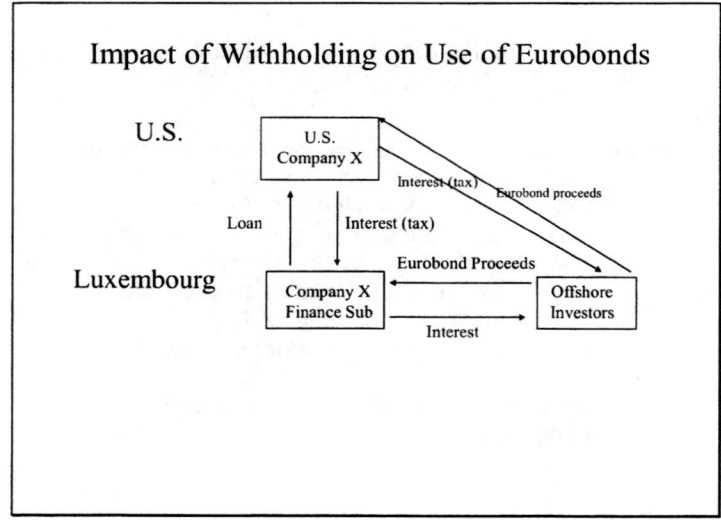

Impact? Have to pay more interest to compensate for taxes, whether on loans from parent or finance subsidiary. **What can company do?** Next slide

Many U.S. companies had European finance subs due to IET (used subs to issue debt to foreigners outside U.S.) and kept them

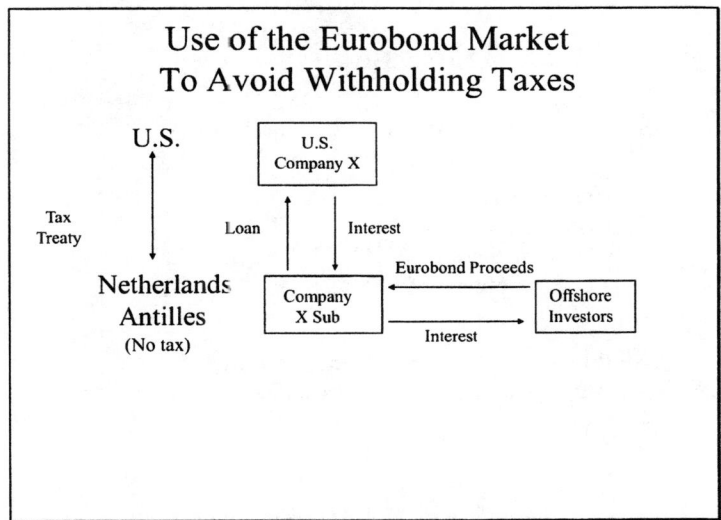

U.S. tax treaty with N.A. provides no withholding tax paid by U.S. company to N.A. borrower.

1. Risk to investors: loss of tax free status either by Netherlands Antilles imposing a tax or if the U.S. imposes a tax and terminates the tax treaty with N.A.
      Solution?: bond provides that issuer will gross up the payment (see next screen)

2. Risk to issuer: gross up is very expensive (25% withholding tax adds 33% to issuer's payments)
      Solution?: call provision. Issuer can avoid higher interest payments by calling
      bonds at a specified price (often par)
This will not completely satisfy either group. Investors will not like this if bonds trading above par (interest rates have declined), issuers will not like if trading below par (interest rates have increased), since will now have to get more expensive funding.

Grossing Up

Assume: $100 interest payment is due (pre-tax)
         25% withholding tax is now imposed

Gross up by $33.33
    Issuer pays $133.33
    Issuer withholds $33.33 (25% tax on $133.33)
    Investor receives $100 (after tax)

Call Provision: Issuer can avoid higher interest
payments by calling bonds at a specified price (often par)

```
┌─────────────────────────────────────────────────────────────┐
│                      Grossing Up                              │
│  Assume:   $100 interest payment is due (pre-tax)             │
│            25% withholding tax imposed (issuer in Switzerland)│
│                                                               │
│  Tax Impact (French investor; France & Switzerland tax interest at 50%) │
│                        Initially      After (No Gross Up)     │
│  Interest paid          $100           $100                   │
│  Swiss tax withheld     none           25                     │
│  Interest before Fr. tax 100           75                     │
│  50% French tax          50            50 (25 with credit)    │
│  After Tax Return        50            25 (50 with credit)    │
│                                        After (with Gross Up)  │
│  Interest paid                         $133.33                │
│  Swiss tax withheld                    33.33                  │
│  Interest before French tax            100.00                 │
│  50% French tax on interest paid       66.67 (33.34 with credit) │
│  After Tax Return                      33.33 (66.66 with credit) │
└─────────────────────────────────────────────────────────────┘
```

Question of whether gross-up would make you better off.

- Withholding taxes are collected by the source country not to help country of foreign taxpayer. Rather the tax is imposed because the source country is concerned that its own citizens (here Swiss) will try to escape tax. So impose tax and then give honest taxpayer a credit. This will put the taxpayer in the same position he would have been without withholding. The source country will tax foreign recipients for two reasons—first, to make sure that foreign recipients who are Swiss taxpayers do not escape tax and secondly to impose equal burdens on foreigners and Swiss. Administratively it would be very difficult to distinguish. The source country will typically give its own citizens a tax credit, so in this example the Swiss will give Swiss citizens a credit against their Swiss income tax for these payments. The issue is with the foreign investor, however.

- It is up to the foreign country as to whether it wants to grant a tax credit—this will reduce its tax but avoid double taxation for its citizens. Some do and some do not. If there is no tax credit, the foreign investor, here in France, is worse off without gross up. After tax return would be 25. But note if tax credit, position would be unaffected, just as a Swiss citizen would be unaffected. Also, if the investor does not pay French tax (cheat), worse off without gross-up, gets 75 rather than 100.

- Gross-up will not restore taxpayer to status quo ante if there is a French tax without a credit; his after French tax return will be 33.33 compared to the original 50. And if there is a tax credit, the taxpayer is better off with gross up than he was before the advent of the Swiss withholding tax. His after French tax return is 66.66 compared to 50.

- So gross-up is designed to put the taxpayer in the same position with respect to pre-tax position in residence country, probably on the assumption that most of these taxpayers do not pay such tax..

All moot because gross-up leads to call of bond. And here the investor's fate hinges on whether the call price is above or below the market price.

U.S. Withholding Taxes Today

- No withholding taxes on debt (30% on dividends, often reduced to at least 15% by treaty)
- But tax of 1% x number of years to maturity, if bonds issued in bearer form, unless
  - interest payable outside U.S.
  - legend indicates bond subject to U.S. tax
  - sold under "arrangement reasonably designed" to ensure securities not sold or distributed to U.S. persons
- Netherlands Antilles finance sub cannot be used to avoid bearer bond restrictions since there is no exemption from this tax in the treaty.

Idea behind U.S. regime: if we know who the registered owners are we can go after them for taxes (particularly with MOUs), prohibition of bearer bonds insures this knowledge.

January 2003 E.U. Withholding Tax Plan

- E.U. countries (Austria, Belgium and Luxembourg) and Switzerland (countries with secrecy laws) agree to withhold tax on cross-border interest payments to individual E.U. investors (15% 2005, 20% in 2007, 35% in 2010)

  Example: Eurodollar bond issued by Luxembourg company pays $100 interest to German investor. German investor receives $80 [$100 - (.20 x 100)] and Luxembourg government receives the $20 of tax—75% of that tax ($15) remitted to Germany, the taxing state (taxpayers can claim refunds from Luxembourg and Germany)

- Other E.U. countries (without secrecy laws): paying agent on bond informs issuer's tax authority of payments to bondholders; issuer's tax authority then tells tax authorities of bondholders of payments made to their residents
- Bank secrecy states (on OECD "grey list" will continue even after G-20 (April 2009) focus on "tax havens". Will only drop secrecy on case-by-case basis where there is fraud investigation, not as a matter of course like U.K.

This E.U. law applies throughout the E.U. plus Liechtenstein, San Marino, Monaco, and Andorra as well as 10 former British and Dutch colonies, and Switzerland.

Discuss: What problem did this try to address? Countries worried about tax evasion, e.g. German citizen does not pay German tax on interest paid to her on a bearer bond issued by a Luxembourg issuer. Germany does not know about payments on bearer bonds because it would not have information from the issuer on to whom payments were made

How would this fix the problem? Germany would either know the German citizens to whom interest was paid through the sharing of information or be assured of collecting the tax through withholding. Note administration of this withholding tax system for the paying agent adds cost to the loans.

Is this a complete solution? (1) the withholding tax might be less than the German tax; (2) will withholding tax countries fully comply? See Germany's dispute with Liechtenstein, and little collection of withholding taxes by secrecy countries, either due to non-compliance or loopholes; (3) if E.U. failed to negotiate tax sharing information with any country, e.g. Grand Caymans, that country could have secrecy and no withholding tax.

How would this affect eurobond market based in U.K.? U.K. Not worried because they do not impose withholding tax and have no problem with sharing tax information. Just the opposite of Switzerland. But why not Grand Caymans? Infrastructure requirements for the market.

Investors concern: For countries that withhold for first time, the bonds provide for grossing up which may allow the issuer to call. Effect somewhat limited because bonds issued before 3/01 were grandfathered.

2006 Update: ECJ decision questions legality of cross-border but not domestic dividend withholding tax.

TEACHING PLAN FOR

CHAPTER THIRTEEN
STOCK MARKET
COMPETITION

POWERPOINT SCREENS FOR FOURTEENTH EDITION

```
                Stock Market Competition
                      Class Outline

  • What do Stock Markets compete over and what are
    the terms of competition?
  • Are electronic better than floor-based markets?
  • Comparison of U.S. and European approach to
    market structure regulation
  • NYSE-Euronext merger
  • Who should regulate exchanges (SROs v.
    government)?
```

This class is about the market for stock markets, the nature of competition among them, and the role governments play in that competition. We will examine the four topics on the slide.

The Biggest Stock Markets

Domestic capitalization, trillions, December 2007

- NYSE   15.7
- Tokyo   4.3
- Euronext   4.2
- Nasdaq   4.0
- LSE   3.9
- Shanghai   3.6
- Hong Kong   2.7
- Deutsche Börse 2.1

Key Parts of StockTrading Process

Buy and sell sides of markets
- "Buy side": investors, individuals and institutions, e.g. Hal Scott and funds (mutual, hedge)
- "Sell side": brokers that provide services to buy side (trade for clients) e.g. Schwab, and dealers (trade for themselves), e.g. Goldman Sachs

• Information about quotes and trades

• Order routing: from customer/broker to trading venue

• Execution of order

• Clearing (matching-confirmation and position netting) and settlement (delivery and payment)

Importance of Trading Rules

- Accurate prices of capital
- Satisfy investor preferences: liquidity, speed and cost
- Provides business to market participants
- Protection of investors

What Do Stock Markets Compete Over?

NYSE-Euronext Revenues 2007

	(millions)	%
Activity Assessment	556	13
Cash Trading	1575	38
Derivatives Trading	661	16
Listing	385	9
Market Data	371	9
Software/Tech. Services	318	8
Regulation	152	3
Other	140	3
TOTAL:	$4,158	

Explain what these fees are, enormous importance of data processing and market information.

Mention UTP (unlisted trading privileges), allowing markets to trade stock listed on other exchanges, e.g. Nasdaq trades NYSE stocks.

What are the important terms of competition (next slide)?

Terms of Competition Among Trading Venues

- Listings
- Liquidity: depth of trading insures price continuity
- Trading Systems (order v. quote markets); technology; matching procedure
- User fees: for listing companies, traders, spread/commissions/fees to customers
- Speed of execution
- Integrity, e.g. insider trading prohibition
- Transparency: promptness of price reporting
  - Normal trades
  - Block trades
- Clearance and Settlement systems, e.g. length of time to complete transfer of shares and payment, guarantees
- Ownership of exchange: mutual (NYSE) or corporate with single owner (AMEX NASD) or public owners (ArcaEx)
- Transaction taxes (none in U.S.)
- Regulation/litigation (e.g. SOX, class actions)

Key Terms: Liquidity

Investors want to be able to buy and sell at a reasonable price without moving the market. The deeper the market, the more assured they are of being able to do so. Ability to trade large size quickly, at low cost, when you want to trade.*

* Larry Harris, Trading and Exchanges (OUP 2003)

Reference on terms of competition.

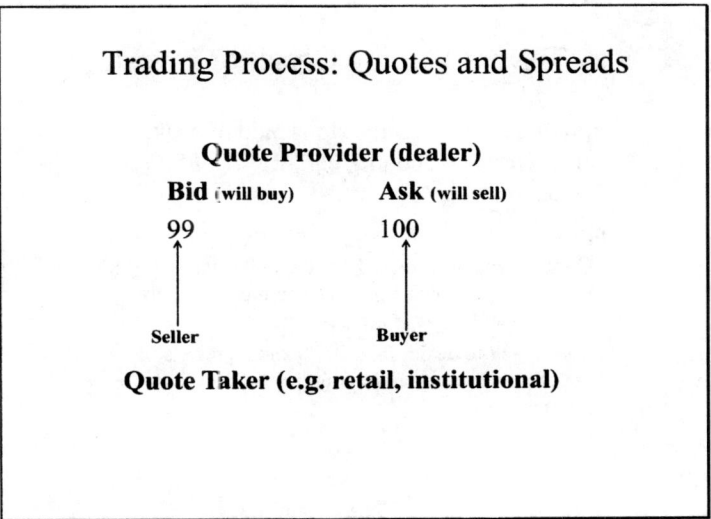

Reference on terms of competition.

Key Terms: Trading Costs for Investors

- Explicit Costs—Commissions paid to brokers (full service or discount), e.g. higher of $25 or $0.025 per share
- Implicit Costs—Spreads, when buy from dealer
  - Quoted spread: if bid is 100.70 and the ask is 100.80, the spread is 10 cents per share (typical for actively traded stock)
  - So you sell to dealer for 100.70 and he resells for 100.80, so you pay an implicit price of 10 cents for intermediation

---

Reference on terms of competition.

Key Priorities in Executing Orders

- **Price**: Execute order against the best price
- **Time**: Execute order against the earliest best priced order
- **Quantity**: Execute order against largest best priced order
- **Speed**: Execute order as fast as possible even if not at best quoted price
- **Public**: Execute order against public before non-public (specialists, floor brokers) orders where both at same price

Reference on terms of competition.

Key Terms: Transparency (Price and Trade Reporting)

- Investors want to know what the prices are (quotes and orders) and what they have been (trades)
- Block Traders, who want to be able to unload their blocks without counterparties knowing the price of the pieces, do not like transparency. However, even with such requirements, they can negotiate the pieces "upstairs" and then execute whole block or peddle pieces of the block anonymously

NYSE and NASDAQ: all trades reported within 30 seconds

Reference on terms of competition.

Differences Among Markets

Types of U.S. Trading Venues

- Exchanges: e.g. NYSE
- Nasdaq: dealer network (National Market Center), was referred to as OTC, SEC approves exchange status on January 13, 2006, previously owned by NASD
- OTC Bulletin Board (less active, registered)—indications of interest, not orders (second market), operated by Nasdaq
- Pink Sheets: privately owned (unregistered shares)—indications of interest not orders (second market)
- Internalization: within a broker-dealer, e.g. Madoff (third market)
- Electronic Communication Networks (ECNs): electronic matching systems, e.g. Posit (fourth market)

NYSE

- Largest market, $15.65 trillion domestic market capitalization
- Merged with Archipelago, public electronic exchange, February 2006, and became public; merged with Euronext 2007
- Floor auction system involving traders plus an automatic execution system—a hybrid evolving into a more automated system, NYSE hybrid automated auction
- Participants are floor brokers (commission brokers employed by brokerage house members and independent members who handle orders for other brokers) and specialists
- The floor auction (traditionally 80% of orders) centers around the specialists (6 firms) who are arranged around trading posts with 400 trading positions dedicated to the trading of particular securities.

NYSE: Specialists

- Maintain "fair and orderly market" which implies "the maintenance of price continuity, with reasonable depth, and the minimizing of the effects of temporary disparity between supply and demand (1987 market crash?) [NYSE Rule 104]
- Execute commission orders for brokers
- Conduct auctions in stocks for which registered as specialist
- Must yield to public orders at same price or better
- See entire system order flow (5 second delay to public on OpenBook; proposal to do real time, SR 34-50275, August 26, 2004)
- 6 total: concentrated, top 3 (LaBranche, Spear Leeds (GS), Bank of America), over 80.1% of dollar volume
- 9% of the total buy and sell volume, 80 % of which is for market stabilization
- Trading ahead scandal, $241.8 million settlement in March 2004 (subsequent criminal convictions/acquittals): manual trading has abuse potential

Electronic versus Floor-based Auction Markets:
Which is Better?

- Price improvement versus speed: auction-floor can give price improvement as compared with speed automatic matching, but maybe NYSE hybrid can do both
- Less room for human mischief on electronic systems
- Electronic cheaper
- Human system less likely to automatically spiral out of control (at least need humans when electronic spirals out of control.

Back-up easier for electronic, see 9-11

Market Structure and Regulation

National Market System

1975 Congressional mandate to SEC: develop an integrated national market system for U.S. exchanges

    Goal: increase liquidity, give retail investors access to the best price

SEC initiatives for all exchanges:

- tape consolidating price & volume of every trade
- composite quote system identifies national best bid and offer prices (NBBO)
- intermarket trading system (ITS), so brokers can route orders to market with the best prices automatically
- Trade-through rule for NYSE stocks (best price in any market)

NYSE and Nasdaq have both proposed to withdraw from consolidated tape reporting and the ITS: let different services compete.

New SEC National Market System Rules
(Adopted June 9, 2005; effective March 5, 2007)

- Trade Through: market receiving order for NYSE or Nasdaq stocks must send it to market with better price. e,g, if Market A receives market bid order and has best ask of 101, must send to Market B with best ask of 100.50
  - SEC Rule permits "fast"(automated) receiving market to execute, e.g. "trade through" better price of (non-automated) market if fast market price is close, e.g. for orders over $100 within 5 cents—SEC rejects investor opt-out
  - Fast market must still send to another fast market with better price
  - Cost of implementation may be $1 billion
- Access: Any market (aimed at ECNs) with 5% of trading in stock must display BBOs and allow all market participants to access those orders at a maximum charge of $0.003 per share (ECNs charge order takers and pay order suppliers)
- No sub-penny pricing
- Data Fees: New system for dividing revenue among markets from supply of quote and trade data

Dark pools, no bid-offers.

U.S. and E.U. Market Structure for Trading Securities and Derivatives

	U.S.	E.U.
Best Execution Obligation	x	x
Reporting of Trades	x	x (blocks different)
Reporting of Quotes/Orders	x	x (blocks different)
Trade-through Rule	x	no
Controls on data fees	x	no
Controls on access fees	x	no
Limits on internalization	x	x
Regulator approves market's rules	x	only at state level
Use of SROs	x	no
Restrictions on short sales	x	no
Level of official enforcement	high	low
Use of class actions	x	rare

Why different approach?

- E.U. less interventionist (or less ability to intervene)
- Different problems: U.S. fragmentation because of UTP and floor-auction alongside electronic; E.U. all electronic and no UTP (unlisted trading privileges)
- SEC investor protection, limit order protection mania on trade-through

Is lack of same rules a problem? Yes for trade-through CLOB idea; maybe good because gives E.U. escape hatch to E.U. trading rules

NYSE-Euronext Merger

- Market Capitalization: NYSE ($26.5T) and Euronext ($4.9T)
- Market Values (5-06): NYSE ($15.6B) and Euronext ($10.4B)
- Trading System: NYSE (floor and electronic) and Euronext (electronic)
- Separate regulation plus MOU
- Regulatory Ring Fencing: NYSE (Delaware Trust) and Euronext (Dutch *stitching*)

Can ring fencing work?
Is it desirable?

Davies to HLS seminar: How can you have one stock market trading under two different sets of rules? Why not?

Who Should Regulate Exchanges?

- Government, e.g. SEC, E.U. Commission/member states
- Exchanges (SROs)
  - Note NYSE creation of NYSE-R, sub of NYSE public, with all independent board (minority from public NYSE))
- Industry SRO, e.g. NASD (merger of NYSE-R and NASD, all broker-dealer regulation at NASD, market surveillance at NYSE)

Concerns:
- Independence of regulators
- Economies of scale in regulation
- Expertise

What impact of public ownership? Could say stronger case for self-regulation because regulatees have less power (but now shareholders) or weaker case since SRO designed for members to regulate selves, not publicly traded company where shareholder interests are at stake.

TEACHING PLAN FOR

CHAPTER FOURTEEN
FUTURES AND OPTIONS

POWERPOINT SCREENS FOR SIXTEENTH EDITION

Class Outline
Futures and Options

- The Mechanics of Futures
- Barings
- Regulatory Response and Future Action

The Mechanics of Futures

A future: contract to buy or sell an asset at a set time in the future for a price agreed at time of contract.

Both parties must perform

- Long position: promise to buy the asset at future date
  - Buys right to underlying security (or its cash value) at agreed price
  - Expects price to rise above agreed price

- Short position: promise to sell the asset at future date
  - Gets right to agreed price when it delivers the security or cash
  - Expects price to fall below agreed price:

    (security is worth, and can thus be bought for, less than agreed price)

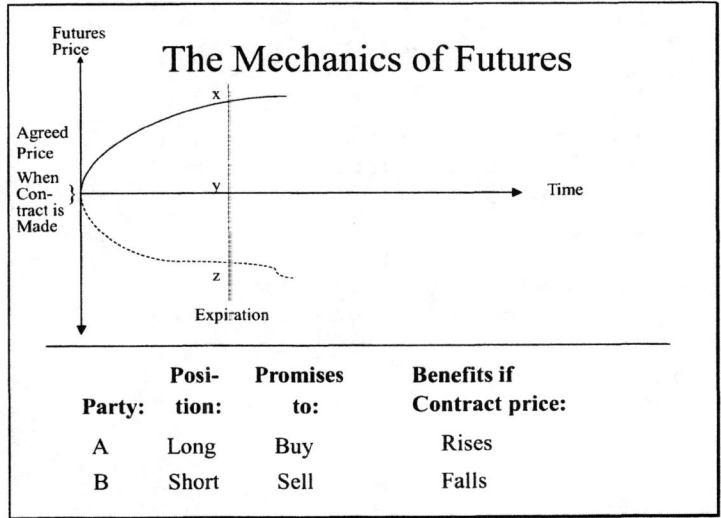

On the chart, the top curve (with the x) shows the futures price rising over time after the contract is made. At the expiration date, Party A, the buyer, pays the contract price (y), receives the security, sells it for (x), and makes a profit of (x) - (y). The Seller, Party B, has bought the security for (x) (if buys at expiration) and delivered it to the Buyer for (y), losing (x)-(y). Or the parties can settle the cash difference between (x)-(y), by the seller paying the buyer this amount.

If, instead, the futures price falls after the contract is made (the lower dotted line), at the expiration date the seller, Party B, acquires the security for (z) (if buys at expiration), delivers it to Party A, receives contract price (y), and makes a profit of (y) - (z). A loses because he gets something worth (z) for (y). Again, this can be a cash settlement so A pays B (y)-(z).

The buyer benefits if the contract price rises.

The seller benefits if it falls.

Exchanges and Clearing Houses

- Design contracts: term and dates, delivery rules (cash/security), strike prices, nominal amounts, increments of price change

- Make trading rules

- Act as counterparty (to reduce risk), so set members' minimum capital and margin accounts (to reduce risk to exchange)

Exchanges create most instruments (unlike stock exchanges), set the parameters for contract trading, become counterparties and control the risks. Since the exchange is the counterparty, it is at risk for non-performance of a trader. Major tool for control is margin.

Note: each futures exchange internalizes the clearing and settlement function whereas outsourced for stock, DTCC, and equity options. **Why?**

Margins for Futures Contracts: Long Party

	Day 1	Day 2
a. Initial contract market value (MV)	$5,000	$4,900
b. Initial margin required (5%)	250	-
c. Buyer's margin account (a/c)	250	250
d. Deduct MV decline (transferred to seller)	-	100
e. Adjusted margin account balance	-	150
f. Required maintenance margin (75% of b)	-	188
g. Margin call (to return to initial margin level)	-	100
h. Margin a/c after call	-	250

Margin limits the risk to the exchange and to some extent speculation. The futures margin is to assure the customer performs. The customer gets unused margin back when the contract expires. The hypothetical on the screen assumes a customer buys a futures contract for $5000. The initial margin requirement is assumed to be 5%. The customer's initial margin is $250. The customer pays this with either cash or highly liquid securities like treasuries.

Maintenance margin: The idea of the maintenance margin is to ensure that the parties can and will perform at the agreed price even though the actual value of their positions changes. In this example, the daily maintenance margin keeps the losing party's margin at no less than 75% of the initial rate (5% here), adequate given the risk.

The futures' value is marked to market daily against the current market value of the futures contract. Here we assume the value of the position falls to $4900 on Day 2. Any loss is fully deducted from the customer's margin account and any gain is added. In the example, the buyer's margin account is reduced $100 and falls below the $188 maintenance level (75% of the initial margin of $250). The buyer must then return the margin account to its original level by paying $100. The entire margin payments of the long party will have been $350. Note: banks often fund margin requirements.

What is the exchange's exposure? Intraday only and only to the extent that intraday price changes exceed the value of the maintenance margin. Marking to original margin level (back to 250) gives the losing party a cushion in the margin account from which small variation payments can be made without a margin call. The margin call restores the cushion.

Margins on Futures for Member Brokers

- Members are responsible to the exchange if customers do not meet margin calls

- Members must also meet margin calls on their proprietary positions

- Members may have intra-day calls and, if positions endanger their own or customers' capital, "super" margin calls

---

Margin rules and practices vary a lot across countries. This is likely to reflect competition among exchanges and suggest a possible race to the bottom. For example, as we shall see, the Osaka Stock Exchange's higher margins drove Barings (Japan) to due much of its trading on SIMEX, in Singapore, where Leeson was trading.

Highlights of The Barings Story

Leeson gambles (1992)

Barings collapses (1995)

ING buys most of Barings

Leeson goes to jail

SIMEX changes its rules

U.K. Parliament investigates the Bank of England

Bank of England loses its supervisory role in 1998

- **How did it happen?**
- **Could it be prevented from happening again on a grander scale?**

Keep these questions in mind.

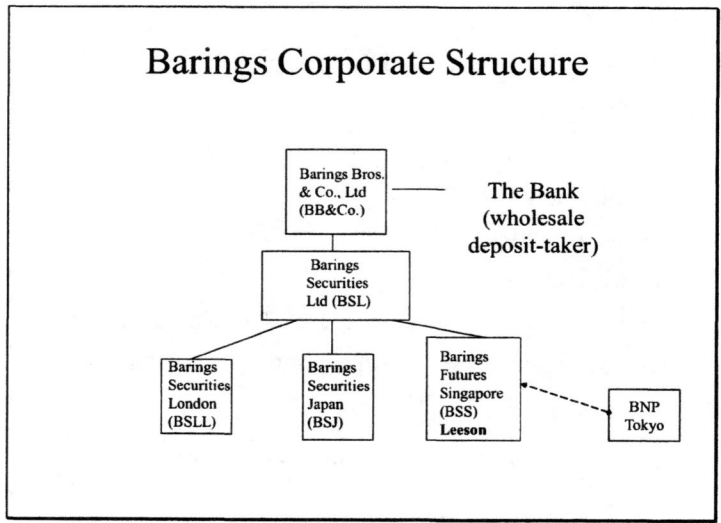

BB&Co., a 230 year old venerable British firm acquired BSL in 1984, and was a difficult cultural fit between British conservative merchant bank and lower class aggressive trading company centered in Asia. Leeson worked for BSS and his clients were BSL, BSLL, BSJ and BNP-Tokyo, a branch of the French bank. During 1992-1994 Barings was integrating BB& Co. and BSL into one investment bank.

Leeson's Authorized Derivative Activities

Trades for Clients: first just execution, later managing positions

 Cash-Futures arbitrage: buy (sell) N225 stocks and sell (buy) N225 index futures—futures business moved from OSE to SIMEX in Singapore (lower margins)

 Inter-exchange arbitrage between SIMEX and OSE on future contracts on N225 and JGBs

 Options on futures

Trades for own account: 200 futures contracts intraday

Explain

Example: Inter-Exchange Arbitrage of Nikkei 225 Futures Contract

	Agreed price	So Lee-son:	Prices con-verge	So Leeson off-sets:	and his profit:
on SIMEX:	98	Sells	97	Buys	1
on OSE:	96	Buys	97	Sells	1

Explain: Leeson could help arbitrage identical financial futures contracts traded on two futures exchanges. This is an example of inter-exchange arbitrage on the Nikkei 225 contract traded on SIMEX and OSE. Barings would look for "temporary price differences between the SIMEX and OSE Nikkei 225 contracts, buying the cheaper contract and selling the more expensive one and then reversing the trade when the price difference had narrowed, or even been eliminated, in calmer markets," according to the BoE. Price differences occurred because demand and supply differed.

Holder of a position closes out by taking the opposite position. So the holder of a long futures contract closes out by taking a short position in the same futures contract.

Leeson's Limits

One SIMEX contract was 500 times the value of the
Nikkei index. If the index was at ¥20,000, a
contract was ¥10 million ($100,000).

- Leeson's 200 contract limit = nominal exposure
  of $20m (200 x $100,000)

- Actual risk was lower: if 5% price shift, risk
  would be $1m

Leeson's Unauthorized Activities

- Exceeded authority with high risk trades in proprietary accounts: Unhedged futures (Nikkei 225, JGB and Euroyen), Nikkei options

- Ignored clients' instructions, manipulated accounts he managed

  - Did not hedge SIMEX side of OSE positions, or pass back to BSJ (his customer) margins SIMEX returned to him, reported non-existent intra-day margin calls; reported paper profits; hid losses in secret account 88888

- Misreported trades to SIMEX and Barings HQ, using his control over back office

---

What would Leeson get out of this fraud? Leeson got bonuses (£115,000 in 1993 and £450,000 planned for 1994). He advanced in Barings. He rose in status, with a promotion and more authority. No report found theft. But losing £560 million in capital is an expensive way to get a bonus and temporary status. Cannot avoid compensating on trading profits, cannot attract traders—need better controls.

> ## Why Did Barings' Managers
> ## Not Catch Leeson?

Up to December 1994:
  (1) Senior managers did not understand derivatives
  (2) Corporate responsibility for Leeson was unclear
       Administrative confusion as BB&Co and BSL integrated
       Style: corporate-finance BB&C (the bank) vs. BSL wheeler-dealer traders
       communicated badly

From January 1995:
  (3) Hard to discipline the big profitmakers
  (4) Leeson's job was simple: how could he get into trouble?

Note that the external auditors missed the fraud. They seem to have relied on Leeson
without verifying his statements. They even missed "Nick and Lisa" on the fax from the
company supposedly verifying a false transaction. BoE also missed boat.

SIMEX and Barings

Barings' share on SIMEX:

Total Volume		Nikkei 225 Contracts	
12/92	2.5%		
12/93	7.7%		
9/94	12.1%	4/94	10%
1/95	12.7%	1/95	40%

What danger did Leeson's fraud pose to SIMEX?

What danger did Leeson's fraud pose to SIMEX?
SIMEX was a counterparty to Barings' proprietary and customer contracts. If Barings were to default, SIMEX must perform. This puts SIMEX and its members at risk. By January 1995, just before Barings collapsed, the large volume of Barings' trades made it a major player on SIMEX. Barings accounted for almost 13% of all trades on SIMEX and 40% of all trading in N225 futures contracts.. Barings' position overall was long on the index, so they would lose if the market fell.

Were SIMEX's rules adequate?
> *Yes:* caught Barings, and returned $33.6m after winding down
> ***Maybe not:*** SIMEX was exposed to risk that the margins would be inadequate. Prices could have fallen 10%-15% in the time it took to wind down, liquidate the positions. It took about 9 days during which time stocks actually went up, helping out SIMEX.
> ***Was SIMEX lucky?*** Did it take 9 days for technical reasons or for Singapore government to buy contracts or underlying stock to prop up market (government had huge resources)?

No: a bigger Leeson could come along.

SIMEX: Inadequate Protection from Margins

SIMEX margin rules:

- Higher if unhedged (Leeson overreported hedged)

- No netting of proprietary and customer positions (Leeson netted)

- Higher for customer than proprietary positions (Leeson misreported customer as proprietary)

How could these evasions be prevented?

- SIMEX could have audited Barings' books: issue of cost and feasibility. Also note that the banks who were funding the margin calls had an incentive to check this, as well as Barings. Cheaper for banks and Barings (outside auditors) to check but may not be as reliable. Also note that auditing hedging positions requires OSE cooperation.
- Could change margin rules, e.g. make customer and proprietary positions carry same margin and/or just generally increase. Problem is competition with margins on other exchanges trading same contracts.

Could have moved faster once discovered discrepancies in Leeson's reports, $100m in late 12/94

The Role of Barings' Lead Regulator

BoE was lead regulator for Barings in two fora:

1) for U.K. financial regulators, BoE reviewed consolidated data about capital and large exposures, and the non-bank units' impact on the bank's risks

2) pursuant to the Basel Concordat, BoE would respond to inquiries from Barings' host regulators about a "material problem"

In neither forum did BoE identify Barings as a concern: why?

BoE had a systemic risk concern since Barings was a deposit-taking bank.

- Failure to enforce its large exposure limits of 25% of capital on BB&Co. loans to BSL on theory of "solo-consolidation". But the two firms were still separate even though they were in the process of consolidating. Bankruptcy of BSL would be hit on BB&Co. capital. The mistake was compounded by the fact that BSL passed the loans on to its subsidiaries like BSS in Singapore. So BB&Co. was really at risk for the Singapore operations to a high percentage of its capital.

- Large exposure limits also applied to margins put up with exchanges—on theory that return of margins was a credit risk on exchange. Margins were put up by various entities of BB&Co, and BoE failed to consolidate (aggregate) these loans for purposes of judging the exposure limits. Inadequate supervision of internal controls

- Relied on auditors rather than own inspection (is this wrong?)

Split regulation problem, SFA (old U.K. Securities and Futures Authority) poor supervision of foreign operations of BSL

The Need for Regulators Around the World to Cooperate

1995 Windsor Declaration calls for exchange regulators to cooperate

1996 Declaration implements information sharing:

Regulator A may ask Regulator B (in another country) about big changes in exchange member's equity, customers' or proprietary margin fees, or contract positions that are a large share of total open interest.

Regulator B will use "reasonable efforts" to get the data.

Regulator A will not let data be used for competitive advantage or violate confidentiality rules

Will this stop a future Barings?

The two declarations address a key gap: the inability of exchanges and regulators to get information when a problem appears. But no regulator or exchange identified Barings as a problem until it was too late to save. The declarations would not have prevented the Barings collapse. Also, these declarations are weak. The first is too general. The second leaves exchanges and regulators too much discretion to ignore a request.

We were lucky Barings was small. The next failure could be of a much bigger bank. One could argue that some central agency must know and reconcile all positions, proprietary and for customers, of the entire bank (including affiliates) worldwide. The declarations fall far short of what is needed. Compare the U.S. requirement of effective consolidated supervision for banking.

However, such extensive reporting is, at the very least, very expensive and possibly not feasible to do in the short time it takes to destroy a bank. In addition, the exchanges compete. They do not want to share all information.

What else can be done (next slide)?

Other Actions to Protect Against an Even More Serious Barings Crisis

- Tighter exchange rules on margins
- More cooperation among exchanges
- Stronger control by the lead regulator
- More cooperation among regulators
- Unified regulatory structures within countries (creation of U.K. FSA)

TEACHING PLAN FOR

CHAPTER SEVENTEEN
PROJECT FINANCE

POWERPOINT SCREENS FOR NINTH EDITION

Project Finance
Class Outline

Topics:
- Overview of project finance and the Pagbilao project
- Major risks of the project for each group of players
- Function of export-import banks and multilateral agencies
- Protection for the senior lenders

Project Finance

Limited recourse finance:

Lenders to the project can only "look to certain assets of the borrower for repayment of their loans and payment of interest"   [Vintner, Project Finance]

Sponsorship
Sponsors -- governmental as well as corporate -- may provide specific support, such as guarantees, by contract

Lecture: Project finance is one form of limited recourse funding, a standard type of finance. The idea is that investors can evaluate the assets and their projected cash flow (including enhancements like performance bonds) of a discrete project in order to calculate the risk, if they invest, and therefore the return they require. Specifically, if the project fails the government of the country in which the project is located will not stand behind the project's obligations generally.

This distinguishes project finance from Eurocredits, the general purpose syndicated loans that greased the skids for the LDC debt crisis in the 1980s. Project finance forces investors to evaluate risk and monitor the borrower's performance. Market forces will enforce an efficient use of resources.

The Pagbilao project is one form of project finance, in emerging markets. Project finance takes place in industrial countries too,where the players are not all the same. For example, export-import banks play a more limited role in industrial countries and multilateral banks do not play a role.

Lecture why a government would want project finance: The government probably lacks both the skills and willingness to build and operate the project. These are generally large, complex projects requiring significant technical and managerial skills at both the construction and operation stage. The government may adhere to a policy of privatization, so not want to undertake a project itself.

The Pagbilao Project in the Philippines

One type of project finance

Chronology

   1993: Start -- Hopewell Group to build two coal generators

   1996: Complete both and start operating

   2021: Transfer plant to government

Lecture: the project began quickly but did not finish construction ahead of schedule (Hopewell blamed Napocor). This is BOOT project: the sponsor will build, own, and operate until 2021, when it will transfer it to the government.

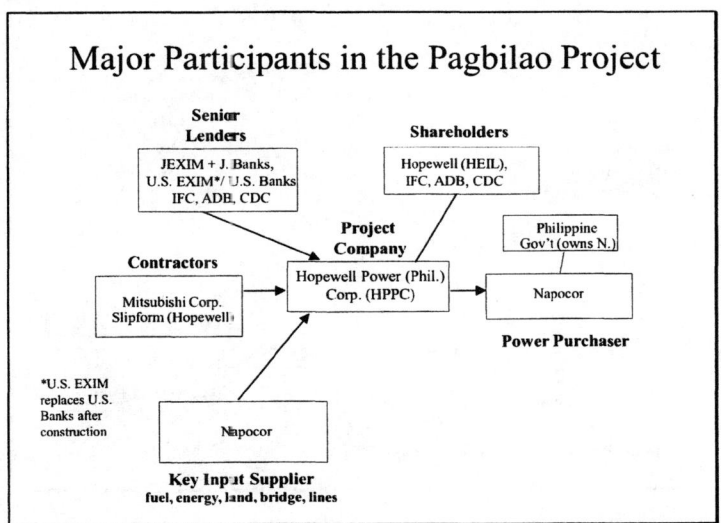

Major Participants in the Pagbilao Project

Senior Lenders: JEXIM + J. Banks, U.S. EXIM*/ U.S. Banks, IFC, ADB, CDC

Shareholders: Hopewell (HEIL), IFC, ADB, CDC

Project Company: Hopewell Power (Phil.) Corp. (HPPC)

Contractors: Mitsubishi Corp. Slipform (Hopewell)

Philippine Gov't (owns N.)

Napocor

Power Purchaser

*U.S. EXIM replaces U.S. Banks after construction

Napocor

Key Input Supplier
fuel, energy, land, bridge, lines

Lecture the major parties:
the *Philippine government and its power supply company, Napocor.* The Philippine government and Napocor are more than just the ultimate purchasers of the plant. They supply important inputs (land, coal), regulate construction and operation, and buy the power.

the *Hopewell Group, which leads the project*, is an equity investor, subordinated lender, and cobuilder. Hopewell is responsible for the building and management of this coal-based power project. Hopewell brings special skills and a strong track record in just this kind of project from China and is familiar with the Philippines. In addition to managerial and technical skills, Hopewell brings finance. Hopewell HK owns Slipform and HEIL, which owns HPPC.

Mitsubishi, the *principal contractor* and a subordinated lender. Mitsubishi brings years of experience with construction of these types of projects. By virtue of its home base, it also brings Japan's export-import bank and the syndicate of banks from Japan that will finance a large part of the project, at competitive (and possibly subsidized) rates. Mitsubishi is making a subordinated loan as well.

several *multilateral agencies* (IFC, ADB, CDC) as equity investors and senior lenders;

two *export-import banks*, as senior lenders and guarantors. The U.S. Eximbank, with a U.S.-based group of banks, is providing a loan for equipment sourced there; and

two *banking consortia*, one based in Japan, the other American.

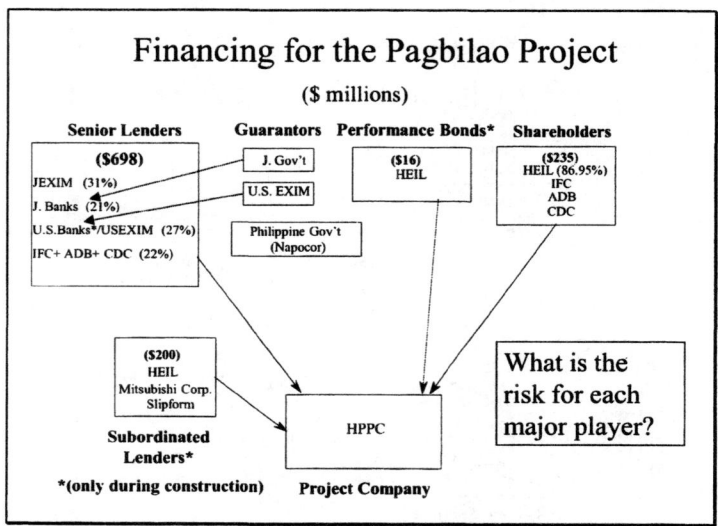

Financing for the Pagbilao Project

Lecture: **the different types and sources of funds for the project.**
Discuss: **What is at risk for each of the major players?** Summarized on next screen.
For the ***government and Napocor***, the biggest concern is that the plant will not be
completed on schedule or at all, and the second concern is that it will function poorly. As
a guarantor of Napocor, government is also at risk.

For ***Hopewell***, the biggest concern is the loss of its equity investment ($205 million) and,
with Mitsubishi, the loss of the $200 million in subordinated debt. Hopewell is also at
risk for the performance bond providing liquidated damages if delays occur or the plants
are below international standards. More generally, both would suffer severe damage to
their reputation if the project failed for reasons within their control and this would hurt
their earning capacity in future projects elsewhere. But they are also at risk if the
Philippines fails to perform for either political or economic reasons.

The ***multilaterals*** have a small equity stake ($30 million). They risk losing it in whole or
in part if the project does not perform as expected or if the host government or economy
make it impossible for them to be paid dividends.

As ***senior lenders***, the multilaterals ($152m), export-import banks (U.S.EXIM $179m,
JEXIM $220m), and commercial banks (Japanese banks, $147m) bear substantial credit
risk ($698 million is the total loan), though they have priority over the subordinated
lenders. The loan is subject to substantial political risk as well as the usual financial and
economic risks that are part of a project.

Insurers insure against many different risks, but these do not increase the financing to
build the project.
Later, in the operations phase, an **international bank** (Bank of America) gives an **L/C** to
smooth cash flow, if short delays in HPPC's payments might otherwise interrupt
servicing of the senior lenders.

Summary of Risks for Major Players

Government and Napocor: plant will not be completed on schedule or at all, or will work poorly; gov't risk as guarantor

Hopewell: equity stake ($205mn) and credit risk as subordinated lender (with Mitsubishi) and for liquidated damages, reputation, political and economic risk

Multilateral Banks: small equity stake ($30mn)

Contractors: credit risk on subordinated loan, penalties for late completion, reputation

Senior Lenders: substantial credit risk ($698mn total loan), economic and political risk

Lecture this summary if necessary.

Lecture how senior lenders protect themselves in many ways. The protection depends on the problem. Some are:

> shift certain risks (such as foreign exchange risk, much of the interest rate risk, and insolvency risk) to others (the government, junior lenders, and equity investors)

limited insurance and substantial guarantees

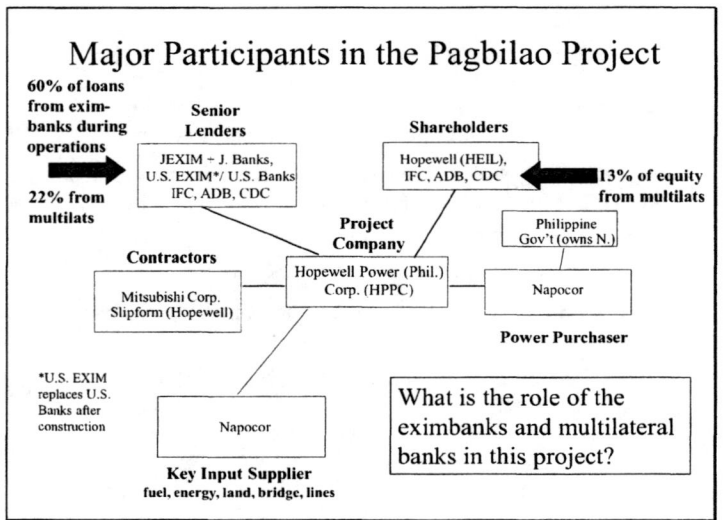

Major Participants in the Pagbilao Project

Discuss the function of the eximbanks and multilateral banks. The obvious role is as the dominant source of funds: 82% of the senior loans and a smaller source of equity. They make it go!

Are they so important that this project would not have happened without them? If the price was right, commercial lenders could have taken a large share, but there seems to be a subsidy in lending by the eximbanks, at least. Eximbanks' job is to promote their country's exports. A lower cost of interest on a loan to fund the purchase of equipment, e.g., could substantially reduce its cost to the buyer.

Suppose the eximbanks and multilaterals had only 8% of senior loans. Would they still play any significant role? Even if their share of credit was small, they would have a vital role ensuring the borrower (and its home government) performed. The Philippines has a continuing interest in staying on the right side of the Eximbanks, World Bank, and Asian Development Bank, in order to get more money from them. Both are important sources of funds for many projects in the Philippines. The government is likely to do much to avoid defaulting on obligations to them.

The eximbanks and multilaterals can blackball a country, making it difficult for commercial lenders to fund borrowers in that country. Their lead is not always effective. The markets will act independently of these official institutions, as shown by commercial lending before 1982 and portfolio investors in Asia before 1997. Not all countries kowtow to the exims and multilaterals. Many, like Nigeria, are in substantial arrears. But the Philippines was in arrears in 1992 and worked its way out to get access to new credit. But this may change with the recent IMF proposals to lend into arrears.

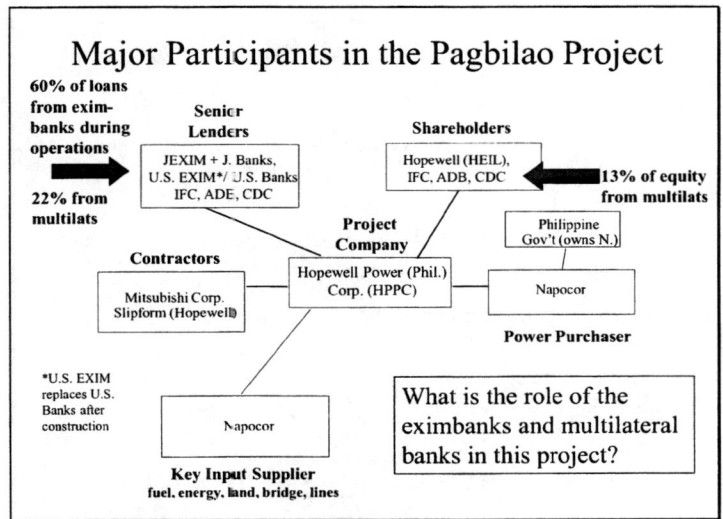

Major Participants in the Pagbilao Project

Would a private bank want an eximbank or multilateral as a co-lender? Yes, most of the time. But perhaps the official lenders would not want to enforce claims against a borrower in default for political or developmental reasons, in circumstances in which the private lenders would want to recover even just a part of the debt. This could be a problem in Pagbilao. The official lenders made over over 80% of the loans and, since 75% of the senior lenders are needed for a suit against a defaulting party, the official lenders would have to approve the suit but might be subject to political pressure.

Export Credit and Multilateral Aid

Eximbanks finance home exports:

- lend to buyers relatively long term, often below market rates (fund 2% of U.S. exports, 32% of Japanese exports)
- link their loans to foreign assistance
- guarantee against political risk--transfer, expropriation, violence
- have large arrears with many countries

Multilateral banks finance developing countries:

- lend for projects and general purposes
- provide technical assistance
- invest in private firms (IFC)

- Should these agencies be involved in project finance?

Is this an appropriate use of public funds? Aren't banks supposed to do this?
Eximbanks in theory provide financing for a country's exports that financial markets will not provide. Long-term finance is a case in point. Many private lenders are often reluctant to take on risk in a country like the Philippines for over 5 years. These loans are 10 years. Eximbanks get paid for their services, as do multilaterals, so the subsidy may be small in many cases.

The same market gap argument justifies the multilateral banks. In addition, the multilaterals (like the World Bank group) are a buffer between the industrial/capital exporting countries and the developing/capital importing countries. The multilaterals can insist on performance criteria that, if put forward by banks (or governments) from any one developed country, could be seen as a form of imperialism.

Should the U.S. government stop funding the multilateral banks?
Yes: they cannot be justified economically.
No: they do fill a market gap; they provide a platform for U.S. policy to work indirectly, since the U.S. and a few other major industrial countries control the multilaterals' activities. Developed countries have a development agenda. Now they believe it is useful for a stable world for poor countries to develop.

What Types of Events Would Put Payments Due to Senior Lenders at Risk?

1. Project is not completed on schedule, or has higher cost, or falls short of standards: reduces HPPC's ability to service debt on schedule

2. Project operates below capacity (limited demand) or at higher cost (inefficiency, input prices rise): HPPC lacks income

3. Peso devalues so much HPPC cannot buy $ to service debt or peso cannot be converted to $

4. New government prevents HPPC from performing

Discuss

Completion Risk and Senior Lenders

Protection: Collateral is the most common way senior lenders
secure their debt

- Pagbilao has land and plant as possible collateral

> How much protection would land and plant give the Pagbilao
> senior lenders?

- Contractors + HEIL finance cost overruns up to $200mn
- 3:1 leverage ratio forces HPPC to get more equity
- HEIL $16mn performance bond if below standard or delay
- HEIL and contractors pay Napocor penalties for delays

Are these the best protection for senior lenders?

Lecture about completion risks

Discuss the usefulness of land and plant as protection: Neither provides the kind of
protection it would give in most developed countries.

> The constitution prohibits foreigners from owning land, so the senior lenders
> could not take ownership. In bankruptcy, the land could be sold to a citizen and
> the proceeds used to meet obligations to the senior lenders. But the land is on
> an isolated island and of limited value.
> The plant is only useful if it produces power. The senior lenders do not want to
> run unfinished power plants in the Philippines and there are not likely to be
> many buyers.
>
> Claims on both would have to be enforced through inefficient and corrupt.
> Philippine courts.

What happens if there are cost overruns: the subordinated loan is drawn, and after that
the shareholders would have to raise more equity. While not providing 100% protection,
the loan amounts to over 25% of the value of the Mitsubishi and Hopewell contracts
($535mn and $167mn) and is substantial.

What happens if completion is late: senior lenders can draw on the $16mn
performance bond from Hopewell and the contractors (Mitsubishi, Hopewell) pay
penalties. If the delay extends beyond February 1997 there is an event of default, which
triggers a call on the loans (if the lenders choose to act) [hold this to later in class].

Risk for Senior Lenders during Operations

Suppose that the Philippines was badly hit by the Asian financial crisis and in late 1998:

HPPC was only selling at 40% capacity,

peso devalued to 40% of its 1996 rate against the $

government was rationing dollars

> • How well are senior lenders protected from these risks by the contract?

Discuss the forms of protection listed on the next screen:

1. **Limited demand:** The *capacity fee* makes Napocor liable to pay more than enough to service the senior debt as long as HPPC can produce 85% capacity even if Napacor does not actually buy the output. The government guarantees Napocor's obligations, making debt servicing a government responsibility as long as HPPC can produce the energy. So the risk here is that the plants cannot operate at full capacity (or even 80%, which was the rate assumed for calculating the fees).

• **Inefficiency raises costs:** the *energy fee* penalizes Hopewell for inefficient operation of the plant and rewards efficiency.

• **Peso devaluation:** Napocor pays $ to HPPC for $ debt servicing. So Napocor bears the risk of devaluation and the government guarantees Napocor.

• **Pesos cannot be converted into dollars:** the trust at Bank of America in New York channels most payments due to HPPC offshore. Whatever is in that pipeline cannot be frozen in the Philippines by the government. The trust builds reserves to put as much in the pipeline as possible. [Go to the trust screen.]

• **Limited inputs:** Napocor supplies coal

• **Guarantees** by government of Napocor

7. **Trust:** creates reserves, holds bank L/C against cash flow shortfalls

---

Contractual Protection for Senior Lenders When Plant is Operating

Funds to service the senior loans: Napocor pays HPPC for its output @ 2 flat fees per KwH.

Capacity fee: formula produces 90% of HPPC's income if HPPC can produce 85% capacity,

servicing loans, equity, fixed operating costs, and infrastructure.

Energy fee: based on power Napocor actually buys, with bonus or penalty depending on HPPC's efficiency.

Background and summary.

Continued Obligations of the Government

The government gives its full faith and credit that Napocor will:
- provide key inputs
- pay 90% of fees regardless of demand
- bear FX risk

In 2000, demand was so low that the plants operated at 40% capacity, but Napocor (with government help) paid fees at 85%.

> Much of the risk is shifted to Napocor and the government. Will this work?

> Is the government still so involved that it insulates management of Pagbilao from market forces?

Lecture the screen: Government has a continuing role to play (screen).

The government chose project finance for Pagbilao to bring economic efficiency to the power sector. It would be removed from the constraints of official bureaucracy and become subject to market discipline. Its private sector managers would have to perform well, at least in theory.

Discuss: Is the government still so involved that lenders to Pagbilao will be too insulated from market forces to evaluate the project neutrally for its creditworthiness?

No: The obligations of the government and sponsors are clearly defined.
The goal of privatization is much more efficiency. Hopewell runs the project for 25 years and is rewarded for efficiency, which is long enough for a productive impact

Yes: The government bears so many risks and is involved in so many ways that shield the project from market forces.

Free land, free inputs, and guaranteed purchase of power remove the project from the market discipline. The lenders are insulated from the collapse of demand since the 1997 financial crisis.

Even the majority of funding is public, since 80% of senior debt is from official eximbanks and multilateral banks and the other 20% during operations (from Japanese banks) has some political risk insurance.

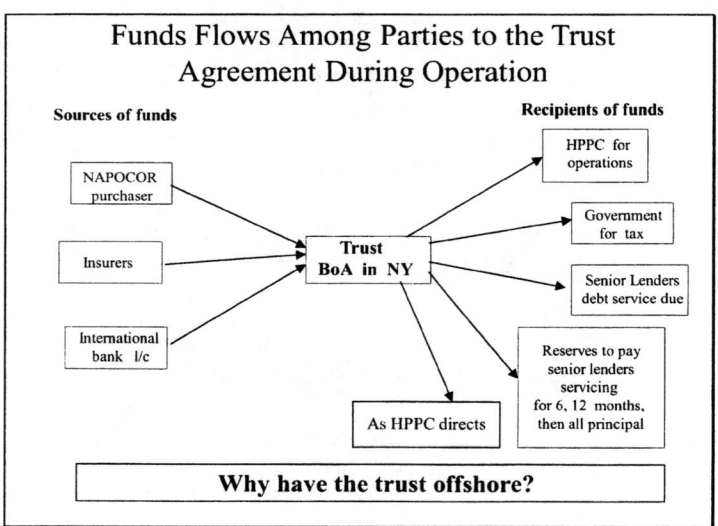

Funds Flows Among Parties to the Trust Agreement During Operation

Explain most inflows are from Napocor paying for the energy. This alone is enough to service the senior debt. If any catastrophe occurs, the insurer must pay the Trust, not HPPC. Finally, an L/C from a major bank (Bank of America) provides a temporary cushion against a shortfall in payments from HPPC that varies according to the size of the Trust's reserves.

Discuss: Why do this? To get the funds out of the Philippines. The lenders want the cash flow. Lawsuits in NY may give more fair decisions than in Philippines courts (the lenders are foreigners). But of course the contracts can choose NY law and specify NY jurisdiction without setting up a trust. In any case, enforcement must be through the Philippines.

Discuss: How much protection does this buy in general? To the extent the cash flow leaves the Philippines, the senior lenders are protected. The priorities put building reserves to pay the lenders above dividend payments to shareholders.
   But future payments by Napocor remain in the Philippines subject to Philippine government seizure.

Discuss: How well does this protect senior lenders? Students could debate --
   Some: the Philippine government guarantees Napocor.
   Not much: once the reserves run out, the flow to the Trust could fall drastically since the dollar reserves of the Philippines will be very low and Napocor is not likely to earn enough the pesos to buy dollars in FX markets, now that their value is halved.

Discuss: What happens if Napocor fails to pay? This is an event of default.

Political Risk

Suppose a new Philippine government that took office during
plant operations is hostile to foreign lenders of any sort. It
decides not to allow Napocor and HPPC to make the payments to
the Trust and service the senior loans.

Is this force majeure?

> • How well are the senior lenders protected?

Discuss: This political risk invokes the force majeure for Napacor and HPPC. The
government's role is clear, so it would come within Force Majeure clause B: "rationing
or allocation ... imposed by ... decree ... or any other event ... within the reasonable
control of ... the government." It requires Napocor to buy the project for the present
value of remaining capacity fees (except fixed operating costs).

Discuss: This clause would not give the senior lenders much real protection, since a NY
decision for the lenders would have to be enforced in the Philippines. Perhaps they could
pursue Philippine assets in the U.S.

**Discuss: are the private senior lenders protected? What if the Eximbanks and
Multilateral lenders are subjected to pressure not to let the trustee sue?**
75% of the senior lenders in both number and amount must give directions to the trustee.
If they do not, the trustee must wait six months. If they do (and the official lenders are
82%) instruct the trustee not to act, the trustee must wait two years and then enforce. Not
so good for the private lenders (mainly from Japan).

Discuss: why would Japanese banks elect to be subject to NY law? It is among the
best developed to protect creditors.

Lecture: If this had occurred during construction, the U.S. bank syndicate could have
claimed against the U.S. EXIM political risk insurance (for transfer risk).

Conclude: Project finance today is structured to limit the senior creditors' risk
substantially, so much so that the government remains obligated to protect against even
falling demand for the output. Much of the revenue stream is moved off shore and
becomes subject to, e.g., NY law.

> But ultimately the project's success and the enforcement of the creditors' claims in
> the event of default must be in the host country. This risk cannot be avoided by the
> foreign lenders.

CHAPTER EIGHTEEN

FIFTH EDITION TEACHING PLAN FOR

PRIVATIZATION AND INSTITUTIONAL INVESTORS

A.   OVERVIEW OF THE SESSION

1. Major Parts of the Classes

Class 1
A.   Introduction
B.   Privatization in General
C.   Mexico
D.   Telmex in 1989-90
E.   Traditional Options: Mexican Stock Market, Foreign Direct Investment
F.   Transfer of Control to the Consortium
       End

Class 2
F.   Transfer of Control to the Consortium (cont.)
G.   The Telmex Offer on World Markets
H.   Buyers of the Telmex L ADR
I.   Conclusion
       End

2. Goals of the Class

The course has three major goals: introduce students to privatization as an important activity in financial markets; introduce students to the role of institutional investors and particularly pension funds in emerging markets; and help students integrate the course as it ends.

B.   QUESTIONS AND ANSWERS

A.   Introduction

The subject for today and tomorrow brings in new players—institutional investors—and an activity—privatization—that has been a driving force in international financial markets.

Privatization is a big part of the restructuring of the world economy. It began in earnest in the late 1970s, with Mrs. Thatcher's then new government. Eighteen years later it continues to employ British civil servants full time and enhance the bottom line of U.K. financial firms. And much of the rest of the world joined in. Privatization has accounted for a large share of cross border financial flows in industrial and developing countries as investors look for new opportunities.

Institutional investors, like pension funds, have been the biggest investors, even in ADSs, which are available to retail investors.

The topics for discussion will carry us into tomorrow's class. We will go as far as possible today.

B.   Privatization in General

B1.   *What is privatization?*

The transfer of productive operations and assets from the public sector to the private: the reading gives this definition.

Why is the definition so broad? This could include opening state-owned timber land to lumber companies.

The text's definition is broad because privatization takes many forms. The critical element is that the state relinquishes its direct control. Normally, private entities get the control, but the Telmex consortium included a French parastatal company. Normally the object of control is productive assets, but some legal scholars speak of privatization of dispute resolution when they refer to arbitration. This is confusing for our purposes.

Our conclusion: rather than use the phrase "privatization," one should speak of the specific type of transaction. For example, the Telmex "privatization" was the government's sale of equity it held in Telmex stock. By some definitions, the Pagbilao project was a form of privatization. When we use it in class, it refers to the transfer of a government's ownership of firms to private investors.

B2.   *Let's focus on the transfer of control in large state-owned firms. Mr. Waddell mentions six types. We will return to these later when we examine the Telmex privatization.*

B2a.   What are the types and how relevant would each be to an industrial country like the one described in Question 1? Suppose the national airline was to be sold.

This country is a leading industrial state with a deep and broad stock market, large banks, sophisticated accounting systems and investors, moderate domestic savings, no exchange controls, good pools of managers, and a legal system that resolves commercial disputes quickly and predictably.

The six types of privatization are:

IPOs: sell directly to the public. This is a major option for the government of such a country, which has the stock market, savers, and capacity to give good information about the firm. The firm must be profitable and have good prospects; IPOs are not for failing firms.

Strategic investors: get bids from "technically and financially capable investors," which usually means leading firms in the industry. For the industrial country, this is an option if the government wants to change management and assure a certain standard of performance. The government can carry out the complex preparation and analysis of bids itself, since it has the skills.

Joint ventures: an investor (often foreign) jointly owns the firm with the government, bringing capital, managerial skills, or technology. This would not be useful to an industrial government seeking to divest itself of ownership in a firm.

Mass or voucher privatizations: the government issues vouchers to its citizens, who exchange them to buy interests in individual firms or, perhaps through a mutual fund, many firms. The government gives something—its shares—in exchange for nothing. The industrial country does not need to do this and can afford the cost in time and resources to prepare individual IPOs.

Build-own-manage: the investor agrees to finance, build, and operate infrastructure projects. Nothing prevents an industrial country from doing this, but the option usually is chosen when the country lacks the skills to build and run the project itself.

Liquidate: sell the assets of a state-owned enterprise that has limited commercial prospects. An industrial government may do so, but would not normally deal with a large state enterprise this way because of the likely political reaction.

Relevance of Types of Privatization to Different Countries

Type of Country

Type of Privatization	G-7 country	Former communist
1) IPO	Most appropriate: Use own capital markets, investors	Not an option: country lacks savings for buying IPO shares and lacks access to foreign stock markets
2) Strategic Investor	Maybe to assure certain performance	Useful: bring capital, skills and a stake to assure good performance; need help analyzing the bids
3) Joint Venture	Not useful since government stays in	Important: typical way to get foreign skills, capital but keep some local control
4) Voucher Privatization	Not relevant: no need for vouchers and give-away	Could be very important: country lacks capital. Seems fair
5) Build, Own, Operate	No: country has this ability	Yes: country lacks skills to do build and run on its own
6) Liquidate	Possible, but not likely to be common	Essential in many cases but politically hard

B2b. **How useful would a former communist country like the one described in 1(b) find each of these approaches if it were selling a large manufacturer?**

This country has no working financial system, a small inactive stock market, banks with minimal capital and bad debts equaling at least 30% of all loans, government officials and a population with limited understanding of how a market economy works, a legal system unequipped to resolve private commercial disputes, minimal domestic savings eroded by serious inflation, and a private sector consisting of only small family owned firms. For it:

IPOs: likely to be impossible for such a country. It cannot issue at home, since it lacks domestic savings. Its large firms are unlikely to be in sufficiently good economic shape or to have good enough information about themselves to gain access to stock markets elsewhere.

Strategic investors: these should be very useful, as they would bring capital and skills in the industry. Their stake would assure their interest in seeing the firm succeed. The country's government would probably need foreign help evaluating the bids, and many investment firms stand ready. The problem would be finding good investors.

Joint ventures: this is a traditional way to tap foreign skills and capital, while keeping some local control. The foreigner could take either the government or a private local partner. The problem may be that neither the government nor a local group partner is able to do the job of local partner.

Voucher privatizations: very appealing for two reasons.

(1) The country lacks savings, so citizens cannot pay and the government may as well give away its shares if ownership is to remain in national hands.

(2) Everyone gets vouchers, so the distribution looks fair.

The danger of diffuse ownership is solved if individuals invest their vouchers in mutual funds, which are supposed to impose shareholder discipline on the companies, demanding good performance. Yet voucher privatizations of large firms have been hard to do in countries like Russia, for example, for political reasons. The public wants to continue getting subsidized services from the large firms. The firms' managers wield political power and do not want to lose their jobs. Individuals who get the vouchers may not understand their value or their poverty may force them to part with them in exchange for very little.

Build-own-manage: this also would be attractive to a country that lacks the skills and capital to build and run projects itself. It has a long history in many developing countries.

Liquidate: this may be essential in many cases, but can be politically difficult for large firms.

B2c.   What do you conclude about the relevance of the different types of privatization to an industrial country and a former communist country?

Subject to the fact that big differences exist within each group of countries:

Privatization is relatively straightforward for governments of industrial countries. The critical question is whether the large firm is viable. If so, an IPO would be a reasonable course, as happened in the U.K. If not, the government would either have to restructure or liquidate it. Other options are available and may even be used, but are not critical.

Privatization is much more difficult for former communist countries. Their need to do it is much greater. But they lack the resources. They must often depend on foreign capital and skills.

C.   Mexico's Evolving Economy

C1.   *Before 1982, Mexico relied heavily on general purpose syndicated Eurocurrency loans. What is their economic function?*

Mexico needed foreign currency and the loans were an easy way to raise it, especially for state-owned enterprises, which were the major borrowers. Foreign savings would help the economy grow faster by financing investment or let people consume more and save less. The loans were convenient because bank syndicates could mobilize large sums (in the billions) quickly and at a low transaction cost. The proceeds could be used by the government in any way because most loans were for general purposes. Mexico could raise lots of money due to its oil wealth.

C1a.   If banks saw, in 1980 or 1981, that Mexico's economy was weakening, how easily could they reduce their exposure?

It would be hard to do. If one stopped participating in syndicates, the others would know. If all stopped, Mexico could not service its debt and would default.

C1b.   How would this affect the real value of their loans to Mexico?

The real value would decline.

C1c.   How easily could one determine the real value of the bank's loans to Mexico?

No secondary market existed for participations then, so book value was the only way to carry the loans.

C1d.   How would this affect the bank's lending to Mexico?

Even if they saw Mexico's economy failing, they have strong incentives to lend more to Mexico and limited disincentives.

As we will see, the dynamic differs greatly when funds are raised in publicly traded markets, like the ADRs traded on the NYSE.

C2.   *The U.S. government worked harder to help Mexico through the debt crisis than it did for any other country. Mexico's government played by the rules, on the whole, deflating the economy and devaluing the Peso, while others like Brazil did not. But would the U.S. government have had any other reasons to help Mexico?*

As a U.S. neighbor, Mexico is special: a collapsed economy would propel even more illegal immigrants from Mexico into the U.S. and the political instability would generate a fear of instability and possibly a Cuban-type regime along the U.S.'s southern border.

An interesting question is whether investors who buy Mexican ADRs on the NYSE could rely on similar assistance from the U.S. government. We'll come to this later.

C3.   *From the sketch of Mexico, would you say it more closely resembles country A (the industrial country) or country B (the former communist country)?*

Mexico has elements of both. It obviously has some pretty sophisticated managers and officials; its stock exchange is small but the largest in Latin America; it has brought inflation down and is growing reasonably well; it has reduced its foreign debt and reduced trade barriers; its private sector seems strong.

On the other hand, its banks are nationalized; the stock market is much smaller than industrial countries' exchanges; inflation is still high at 30%; it still overvalues the Peso against the Dollar; much of the economy remains dominated by the government; and its single party government is under attack.

Mexico is a leading "emerging market." This suggests the stock market and the country itself are moving toward the situation of western industrial states. This implies that countries are arrayed along a spectrum, from former communist countries to Mexico to countries like the U.K. Forget stock markets; we haven't looked at them yet. Just look at the countries. Is this a spectrum or does Mexico seem basically different from either of the other types and likely to remain so?

It is not obvious that Mexico (or many other "emerging markets") is a young U.K. or more evolved than an ex-communist state. Its political system is very different from any industrial country. The country has depended on oil for years and we have no evidence the manufacturing sector is thriving. It is a low wage economy. Social problems are "appalling." It seems very dependent on the U.S. The idea that the country is emerging into an industrial state is misleading. Small states, even prosperous ones, differ from large ones. This affects investors.

D. Telmex in 1989/90

D1. *Why was Telmex nationalized? We know that in 1972 Mexico's president pursued a strategy of direct government intervention. What else might explain why the government took control of Telmex then?*

The communications industry is one of the economy's commanding heights. The idea in Mexico, and many other countries including France, was that the private sector, and particularly foreigners, could not be trusted to manage those commanding heights in the broad interest of the country. The government must take control for the good of all. Other sectors included banking and energy. The power sector is another, as we saw with Pagbilao.

D2. *The reading in section B lists several goals of privatization. Which might have motivated President Salinas to sell the government's stake in Telmex in 1989?*

The four goals, and their relevance to Salinas' decision, are:

a. Reduce the government's role in the economy: this seems to have been important to Salinas, but not merely as a general philosophy.

Telmex is a mess and needs radical change to give Mexico a good communications system.

b.   Level the playing field: this was not a goal, at least in the medium term, since Telmex retains its monopoly at least through 1996.

c.   Finance the government's budget: this was a major goal, though students may not see it immediately. The government's budget deficit in 1990 was $7.7 billion and it was 3% (modest compared to many countries if it is accurate, though students may not know this). Inflation is still 30% and the government is worried about it. The sale of Telmex will bring the government over $3 billion over two calendar years (1990 and 1991). Half the proceeds would reduce the 1990 deficit by almost 20% and the other half would probably have the same impact on the 1991 budget.

d.   Broaden domestic share ownership: this was not a goal, since the new shares were distributed to existing shareholders and since so much of the offer was abroad.

D3.   *How might these goals—to restructure Telmex and raise funds for the government—affect the government's choice of privatization options?*

The government will want to choose options that will make Telmex more efficient and productive and will maximize the government's return. We'll shortly see how this worked.

D4.   *The public already owned 44.1% of Telmex shares and 60% of this was already traded through ADS on NASDAQ. How might this have affected Salinas' options?*

Telmex had a track record already on Mexican and U.S. markets. Mexico did not need to educate either public from scratch. This is an advantage.

On the other hand, the government had to be careful not to alienate existing shareholders in Mexico and the U.S. Its discretion was limited by their presence. For example, Telmex could not dilute the share of existing shareholders.

E. Traditional Privatization Options to Sell the Government's Telmex Stake

E1.   *The Mexican stock exchange: could the government have sold its Telmex shares on the Mexican exchange?*

Not if it wanted to raise $3 billion. True, the exchange has developed a lot in the 1980s. It went through a wrenching period in the early 1980s when the economy collapsed. The government has improved the institutional infrastructure: a new securities law, restrictions on insider trading, a central depositary, for example. But in 1990, the Mexican exchange's total capitalization was the equivalent of only $33 billion. A $3 billion offering would have swamped it.

E1a.   How does Mexico's exchange compare to that of an industrial country?

It does not come close to the world's major exchanges (U.S., U.K., Japan) and while it comes closer to smaller exchanges like the French or Canadian, it is still far off in size. In 1990, the capitalization of Mexico's stock exchange is 1% that of the U.S. and 14% that of Canada. In 1991, its 209 listed companies are 3% of those on the U.S. exchanges and 25% of the French.

On the other hand, given its growth and the regulatory and institutional infrastructure, Mexico's exchange is not remotely like that of a former communist country.

E1b.   Suppose the Mexican exchange could have absorbed a $3 billion offer, would the government have wanted to place it in Mexico?

No. The government doesn't just want more Pesos. It wants hard currency. Mexico has an $80 billion foreign debt and big debt service payments each year. It will probably run a trade deficit, so it will need Dollars to pay for imports too.

E2.   *If Mexico needs foreign exchange, why not just sell the government's entire stake to foreign direct investors, like an AT&T?*

Foreign direct investors buy control of local companies. But the government cannot just transfer all its shares to foreign investors because the law forbids non-Mexicans from owning more than 49% of a Mexican telephone company.

E2a.   Lots of countries have been eliminating limits on foreigners' investment, but Mexico hasn't done so and in the Telmex transactions did not repeal its laws. What might account for this?

Uncle Sam, up north. The Yanquis are seen as a major economic, political, and even cultural threat. These laws cannot easily be repealed.

E2b.   Does the government need to sell its entire stake to get a foreign controlling shareholder?

No. As the actual Telmex deals show, the government can sell control by transferring less than a full 51% stake in Telmex and can then raise more money by selling non-voting shares as well (as we discuss in more detail soon). This privatization is rather sophisticated.

F.   The Transfer of Control Over Telmex to the Consortium

Turn to the Telmex privatization.

F1.   *What was the first stage of the Telmex privatization in 1990-91?*

The transfer of the government's AA shares, which had 51% of the vote, to a consortium of three groups of investors.

F1a.   Before this transfer, what was the government's share in Telmex?

It owned all the AA shares, giving it 51% of the capital, and another 4.9% as A shares, for a total of 55.9% of capital. [Use following table, 1989-90 column.]

Evolution of Telmex Capital Structure
(ownership of total capital (percent)

	1989-90 Ownership before the L issue			**Step 1. L share** Ownership after the L issue		
Shareholders	AA	A	Total	AA	A	L
Government	51.0	4.9	55.9	20.4	2.0	33.5
Public	----	44.1	44.1	----	17.6	26.5
Total	51.0	49.0	100.0	20.4	19.6	60.0
votes	51.0	49.0	100.0	51.0	49.0	----

	Step 2. Sell control. Ownership after the Sale to the consortium				**Step 3. Global offer.** After ADS offering, before A to L conversions			
Shareholders	Total	AA	A	L	Total	AA	A	L
Government	26.0	----	2.0	24.0	9.5	----	2.0	7.5
Gov't for consortium's option	5.1	----	----	5.1	5.1	----	----	5.1
Consortium	20.4	20.4	----	----	20.4	20.4	----	----
Telmex employees	4.4	----	----	4.4	5.8	----	----	5.8
Public	44.1	----	17.6	26.5	59.2	----	17.6	41.6
Total	100.0	20.4	19.6	60.0	100.0	20.4	19.6	60.0
votes	100.0	51.0	49.0	----	100.0	51.0	49.0	----

Shares	Exchange	Shares	Exchange
A	Mexican	L	Mexican
A ADS	NASDAQ	L ADS	NYSE

F1b.   What was the first step toward this transfer?

Telmex created a new share, the L share. Each AA and A share received 1.5 L shares in a share distribution. See table, Step 1. [Note it rounds to one decimal place.]

F1b(1).   What has actually changed?

After the L distribution, the total share of the government and public remained the same (55.9% and 44.1%), but both hold L shares and the portion of AA and A shares in total capital has diminished to 20.4% and 19.6% or 40% overall. The ratio of AA and A shares to L shares is 1:1.5, which reflects the 1:1.5 L share distribution.

F1b(2).   So what is the government's stake now?

From table: all AA shares (or 20.4% of capital), some A shares, and the majority of L shares (or 33.5% of capital).

F1b(3).   Have the shareholders' relative voting rights changed?

No. The government still holds 51% through its ownership of all AA shares and 4.9% through it's a shares (A shares control 49% of the votes and the government holds 10% of the A shares (2/19.6). The public still holds the rest, 44.1%.

F1c.   So what was the nature of the transfer to the consortium?

The government sold all its AA shares to the consortium (Step 2 on the table).

F1c(1).   What is the government's stake after the transfer?

It holds no AA shares, it still holds A shares (2% of total capital), and it holds L shares equal to 24% of capital because it also transferred some L shares to a fund for Telmex employees (4.4% of all shares) and set aside another 5.1% for the consortium to buy through an option.

F1c(2).   Is the public's stake in Telmex changed?

No.

F2.   *Which of the privatization options described earlier does this resemble?*

It combines two options: it is a sale to a strategic investor. The winning consortium consists of two foreign telephone companies and a local group of investors. They buy control of Telmex. Their shareholding gives them a stake in the profits and a strong interest in making Telmex perform well.

It resembles a joint venture since the government remains in with a 26% stake. It is a weak one: the government relinquished any direct voice when it sold all its voting shares. It does not share control.

F2a.   What would the consortium members bring in addition to money?

The foreign phone companies bring experience in activities Telmex needs, after years of neglect. Bell's customer service skills would help Telmex expand and strengthen its customer base, which is critical. Cellular phone technology may substitute for a shortage of phone lines. France Telecom rapidly modernized France's phone system, which is Mexico's prime need. Bell is Mexico's neighbor; it may be able to extend economies of scale from its U.S. operations at least to Northern Mexico. Grupo Carso may have experience in related industries like real estate, but not telecommunications.

F3. *Why did this transaction take this form?*

To keep control with Mexicans. Although the AA shares are only 20.4% of total capital, they have 51% of the votes. Only Mexicans can hold AA shares.

F3a.   But the consortium has two foreign members and only one Mexican group. How does this assure Mexican control?

The shares are held in trust, as required by law, for the beneficial members of the three consortium members. The Mexican group owns 51% of the AA shares. And these investors are not even united: Grupo Carso holds 28% and 50 other Mexican investors hold 23%.

So Mexican investors holding only 10.3% of total capital (51% of the AA 20.4%) control the votes in Telmex.

F3b.   Does this new capital structure reflect the spirit of the Mexican foreign investment laws?

Students could argue both ways.

It keeps the spirit of the laws: Mexicans still have voting control. The foreign strategic investors were willing to accept only 49% beneficial ownership of the AA shares in the trust. The A holders still have 49% of the voting shares, which they had before. The L holders will accept no voting rights. This is ingenious, the best of all possible worlds.

It violates the spirit: the "controlling" Mexicans will be in bed with the 49% foreign partners, who have the expertise to manage Telmex and on whose opinion the Mexican AA investors will depend to exercise their control. The Mexican investors' interests have more in common with their foreign investor partners than with Mexican holders of A or L shares. This was a tricky device to get around the foreign investment laws.

Bottom line: you cannot legislate control. An example was IBM's experience in India some years ago. Indian law changed to forbid IBM from owning its subsidiary there 100%. IBM sold its stake to a local investor, which became the service company for IBM equipment and IBM imports. The service company depended on IBM so completely that IBM retained effective control. Control can be exercised even without shares. It rests with the party that has the leverage.

Telmex needs foreign expertise, so the providers have control even without the majority of shares.

F4.   *Is the government worried that the AA shareholders might abuse their control?*

Yes. It set performance standards in the new concession and retains a strong regulatory hand.

F4a.   Should the consortium members be concerned about the government's continued power?

While the government's ability to intervene is relatively well defined, some general powers should be a concern.

The performance standards require Telmex to meet targets in the growth of phone lines, rural services, phone booths, and speed of installation by 1994, 1995, 1998, and 2000. Failure to meet the targets allows the government to terminate the concession. This seems fair.

The government as regulator distanced itself from business decisions but may intervene in certain circumstances. The distancing resembles the way industrial governments regulate a utility monopoly. The Mexican government will monitor prices for basic services, which are subject to a cap on the price of baskets of services, within which Telmex can set prices for individual services at its discretion. This seems a good move toward market forces. The government retains the power to change these rates "in the public interest," however, which sounds open ended.

The government may also take over management of Telmex to protect internal security or the Mexican economy, in situations like a labor dispute. This also sounds open ended.

The Concession

Government's powers	Consortium gets
1. Regulatory	1. Monopoly to 8/96 on long distance
Rates: Review	
Set in public interest	
Capital: Approve	
2. Performance	2. Rational regulation
standards:	
Most start in 1994	
Terminate concession	
if not met	
3. Manage Telmex to	
protect:	
Internal security	
Mexican economy	

Consortium needs
Repay investment ($1.8bn) in 1991/2/3/4 = 25% return on assets each year for 4 years
(Goldman estimated a 37% ROE in 1991)

F4b.   What does the consortium get in exchange for this?

A monopoly in Mexico's domestic and international long distance phone services until August 1996. After that, the government may grant other concessions. So Telmex may manage to extend its monopoly, politics permitting. Much money could be made here, even with regulated rates.

The government rationalized its rules governing communications, it now taxes revenue rather than imposing excise taxes, and it even requires Telmex to end cross-subsidization of services, which protects Telmex from political pressure for uneconomically low rates for powerful consumers.

F4c.   Is this a gold mine for the consortium?

We cannot really tell. The question is whether the rate ceilings and performance standards offset the benefits of the five year monopoly. Most of the standards measure performance at the end of 1994, four years in. If Telmex reaps monopoly profits in the first three years, perhaps much of the investment will be repaid before Telmex performance is even judged.

How could the consortium protect itself? Get the investment back fast. The consortium paid $1.8 billion, giving a premium for control over the 20.4% of $5.3 billion in total capital that it bought. To recoup this in four years, it would need to receive roughly $450 million each year in dividends. Its 20.4% interest means that total equity would have to earn five times $450 million or $2.25 billion each year. This is a 25% return on assets of $9.6 billion in 1990 and is a 42% return on equity (dividends are tax free to non-residents of Mexico). In fact, Goldman estimated in 1991 that Telmex would earn a 37% return on equity. So consortium investors might have concluded in 1990 that they could repay their investment before the monopoly ended. A 25% return on assets from a monopoly does not seem impossible.

On the other hand, the concession required large investments and the government would be watching Telmex closely. It is not obvious that the Mexican government failed to negotiate tough enough terms.

F5.   *Suppose the consortium manages Telmex successfully and the company is very profitable. Should it have any worries?*

A popular backlash against the new Telmex is possible, since it touches almost everyone. But what could the public do? Repudiating the agreement, even after a political upheaval (such as the PRI's loss of power), would close foreign securities markets to Mexico. The agreement does not forbid high profits; that was the point of continuing the monopoly.

A new government hostile to foreign investment or to the Telmex consortium would have to show a failure to meet the targets (most of which are at the end of 1994 or later) or another contractual breach to terminate the contract.

A hostile government could intervene in rate setting or to protect national security or the Mexican economy and take effective control from the consortium. Labor problems could be created, for example; Telmex is the largest non-government employer, so it would be prominent and vulnerable. This seems a more serious threat. This too would probably discredit Mexico on foreign exchanges.

G.   **The Offer of Telmex Shares in World Markets**

G1.   *What is the 1991 offer of Telmex shares in world markets?*

The government sells some of its remaining L stock in Telmex: it sold 16.5% of the total capital, most to the public. A small part goes to Telmex employees (1.4%); we will ignore it. See the Table.

> **G1a.   How does this affect the government's stake in Telmex?**

It holds A shares (2%) and L shares (7.5%). The A shares have voting rights.

> **G1b.   Where will the stock sold to the public be listed?**

On the Mexican Exchange and the New York Stock Exchange. The offer places many more on the NYSE.

<pre>
L shares   =   100 mm on Mexican exchange (in Pesos)
L ADSs 70 mm   =   1,400 mm on NYSE (in Dollars)
  1 ADS = 20 L shares
</pre>

G2.   *Investors could buy rights to L shares on either the Mexican exchange or NYSE. Why would they choose to buy on one exchange over the other?*

Currency: the investor may want a peso or a dollar asset.

Liquidity: the NYSE is a much bigger and more liquid market. The investor could dispose of the shares more readily there.

Convenience: an investor based in Mexico might prefer the Mexican exchange, a U.S. investor the NYSE.

G3.   *A shareholders can exchange their shares, one for one, for L shares after the issue. Telmex will rescind the A shares and issue L shares to replace the A shares.*

> **G3a.   We know investors trading Telmex A shares in Mexico did not switch to L shares in Pesos after the May 1991 closing. What would account for this?**

They want to be in Pesos, which they are already with the A shares and they gain nothing by switching to L shares:

They have a vote: They were in Mexico, could know the situation better than many NYSE investors, and might want to influence Telmex because they were Mexican citizens. But the A shares only have in total 49% of the vote, so A shares do not bring control. At best, a block of A shares might get a minority director.

They get only limited additional liquidity if they stay in pesos but switch to L shares. With the A shares, they also had a vote. The L shares traded on the Mexican exchange only gave a peso exposure and no vote.

<u>Switch from A Shares to L Shares</u>
If hold As on Mex. Exchange: no switch to Ls on Mex. Exchange
  Peso exposure in A and L
  Voting power in A, not L
If hold A ADSs on NASDAQ: switch to L ADSs on NYSE
  Liquidity

G3b. Why did investors trading ADSs in Telmex A shares on NASDAQ switch to L ADSs after the May 1991 closing? What do they gain?

They gain liquidity for two reasons. (They are already in Dollars, so currency exposure is no motive.) Fewer A shares are outstanding than L Shares (which are 1.5 times both AA and A shares). They are traded on NYSE rather than NASDAQ, a smaller market for smaller issuers. Liquidity means the L ADSs are more readily sold at any time than the A ADSs.

What do the A ADS holders lose by switching? The right to vote. But A shares were minority shares, together accounting for only 49% of the vote, so the loss may not be major.

G4. *Which privatization option, described earlier, does this offer resemble?*

The IPO.

G4a. What would have motivated the government to take this route?

To get access to one of the largest pools of capital in the world and get the best possible price for the shares it was selling. Mexico's ability to do this makes it look more like an industrial country and not at all like a former communist one.

G4b. Since the government gets all the funds from the sale, does this offer benefit privatization in Mexico at all?

Yes, since other Mexican state owned enterprises may be privatized the same way and want access to global equity markets. This offer will pave the way.

G4c. Does the offer benefit Telmex?

Telmex gets no money, but it gets an international reputation that it can use later. The international attention it will get from L shareholders may also encourage it to greater efficiency and stronger performance (to the extent foreign investors care, as we discuss below).

G5.   *What is likely to be the relation between the L shares traded on the Mexican stock exchange and the L ADSs traded on the NYSE?*

Arbitrage, specifically permitted in this case by Mexican law, will keep the prices in equilibrium, taking into account foreign exchange costs.

G5a.   Will trading on one exchange dominate the other?

Students may say quickly that NYSE trading will lead Mexican trading because NYSE is a much bigger market and we know that on active days up to 85% of all trades occur on the NYSE. Today, fund managers say more trades occur on the NYSE than Mexico's exchange and that NYSE drives trading in Mexico.

G5b.   Note: The majority of L shares was not offered to back up the L ADSs. The government only offered 1.4 billion for ADSs, only 22% of the 6.4 billion. But this did not mean that the majority of L shares would be traded on the Mexican exchange or that Mexico's trading would drive NYSE trading.

We know most A ADSs switched to L ADSs. The A ADSs were 60% of all A shares. Each A ADS was entitled to 1.5 L shares in the distribution. If many A shares switched to L ADSs after the offer, many more than 1.4 billion L shares are represented by L ADSs on the NYSE.

H.   Demand for the Telmex Offer

H1.   *What would account for the relative distribution of the tranches among the four regions?*

USA = 55%. The listing is on the NYSE. Mexico is probably better known to U.S. based investors than those elsewhere.

International (mainly U.K. and the rest of Europe) = 31%. U.K. and Europe have trade and investment ties with Mexico, so know the country.

Mexico = 7%. Mexico's exchange is 1% the size of the NYSE, as discussed, so has less capacity. The government wants to raise Dollars not Pesos, so wants to place most outside Mexico

What explains Japan's share? Were Japanese investors uninterested on the road show? More institutions showed up in Tokyo than in any other city except New York. But Japanese investors took only 6%. In 1991, Japan's financial crisis is severe, as we saw earlier in this course. Investors are pulling back from their international exposure.

H2.   *What might account for the allocations relative to demand?*

The offer was oversubscribed by ½ to 1 times in leading European countries and by 2 times in the U.S. institutional investors, particularly pension funds, have begun to realize the benefits of investing fund assets outside the home country. This is true in each, but more so in the U.K. than Germany, for example.

H2a.   What accounts for the high U.S. demand?

Two possible reasons: (1) the large size of institutional investors' assets compared to other countries ($3.7 trillion in 1992 for the U.S. pension funds and barely $1 billion for any other country or (2) a decision by the offerers to allocate relatively more to non-U.S. countries in order to make the offer more global. There is a marketing element here.

H2b.   Why are pension funds interested in Telmex?

H2b(1).   Does Telmex itself look good?

Telmex has great prospects: it is a leading company in a recovering developing country. It offers an infrastructure play: Mexico must develop its infrastructure and telecommunications are critical. The shortage of lines is dramatic (Mexico ranks 13th in GNP but 83rd in phone lines per capita) and the need to invest great. This has to be a growth industry and the consortium has a monopoly that looks like a license to print money for five years. Growth potential is enormous.

H2b(2).   Does the fact that Telmex is listed on an emerging market make it attractive or not?

Attractive to a point. Diversification is a key investment policy for pension funds. One problem of investing in other industrial countries' stocks is that their price movements are correlated with each other. A U.S. pension fund does not fully diversify when it buys U.K. shares because when the U.S. market declines it is very likely the U.K. market will also fall. Emerging stock markets' prices are historically much less correlated with industrial markets.

H2b(3).   Why are emerging markets less correlated with industrial exchanges?

Developing economies have been less integrated because of trade restrictions, exchange controls, government involvement in the economy. Their exchanges' prices have been less correlated for the same reasons: exchange controls and foreign investment limits inhibit foreign fund flows and the domestic economy follows a different cycle. A U.S. pension fund can buy diversity.

H3.   *So how important is control over Telmex—through voting shares—likely to be to pension funds?*

Pension funds are portfolio investors. They do not buy shares with a view to exercising control over the company. If they do not like the company's performance or prospects, they sell the position and invest elsewhere. Pension funds work through professional advisers who manage a part of the portfolio according to agreed risk and reward objectives guided by portfolio theory. The advisers are interested in numbers, not control.

However, pension funds are subject to fiduciary standards of prudence. The absence of voting power in a share may make it more risky and less prudent an investment. The lack of voting power concerns fund managers. At the very least, the share sells at a premium.

H4.   *Q. 4 lists items that are said to affect pension funds' interest in emerging markets. Would these have been significant in the Telmex offer?*

Many items Mexico's government fixed: there are no restrictions on capital inflows or repatriation. During the 1980s, the government strengthened broker networks, promoted transparency by requiring more data about the market, and let the exchange grow reduce illiquidity. It also increased the range of financial instruments (not in the readings).

H4a.   Does this solve the problem for the pension funds?

H4a(1).   Exchange controls.

Mexico may reestablish exchange controls in a crisis, as it did in 1982.

But why care if you invested in ADSs, which are traded in dollars? An indirect foreign exchange risk persists. For example, dividends must be paid from Mexico.

H4a(2).   Stock market abuse

We don't know how safe Mexico's exchange is now after the reforms, so manipulation or abuse must be a concern to pension funds.

How could a fund manager check for abuse on the Mexican exchange? Some look at CNV's prosecution of insider trading, asking if it is more than a show. They rely on their custodian and subcustodian for information about fraud in share certificates, price changes, or false pricing at close. They look for electronic settlement, which reduces the opportunity for fraud. Compared to many other markets, Mexico's looks good (not in text). Some are even stricter: Malaysia's is an example.

H4b.   But how much would a pension fund manager really care about these matters? Suppose manipulation was a major possibility. How would it matter?

Some fund managers simply weigh risk and return, and price for this risk.

Other fund managers may be less interested in stocks trading on higher risk exchanges, which would reduce demand.

If Mexico were seen as a riskier exchange, how would this market reaction affect government policy? It would encourage the government to tighten its regulation of the exchange to reduce the risk premium. Local brokers might even approve if they saw greater business as a result of more foreign interest in the exchange.

H5. *From the Mexican government's point of view, how does this form of foreign investment in the country differ from foreign banks' lending to Mexico 15 years ago?*

Like the banks, portfolio investors are not interested in control. Thus they can buy L shares, without a vote.

Unlike the banks, the market value of portfolio investors' stakes in Mexico is known. If Mexico's economy weakens slowly, the portfolio investor has no incentive to invest more to shore up its earlier stake. The banks did. They dug themselves in deeper and reduced the urgency for a policy change by the Mexican government. The government may not like this new situation, but the country should be better off in the long run.

I.   Let's Turn to the Peso Crisis That Started in December 1994.

I1. *Why would the sharp Peso devaluation hurt the price of the Telmex L ADS, which was traded in Dollars on the NYSE?*

The ADSs are denominated in dollars, not Pesos. But any dividends Telmex pays in Pesos now buy 50% fewer Dollars.

I1a.   What is the link between devaluation and Telmex's future earning prospects?

There are several reasons the Peso's decline would hurt Telmex's prospects.

a. To the extent Telmex buys capital equipment from the U.S., essential to upgrade service, the cost in Pesos just doubled.

b. Calls out of the country will diminish to the extent that the customers' costs reflect costs in foreign currencies (e.g. payments to American long distance company).

c. It would reduce Telmex's revenues as customers' spending capacity falls. Real incomes just took a nosedive; the Peso buys much less abroad and Mexico has been importing much more than it exports. Incomes will fall further as the Mexican government's austerity program takes hold. Government expenditures will be cut back, reducing incomes directly (for those who have been selling to government) and indirectly (as aggregate demand falls). The austerity program is needed to reduce the growth in demand and the high inflation.

d. Telmex's Peso cost of borrowing abroad just doubled. If the austerity program includes tighter monetary policy, the cost of borrowing in Pesos will also rise.

The Peso value of Telmex's Dollar earnings from long distance just doubled, but that advantage still left P4.3 billion in FX losses. The fact that

Telmex's huge profits offset all but P390 million in the first quarter of 1995 is not reassuring for the long run because Telmex soon faces competition.

I1b.   Even if the link to Telmex's performance were not so direct, would its ADS price be affected by the devaluation?

Many investors buy Telmex ADSs as a play on Mexico. Much fund investment is driven by quantitative measures and relies on various share indexes, so the performance of an individual stock's issuer is less important than the movement of the index. Telmex would be one of several shares representing Mexico. Major economic or political events like the Peso collapse would affect Mexico and the Mexican part of the portfolio and could prompt the funds to sell, pushing down the price of the L ADS.

I2. *What lessons should an institutional investor draw from the Mexican rescue package?*

I2a.   How does this package compare with those for the 1982 debt crisis in Mexico?

Similarities:

a. Process: U.S. still leads, tries to bring in banks and other G-5 countries, IMF, BIS. Congress is hostile.

b. Content: combines aid and commercial credit; requires Mexican austerity program.

Differences:

a. Process: In 1995—

1) U.K. and Germany do not join enthusiastically;

2) No small group of Government insiders successfully managed the package, compared to Volcker's tour de force;

3) No small number of financial institutions can speak for all, as a handful of leading banks from each major lending country did when they acted as a steering committee for the 100s of lending banks in the syndicates.

4) Congressional opposition was much more successful despite the Congressional leaders' support.

Content: In 1995—

1) Help is shorter term (the 3-5 year swap compares with long-term Eurocredits exceeding 10 years after 1982);

2) Requires Mexican oil receipts as a guaranty.

3) No debt service moratorium (yet) by Mexico.

4) Investors are not forced to renegotiate their terms, as the banks were in 1982.

I2b.   What would account for the differences?

Commercial banks in the U.S. and elsewhere are not so exposed in 1995, though they surely held some of the Mexican debt (Tesobonos [Dollar] and cetes [Pesos]). Overall volumes are smaller.

U.S. political situation is different: a weak President Clinton faces a hostile landslide Congress; in 1982, Reagan was strong and the Congress was divided.

I2c.   Who was being helped by the rescue package? Were the new members of Congress right that this was a bailout of investors who should have known better?

Mexico is being helped short-term but not long-term. The bailout prospects confuse market signals. Mexico's economic health requires markets fully aware of the risks so they can give more nuanced price signals so Mexico can adjust more gradually.

Investors in Mexican Dollar and Peso paper are being helped. The aid allows a defense of the Peso and helps service the Dollar debt. But investors in the Telmex L ADS immediately took a big hit: the price quickly fell to one-third of its 1994 high. The banks in 1982 were not hit so severely so fast.

I2d.   How, if at all, should the package affect investments in:

I2d(1).   Mexico?

Expect aid packages in the future, but not in ways that appear to bail out investors or, perhaps, require Congressional approval.

Moral hazard is therefore a danger. If Mexico's government can avoid economic adjustment at critical times, such as before major elections, the market price of Mexican securities may not fully reflect the risk because investors expect the U.S. government to help Mexico in a crisis.

I2d(2).   Other Latin American countries?

No other Latin American country is as important to the U.S. as Mexico.

I2d(3).   Asia?

Asia is too remote, particularly after the collapse of the Soviet Union.

I2e.   To what extent can governments of major industrial countries be expected to support an emerging market?

The U.S. government was implicated in Mexico's crisis. It wanted a smooth election and transition and therefore would not have wanted devaluation before the election. It may have expected the inevitable devaluation to come between the election and December 1995, as happened in earlier years (such as 1982). Salinas seems to have wanted to head the World Trade Organization and, to preserve his reputation, refused to devalue then (not in text).

I3. *What lessons should an institutional investor draw from the tequila effect?*

I3a.   Where was the contagion serious? Why?

Latin America was most seriously hit. Bad economic management may account for some of the collapse but not all (to judge from the later recovery of some countries faster than others).

I3b.   How capable are investors to distinguish among countries?

Investors were not subtle in their judgments at first. Chile and Malaysia were lumped in with Brazil and Argentina which, unlike the first two, had serious macroeconomic and political problems. The Latin American index fell as much as the Mexican index, though only Mexico was in crisis (some of the fall would be due to the Mexican stocks in the Latin American index).

Within a month the market began to discriminate in several ways:

1) Chile's market did not continue to fall after January, unlike Brazil and Argentina, nor did Malaysia's fall as much as the Philippines'.

2) Country fund investors withdrew in smaller proportions than the price decline, suggesting many expect recovery and will wait out the price decline.

I3b(1). When investors move as a herd, why do they do so?

Investors need to anticipate the market and get out before a prices collapse. In anticipating it, they may contribute to the decline in prices. For emerging markets, information is limited and the markets are thin, so a small shift in demand based on little data can move the market a lot.

I3b(2). To the extent that investors move as a herd, is the behavior similar to that of the banks that make syndicated loans to developing countries in the 1970s and early 1980s?

Like banks, investors contributed to the crisis by withdrawing. Those that did not roll over Tesobonos or Cetes repatriated their investment, further reducing the value of the Peso against the Dollar. The banks also did not roll over their loans, which previously had been used to service outstanding debt, and spread the crisis from Mexico across Latin America.

Unlike banks, the investors in 1995 were able to withdraw. Banks were forced to stay in for the workout.

I4. *In April 1995, does the Telmex L ADS look attractive?*

That depends on your reading of the prospects of Mexican recovery and of Telmex after 1996, when competition may begin. The latter is less important to the extent that investors will continue to treat Telmex ADSs as a country play.

Telmex ADSs should look very cheap at only $25-$30, compared to a $74 high in 1994.

I4a.   How would recent Mexican government policies affect the value of the ADS?

Policies toward Mexico: the austerity program hurt Telmex, as we saw earlier.

Policies toward Telmex: the government seems serious about increasing competition. Its desire to help Telmex (a major factor in the stock market and the economy) seems weaker than its desire to strengthen communications. Telmex's era of high profitability seems at an end.

I4b.   To what extent have investors in the L ADS diversified away from U.S. risks?

The Mexican economy will continue to be managed separately from the U.S. economy. Telmex and the other companies will have their own performance.

But as pension funds and others buy Mexican ADS, the Mexican market will be more closely correlated with the investors' other markets and the very diversity they were seeking will diminish.

1) Arbitragers will keep the ADS Dollar price and the Mexican shares' peso prices almost identical. We know that trading on the NYSE, with its much greater volume, drives the price of the L shares traded on the Mexican exchange. So the two markets are linked.

2) Telmex shares account for much of the trading on the Mexican exchange (18% of Mexican market capitalization and 26% of Mexico's stock index) and the NYSE (in volume, Telmex L ADSs ranked as the most active stock in the NYSE in 1994 (no. 2 was GM) and the most active in the first quarter of 1995). So the markets are likely to move together more than they would in the absence of these parallel listings.

J. Conclusion

1.   The Telmex offer was remarkably successful and the ADS now has a leading position in U.S. financial markets.

In late April 1994, Telmex was the third most actively traded listing on the NYSE. Options on it were the most actively traded options in the United States.

2.   Telmex is so big in Mexico that it represents 30% of the Mexican stock index and 7% of the IFC emerging markets index.

This raises a problem for funds using the indexes, since Telmex may exert too great an influence on the indexes. Some managers therefore adjust the indexes.

Relationship between risk and control
for different types of cross-border investment

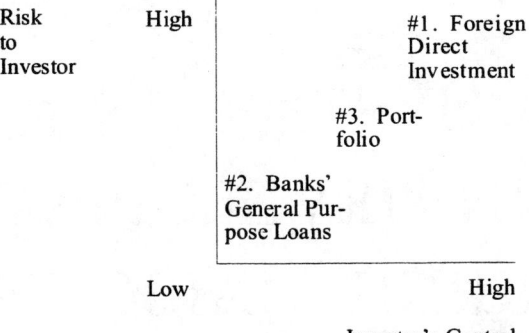

3. Pension funds are just one type of institutional investor in emerging markets.

Mutual funds have become major players. Country funds were slightly larger investors in emerging markets during 1990–92 than investors through ADRs. Many other mutual funds, such as international growth funds, also buy the shares and ADRs. Vanguard's international fund, for example, allocated 3% of the total portfolio to Mexico in 1993. Part was in Telmex ADSs.

4. Portfolio investment promises to grow, for reasons described in the reading. It seems to be a much better form of investment than general purpose bank loans because investors can see its market value and governments can respond. It allocates risk and control in a more acceptable way than bank loans or foreign direct investment. [Source: D. Lessard]

TEACHING PLAN FOR

CHAPTER TWENTY
FINANCIAL SYSTEM REFORMS IN DEVELOPING AND EMERGING MARKETS

POWERPOINT SCREENS FOR THIRTEENTH EDITION

Need For International Banking Standards
Class Outline

- **Why, if at all, do we need international banking standards?**
- **Should developed and emerging market countries have the same standards?**
- **Should the IMF have a major role in promulgating, monitoring and/or enforcing international banking standards?**

Need For International Banking Standards

- Cost to countries of resolving crises, $250 billion estimate as of 1997 (most cost Japan, $90 billion as of 2003)
  - Developed or developing country problem or both
- Cost in part borne by international system through lending/bailouts and spillovers
- Why focus on country banking standards?
  - Relationship between financial crises and the banking system
  - Are spillovers the result of domestic or international bank failures? (Japanese banks versus BCCI)

International Banking Standards: Definition and Effectiveness

- What are they? BIS Core Principles
  - Very general: competent and independent supervisory system with adequate compliance powers
  - Soft law: not binding on countries but surveilled through IMF FSAP program
- Effectiveness?
  - Core principles assume legal and institutional infrastructure (see Beck and Levine 2003 for importance) often not present and assume that one size fits all (United States and Ghana)
  - Caprio (2004) multiple country study for World Bank: market discipline more important, requiring disclosure, protection of investors; increasing power of supervisors can be detrimental (extract rents)
  - Gros (2003) Presence of foreign banks important (better service provider, agent of technology transfer, can support currency pegs)

TEACHING PLAN FOR

CHAPTER TWENTY-TWO

CONTROLLING THE FINANCING OF TERRORISM, TERRORISM INSURANCE, AND FINANCIAL TERRORISM

POWERPOINT SCREENS FOR SIXTEENTH EDITION

Class Outline
Fighting Terrorist Financing

• Money Laundering and Terrorism Financing
• 9-11 Profiles
• Patriot Act
• Taking Stock—an evaluation

Money Laundering Operations

- The cash proceeds of the illegal activity must be converted to bank deposits in order to shrink the huge volumes of cash generated
- Money launderers must conceal the true ownership and origin of the bank deposits, the proceeds of illegal activity
- Criminals must be able to convert their deposits into legitimate investments

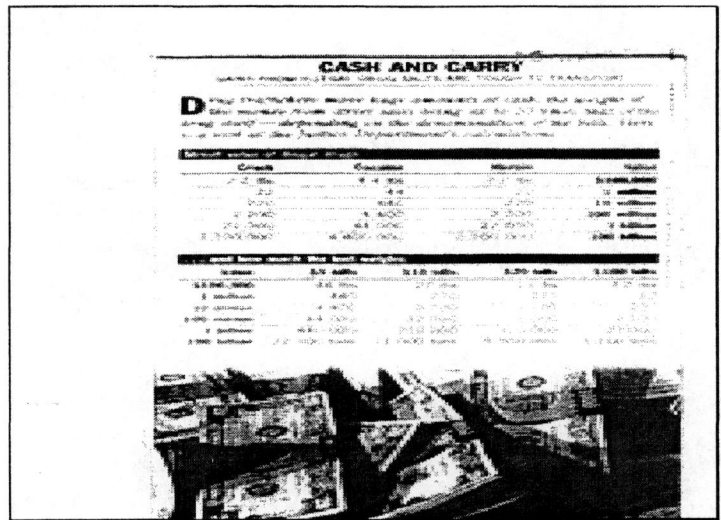

Money Laundering v. Terrorism Financing

	Money Laundering	Terrorism
Source	Illegal-cash	Legal-bank transfer
Amounts	Large	Smaller
Origin	Major markets	Non-major markets

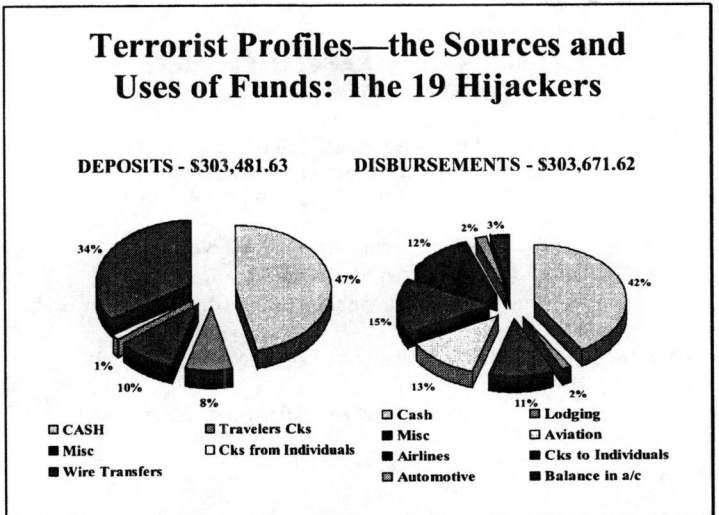

Terrorist Profiles—the Sources and Uses of Funds: The 19 Hijackers

DEPOSITS - $303,481.63   DISBURSEMENTS - $303,671.62

**HIJACKERS' FINANCIAL PROFILE:
THE OPENING OF ACCOUNTS**

– Accounts were opened with cash/cash equivalents (i.e. travelers checks which in some cases were purchased by other hijackers) in the average amount of $3,000 to $5,000

– Identification used to open the accounts were visas issued through Saudi Arabia or U.A.E.

– Accounts were opened within 30 days after entry into U.S.

– All accounts were normal checking accounts with debit cards

– None of the hijackers had a social security number

**HIJACKERS' FINANCIAL PROFILE:
THE OPENING OF ACCOUNTS**

- Hijackers tended to open their accounts in groups of 3 or 4
  individuals
- Some of these accounts were joint accounts with other
  hijackers
- Addresses used usually not permanent (i.e. mail boxes etc.)
  and changed frequently
- Hijackers would often use the same address/telephone
  numbers on the accounts
- Occupation on opening statements would usually be "student"

**HIJACKERS' FINANCIAL PROFILE:
THE OPENING OF ACCOUNTS**

- No savings accounts or safe deposit boxes were opened
- Hijackers would open their accounts at branches
  of large well known banks
- Majority of hijackers (12) opened accounts at the same bank

**Would this profile allows us to identify
future terrorists from bank records? Not likely**

Preventive Techniques

Old Anti-Money Laundering Techniques

- Suspicious Activity Reports (SARs): profiling
- Currency Transaction Reports: cash transactions over $10,000: deter cash conversion and facilitate tracking
- Wire Transfer records (Travel Rule): facilitate tracking
- Asset Freezes

New USA Patriot Act Anti-Terrorism Techniques

- Section 326: Know Your Customer (verify identities and check against terrorist lists)
- Section 314(a): Information sharing with law enforcement officials
- Section 311: Special Measures
- Section 312: Due Diligence for Private Banking and Correspondent Accounts

Taking Stock—How Effective are the Current Measures in Stopping Terrorism?

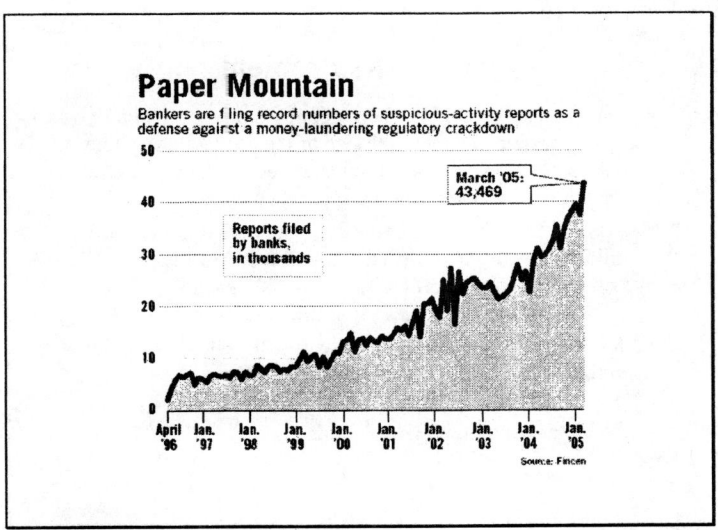

Paper Mountain

Bankers are filing record numbers of suspicious-activity reports as a defense against a money-laundering regulatory crackdown

Reference: Mostly money-laundering, terrorist reports are few, 1046 in 2004.

The SARs Problem

- Banks must file a SAR when it believes it was a crime victim or (depending on the size of the transaction) where it suspects there are illegal funds, funds designed to evade regulations, or funds with no apparent purpose
- Riggs Affair: 2004, Riggs, a D.C. bank, civil fine of $25 million for failure to file a SAR with respect to funds transfers of foreign officials, and in 2005 pleads guilty to criminal charge and fined $16 million
- Am South Affair: 2004 civil fine of $50 million for failure to file a SAR with respect to a Ponzi scheme
- Arab Bank (Jordan) Affair: 2005 civil fine of $24 million for use as conduit of Hamas funds

What concerns about SARs?
Overreaction to money laundering will cause glut of SAR filing that will make it harder to detect terrorist financing (but separable), make terrorists or their banks hold accounts outside U.S., and fines could also lead to bank failure and systemic risk, criminal prosecution of bank could cause bank failure, leaking of information although regulators not supposed to release (privacy).

Federal Reserve Board Proposal of December 7, 1998: KYC - Sampling of Comments

Profiling every individual, based on distrust, is akin to Hitler, in his efforts to purify the German race by identifying Jews, using this same profiling method

I deeply resent and fear the government requiring banks to create a system to detect transactions they deem to be "unusual" for me and then to investigate the circumstances of my transaction in order to determine whether the bank should report me as a possible criminal. This is a recipe for abuse. Hitler or Stalin could not have come up with a better system.

KYC - Sampling of Comments

Whose brain dead idea was this anyway? Perhaps those that came up with this idea should be required to pass an IQ test in order to be employed in a regulatory agency. It is obvious to me that those of you supporting this idea would not be able to muster a score meeting even an elementary level of functioning intelligence. Also, it seems to me that some of you seriously need to get a life outside of your job.

You know the constitution of the United States? Whose _____ idiotic idea was this anyway? I tell you what, if this program goes into effect, you can kiss my ____!

KYC- Patriot Act Section 326

- Banks must:
  - verify identity of a person opening an account
  - maintain records of doing so
  - determine whether the person is on any official terrorist list
- Verification requirements:
  - Obtain standard information: name, address, SSN, etc.
  - Within a reasonable time of account opening verify this information by comparing it to a drivers license or a passport
- Relaxed requirements from initial proposal, requiring examination of a customer's business, due to concern with cost (not privacy)

Reference

Patriot Act Section 312: Special Due Diligence
on Correspondent Accounts

Each financial institution that establishes,
maintains, administers private banking accounts
and/or correspondent accounts in the U.S. for a
non-U.S. person shall establish appropriate due
diligence [risk-based approach by regulation], and
when appropriate, enhanced due diligence
policies, procedures and controls that are
reasonably designed to detect and report instances
of money laundering or terrorist financing

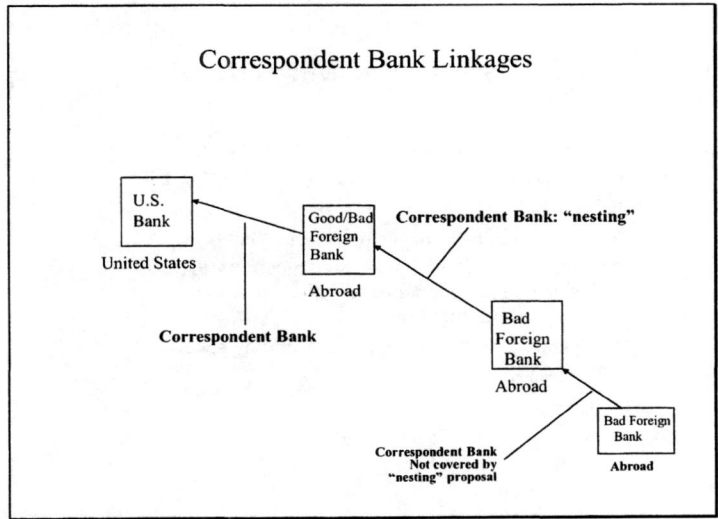

Correspondent Bank Linkages

Special Due Diligence

If correspondent account is requested or maintained by or on behalf of a foreign bank operating

under an "offshore" banking license, e.g. Caymans

banking license issued by a foreign country that has been designated noncooperative with international anti-money laundering principles

designated by the Secretary as warranting special measures

THEN - -

USA Patriot Act - Special Due Diligence

- Ascertain for each foreign bank, the shares of which are not publicly traded, the ownership
- Conduct enhanced scrutiny of such accounts to guard against money laundering and report suspicious transactions
- Ascertain whether foreign bank provides correspondent accounts to other foreign banks and if so identify those foreign banks and require due diligence information from them
- U.S. banks may cut-off certain foreign banks for fear that they might be charged with failure to police them

Section 311: Special Measures

- Certain jurisdictions, institutions or transactions can be designated by Treasury Secretary as posing particular terrorist financing concerns. Factors with respect to jurisdictions:
  - terrorist activity
  - bank secrecy
  - poor bank supervision
  - high volume of financial transactions/real economic activity
  - designated as "offshore haven" by international experts, e.g. FATF
  - corruption
- Designation results in enhanced record keeping requirements with regard to designees
- Can also ban transactions with offending countries' banks or with particular banks, e.g. 2006 ban on U.S. banks holding accounts of Bank Saderat, one of the largest Iranian owned banks, accused of aiding terrorist organizations, e.g. Hezbollah and Hamas.

Taking Stock—Effectiveness of Current Measures

- Have these measures been effective in preventing terrorism? Some data from Reuter and Truman (2004):
  - Cost of regime estimated at $7 billion per year
  - Terrorism regime froze $300 million in terrorist assets from 2001-2004; assuming a 33% success rate, $20 million a month still goes to terrorists— does this suggest these measures are not justified?

P. Reuter and E. Truman, *Chasing Dirty Money*, Institute for International Economics (2004). Costs a pure guesstimate. How to measure benefits, data does not capture value of deterrence and ex-terrorist event tracking down through money trail.

**Taking Stock—What Additional Measures
Could we Take?**

Reference next page

Taking Stock—Additional Measures

- Ban correspondent accounts of foreign banks (all accounts of foreign customers would be held directly by U.S. banks): cost concern and charge of discrimination against foreign banks
- Computer monitoring of all account activity against terrorist profiles: concerns of cost and reliability—reported plan for Treasury access to wire transfer logs
- Identity cards
- National registry of bank accounts available to other countries or banks
- No cash
- Ban informal payment systems such as Hawala: must make alternative "formal" low-cost banking service available
- More international coordination and sanctions

APPENDIX

PAGE CHANGES FROM 19TH EDITION

This Appendix identifies pages in the Nineteenth Edition with text that differs from text in the Eighteenth Edition. Differences include additions and deletions of text, and shifts of text from one part of the chapter to another.

Chapter in Both Editions	Changed pages in Nineteenth Edition
1	Thoroughly revised throughout
2	Thoroughly revised throughout
3	Thoroughly revised throughout
4	Thoroughly revised throughout
5	430, 433-434, 437, 440-441, 443-487,489-493
6	494-496,498-499,502,506-508, 513-514, 518-519, 521, 526-528, 530, 532, 534-539, 542-545, 548-550
7	554-555, 559, 562-565, 568-569, 571, 573, 576, 579-580, 582-589, 591-594, 596-600, 605-613, 617, 620-622
8	624-626, 629, 631, 638, 640-645, 647-651, 654-655, 657, 659, 660, 663, 668
9	680-681, 684-686, 690, 695-696, 700-701
10	720, 726-730, 739-740, 745, 747-748
11	No substantive changes
12	Thoroughly revised throughout
13	No substantive changes
14	No substantive changes
15	Thoroughly revised throughout
16	1054, 1057, 1061, 1071, 1073, 1078, 1081-1082, 1084-1088, 1090-1092, 1097, 1100-1103, 1105, 1110-1112
17	No substantive changes
18	No substantive changes
19	1171-1174,1181-1182, 1184, 1186, 1189, 1195, 1204, 1210-1212, 1214-1215, 1220, 1222-1224, 1227-1229, 1231-1235, 1237, 1241-1243, 1247-1255, 1258-1261
20	No substantive changes

21	1281-1284, 1289-1290, 1293-1295, 1298, 1301, 1303-1305, 1311-1312, 1315-1319, 1321-1339
22	No substantive changes